YALE INSTITUTE OF SACRED MUSIC

Colloquium: Music, Worship, Arts

D1227422

COLLOQUIUM: MUSIC, WORSHIP, ARTS
Published annually by Yale Institute of Sacred Music
Martin D. Jean, *Director*
409 Prospect Street
New Haven, CT 06511
www.yale.edu/ism

JOURNAL
Editors	Bryan Spinks and Margot E. Fassler
Publication Manager	Melissa Maier
Copy Editor	John Leinenweber
Editorial Assistant	Gale Pollen

DVD
Faculty Consultant	Margot E. Fassler
Producer/Editor	Jacqueline Richard
Technical Supervisor	Sachin Ramabhadran
Photography	Sidney Symington and Bernard J. Owens

GRAPHIC DESIGN AND PRODUCTION
Maura Gianakos
Yale *RIS*

COVER: Semana Santa—Good Friday at historic San Fernando Cathedral, San Antonio, Texas, during the solemn celebration of the ancient and timeless Mozarabic-Roman Catholic-Mestizo Holy Week rituals, one of the few places in the world where these multicultural traditions of time immemorial continue to flourish. Photo by Manual Medellin, 1991.

Director's Welcome

The Colloquium is the lively enterprise at the heart of the Institute's mission. At this weekly meeting, scholars, ministers, church musicians, performers, and artists — present and future — engage each other. In this space, we attempt to make more permeable the natural frontiers of our disciplines. Here, at the very least, musicians and artists can learn of the liturgical and theological contexts from which the tools of their trade come. Scholars and ministers gain a much broader understanding for how theology is done beyond the saying and writing of texts.

This conversation reinvents itself with every new topic and every new group of students, and with this journal and DVD we extend this conversation to you, our readers and viewers. We hope that you will find truth and insight between the covers of this second volume of the Colloquium journal, and that this knowledge will help you in your work, whatever it may be.

Martin D. Jean
Director, Yale Institute of Sacred Music
Professor of Organ

Colloquium: Music, Worship, Arts

The mission of the Institute states that we sponsor a "vital interdisciplinary program that brings musicians, presiders, and scholars together for common conversation and formation," and this new volume of Colloquium continues to demonstrate some of the ways in which this part of our mission is fulfilled. Film has become a regular part of our classroom teaching, and we continue to build a film archive. Ronald Grimes discusses the delights and dangers of film in his Aidan Kavanagh Lecture. His discussion reminds us that just as what is regarded as important in a liturgical text may reside less in the text than in the mind of the scholar, so all films are made to highlight what was significant to the camera person and subsequent editors.

As invaluable as film is, it is never a substitute for actual worship, and as contemporary as it may be, a film becomes history. Our Colloquium presenters remind us that consideration of contemporary practices cannot long avoid discussion with the past — with history. Archbishop Rowan Williams's recent book *Why Study the Past?* argues that good history is a moral affair because it opens up a point of reference that is distinct from us, yet not wholly alien. The past can then enable us to think with more varied and resourceful analogies about our identity in the often confusing present.

Markus Rathey puts Bach's *Mass in B Minor* in historical perspective for us, and Michael Hawn illustrates how particular hymns have been rewritten and adapted for newer times and situations. The importance of sound theological reflection is brought home to us by John Witvliet's reflection on Trinitarian theology and worship, and the need to engage with both a global culture and a postmodern culture is underlined by I-to Loh, Quentin Faulkner, John McClure, and Carol Wade.

This issue includes a new section, Authors' Perspectives, in which Institute faculty and invited scholars who work in sacred music, ritual studies, and the arts speak about their new work.

The editors are grateful to all our contributors, and to the students, faculty, and staff of the Institute for their work on this journal.

Bryan D. Spinks
Professor of Liturgical Studies
Chair of the Program in Liturgical Studies

Margot E. Fassler
Tangeman Professor of Music History and Liturgy

CONTENTS

I. Technology, Creativity, and Authority in Ritual and Art

YALE INSTITUTE OF SACRED MUSIC

Colloquium: Music, Worship, Arts

VOLUME 2

Technology, Creativity, and Authority in Ritual and Art

An illustration from City, Temple, Stage: Eschatological Architecture and Liturgical Theatrics in New Spain, *by Jaime Lara. Photo by Jaime Lara*

Shooting Rites

RONALD L. GRIMES

The Kavanagh Lecture delivered October 16, 2003

"SHOOTING RITES." PACIFISTS WOULD NOT LIKE the title. After Columbine, the gun metaphor rings violent, especially if the implied subjects in front of the camera are humans. Feminists would likely join the pacifists if the assumed shooter-photographer were leeringly male, and the one upon whom the predatory photographic gaze rested were delectably female. And the post-colonialists would undoubtedly join these other two groups if those shot were objectified, or patronized by either the shooting or the viewing of the shooting.

One would think that a ritual-studies scholar could find a more venerable subject, such as ritual and the sacred, ritual and political power, ritual and racism, or ritual and cognitive psychology. I thought I had cornered a wonderfully obscure topic until someone called my attention to the popular TV series, *Six Feet Under*. Its funerary voyeurism creates a cultural climate in which rites shot are *au courant*.

Rites are eminently photogenic. After tall mountains, bright flowers, and towering skyscrapers, what else attracts as much photographic attention as a wedding replete with flowing costume and energetic dance? Or an initiation stained with blood and climaxed with hugs and tears? Pilgrims and explorers have long lugged home souvenirs testifying to their presence at exotic scenes in foreign places — what better way to package a culture for export than shooting people's ceremonies and celebrations?

Lots of people shoot rites. Tourists shoot them, hoping to import the local color (duty free, of course). Family members shoot rites of passage, pickling collective memories in order to preserve a sense of belonging. Ethnographers shoot rites in order to salvage indigenous practices before they are gobbled up in the maw of globalization. Documentary makers shoot rites to entertain television audiences (and perhaps, accidentally, educate them). Feature-film makers sometimes shoot rites, usually as framing for more dramatic, non-ritualistic actions. Journalists shoot rites too, but only on occasions when they serve as backdrop for local social dramas or global political events. Religious broadcasters shoot worship, song, and other ritual activities in order to make converts of outsiders, extend sacred space into domestic space, and provide a visible product in return for donations. Even worship leaders and liturgy professors occasionally shoot rites as ways of teaching or evaluating liturgical skills.

But what does shooting rites do? What does it do to the rites shot, the people who shoot them, and those who enact them?

Shooting Documents

To shoot a rite is to render it an object of study. During my first field research in 1973, I took pictures. For one thing, tourists did that, and a camera helped me blend into the crowd. For another, anthropologists were supposed to record what they observed, and I was a religious-studies scholar being adopted, under Victor Turner's tutelage, into the anthropologists' clan. So I shot the Masses, pageants, and parades of the Santa Fe Fiesta as a form of quick, visual note-taking. The Fiesta was an annual, complex, multi-location event crammed tightly into a few autumn days. I shot its rites and performances because I did not have time to observe them carefully. Shooting was a kind of shorthand, as well as a substitute for really seeing.

Unlike texts and paintings, pageants and ceremonies do not sit still. They are not quite "there." Like all performing arts, ritual enactments evaporate in the doing. So shooting is a way of making them hold still so one can analyze them—turn them this way and that. Shooting freezes action, helping a scholar notice details after the action dies down.

But my Fiesta slides, the visual documents created when I first began to study ritual, soon gathered dust, only a few of them making their way into a book. In the book the function of those photos was to testify that I had been there, taken it all down, and completed the anthropological rite of passage called fieldwork. The photos, ensconced in *Symbol and Conquest*,[1] a proper book, were sucked into the service of what was considered real, which is to say textual, scholarship. The pictures, never really valued in themselves, were put to work procuring tenure. So, in the end they were worth the investment in camera and film, although I never really studied those slides as people would today if they were serious about visual anthropology and material culture.

Shooting Reveals

In the early 1990s, almost twenty years after I studied ritual and drama in the Santa Fe Fiesta, a film maker named Jenny DeBouzek went to New Mexico to make a video based on *Symbol and Conquest*. Her video, *Gathering up Again: Fiesta in Santa Fe*,[2] captures a crucial behind-the-scenes event. The story it tells is this:

Randy, a Pueblo Indian, lives in Los Angeles. One summer he returns to New Mexico, and one of his Hispanic friends invites him to play Chief Domingo in a traditional pageant that celebrates … well, that is the question. If one believes local Pueblo people, it celebrates the conquest of Indians by Spanish conquistadors; if one believes certain bishops and clergy in Santa Fe, it celebrates the conquest of war itself by men of good will, regardless of race, color, or creed.

Since Randy now lives in California rather than in one of the New Mexico pueblos, he does not realize that most Pueblo people have been quietly boycotting the Fiesta pageant, that no Indian has played Chief Domingo for several decades.

It is the day of the *Entrada* pageant, the ideological heart of the Fiesta, and, it seems, there has not been a full dress rehearsal. Randy arrives, greets his buddies, sees their ragtag, stereotypical "Indian" costumes, puts up with their mock threats about making "Indian" jokes, and prepares to perform. Then we watch as the meaning of the play and his part in it begins to dawn on him. He is humiliated and embarrassed. The camera notices him offstage crying. At one point it seems that an organizer actually has to push him onstage to finish playing his demeaning part. Interviewed after the pageant, Randy admits that if he had known what was going on, he probably would not have participated at all.

Gathering up Again threatened the local sensibility in a way that *Symbol and Conquest*, a mere book, could not. The video did not merely refer to religious and inter-ethnic difficulties, it re-enacted them, making them present. The video had the capability of renewing the event over and over again. Before our very eyes we watch Randy awaken, his Spanish and Indian cohorts feel shame, and the pageant begin to unravel. The real drama is not onstage but backstage. We not only witness Randy's humiliation but also hear an utterance that one does not hear in Santa Fe: "I was ashamed of being Spanish."

When the state school board began to consider distributing the video to public schools, there was an enormous political outcry in Santa Fe, so much so that the director felt she had to move to another city.

Shot rites, by revealing backstage activity, can threaten or transform them, with the result that ethical and political debates are inevitable.

Shooting Validates

Shooting a rite can amount to a declaration: "This event is really important; this is real." Think about weddings. Video documentation and portrait shooting not only disrupt them but also validate them. Norma Joseph, a friend, and a religious studies scholar at Concordia University, once described a scene from a Jewish wedding in Detroit. The videographer was shooting the photographer shooting the wedding party, all of whom were carrying throw-away cameras which had been handed out so everyone could help *capture* the fleeting, "precious moments." The reflexivity, she observed, was three layers deep.

"Capturing" sounds less violent than "shooting." The dancing, marrying human animals in Detroit were not quite shot like game. Shots fired by a videographer are not like bullets that kill, but like tranquilizer darts. They are for our own good, right?

Most rites of passage require witnesses. A fleshy, merely human pair of eyes is a fallible witness, but the eye, amplified through a lens and dramatically followed up by a distinctive click or a telling whir, creates "evidence"; it makes "memories." The act of shooting renders the one who holds the machine godlike, a manufacturer of eternity. Documenting a performance is no longer an act imposed on a rite by an outsider. Rather, it is part of the ceremony itself.

Like Kabuki theater performances, the scenarios of contemporary Japanese weddings are laced with dramatic pauses built into processions so that viewers, including those with cameras, can take in the costumes and postures, the whole scene, without being distracted by the mere busyness of bodily movement. To the Japanese eye the stilled photographic moment is more sacred than the moving cinematic one. The Japanese wedding performance is constructed to facilitate the shooting, and the shooting validates the ritual act.[3]

Of course, it is not only in Japan that photos and videos have come to possess the validating power usually ascribed to marriage licenses and tombstones. Because shooting itself can become ritualized, the co-opting of scholarly visual materials is always a danger.

Shooting Publicizes

Did you watch Princess Diana's funeral? The day of Diana's funeral I was in the Bay, a Montreal department store. There, for all the word to see, was a bag lady surrounded by a circle of big-screen TVs. She was weeping shamelessly.

Not to have shot the ceremony would have deprived royalty of an opportunity to be publicly contemplated; not to have shot the ceremony would have deprived the world of a moment of togetherness. Not to have shot and then disseminated Diana's funeral would have been to cheat that lady and the rest of us of a chance to grieve, and, yes, to gawk. Without the shooting, the funeral rite would have lost most of its public accessibility. Without the shooting we fathers would have lost an opportunity to discuss dying princesses with our daughters.

A Ghanaian graduate student conducting field research on his countrymen's funeral rites in Toronto discovered that they were regularly shot, and that the videos were shipped back to Ghana.[4] Why? Because tradition requires inheritors to participate in funerals, and video participation is one way of discharging that duty across an ocean.

Like Kodak, Microsoft now capitalizes on the fact that even in ritually inept cultures rites of passage must be shared. The "share this folder on the network" command now provided by *Windows XP* enables you to discharge your kinship duties. No sooner do we return from a wedding or funeral, having shot it on a digital camera, than we can share the entire folder with all the distant relatives, and even the entire web-watching world, if we are so inclined. Why? Because shooting validates.

Shooting Mystifies

A shooter looks through a viewfinder, screen, or lens, and by doing so focuses on some things while cutting others out. The power to define which things are out of bounds and which things are central is an enormous, mystifying power.

Since I work more often with artists than with advertisers or scientists, most of the photographers of my acquaintance regard their instruments as aids for contemplation. When they walk the streets or hunt the woods with the intention of shooting, they slow down, attending to the details of things. They contemplate what most of us hurry past. For them, shooting is an act of selection, and selectivity helps them attend to what appears—to attend fully, as one does in meditation practice.

But selectivity and focus cut both ways. They also blind the beholder. Shooting hides countervailing activities and disguises blemishes. With digital editing one can now disguise and manipulate right down to the pixel level. Consequently most of us are unable to tell which things were "really there" and which things are edited in, or out.

Rites, like photos, enable participants to contemplate what is really real, to encounter mystery, but they also mystify. Rites, like photos and film, cloud the sources of authority, shielding them from criticism. Ritualizing, like shooting, is one of the primary ways of constituting authority. Those with ritual and photographic know-how have more authority; those lacking such knowledge have less.

Authority is not only constructed *in* ritual and *by means of* ritual but also *about* ritual. In A&E's *Ancient Mysteries* series on television there was an installment called "Sacred Rites and Rituals."[5] Leonard Nimoy, the narrator, exudes the cool Vulcan rationality that he embodied as Spock on *Star Trek*. He frames rites as examples of exotic violence. In addition, the ritualists have no names. These rites, the script has him say, "challenge logic." Ritualists' actions

are made weird by the process of cinematic decontextualization.

As a person interviewed in the series, with the albatross of attributed expertise around my neck, I was sucked into the vortex along with Nimoy. I was shot into complicity with the script's interpretive strategy, even though I would have dissented vigorously from much that Nimoy said. For the last decade I have been involved, as on-screen "expert" and behind-the-scenes advisor, in the production of films and plays dealing with ritual. My protests notwithstanding, I am presented in television documentaries as knowing everything about rites, ancient and modern, Eastern and Western.

Behind the scenes, my job, as two producers put it, is to keep them honest. Often when I see the results I think I have failed my task. The "honor" of becoming an authority for documentary television is itself a kind of ritual dismemberment. Hours of interview, and pages of notes, research, and advice, are sliced paper thin, becoming salami for fast-food visual consumption, and are then used to warrant producers' and advertisers' values. Producers may listen dutifully, even enthusiastically, but when the interviewing and editing start, almost all the advice is ignored. In the end, the genre—television documentary—falling prey to the prevailing cultural images of ritual, determines the outcome, the presentation that the public watches. The genre and the cultural prejudices exert canonical force.

Almost none of this made-for-TV shooting leaves me proud of the final product. So, inevitably, I follow up the supposedly creative film-making task with a critical, scholarly one. An airing usually necessitates an article—just to protect myself, if nothing else. Being shot into the stratosphere of expertise, one is forced to ask questions that neither theology nor ethnography prepares one to ask: As public intellectuals, are we responsible for the pap that airs in our names? Are we morally obliged to traffic with TV image-makers? Should we not lock ourselves instead into ivory towers and write responsible books?

Shooting Constructs

The *Harlem Book of the Dead* is a beautiful, disturbing volume.[6] From the 1920s through the 1960s the funerary photographer James Van Der Zee shot the Harlem dead. Photographing them was both a sign of respect and a way of engendering hope. When it became technologically possible to superimpose images of Jesus on a coffin lid, or a band of angels above a corpse, for the bereaved found it easier to embrace the evangelical opportunities lurking around death.

The one photo from the *Harlem Book of the Dead* that stops me in my tracks is of a mother, a father (smiling, no less), and a child sitting for a family photo. Nothing unusual is going on, except that . . . the child is dead.

Toni Morrison says of Van Der Zee's photos, and of this tradition of mortuary photography, "How living are his portraits of the dead."[7] The right photograph not only memorialized the deceased, created an ancestor, and preached a sermon, but it also painted an icon, an aperitif of the resurrection. Shooting was a way of constructing sanctity.

Of course, only a little reflection is necessary to recognize that the eternity afforded by shooting devices is a little less enduring than that promised Muslim and Christian faithful. Photos, after all, fade. Even CDs and DVDs, across time, deteriorate. The "never" in the claim, "The image and sound quality of DVD never decline with age," is like the "never" in "I'll never get pregnant," or "We will never attack another country first." It is a pious aspiration, not a fact.

When my children were younger I would interview them on video, hoping to discover what was behaviorally sacred to them. I would ask, "If the house were on fire and you had time to grab only one thing before running out,

what would it be?" One afternoon they turned the tables, asking me what I would snatch. I heard myself answer, "The video tapes of your birthdays, holidays, trips, and these interviews." The kids are older and interviews are harder to extract now, but the family watches these videos over and over again. Ritually, each new round of sibling wrangling, each little bit of kid metaphysics, is met with hoots, laughter, and "Here it comes, the part where . . ." One does not have to be a ritual-studies scholar to understand why the family Bible or the collection of crucifixes would be left to burn while the family photos would not. Even flawed family shooting rites produce icons, constructions that embody the ultimacies to which they point.

Shooting Dramatizes

The anthropologist Victor Turner taught a generation of anthropologists that ritual is nothing if not dramatic.[8] He made this claim not as an observation of a fact but as a matter of definition and theory. Many scholars continue to echo his assumption. I no longer share it. Although ritual and drama may be first cousins, and rites are photogenic, we are not well served by the assumption that rites are *necessarily* dramatic. Many rites are sedentary, repetitive, and boring—marked by a rhythm quite unlike the climactic actions that the Euroamerican West expects of drama. Try to make a film of a rite and you will often discover how undramatic ritual can be.

But never mind. By shooting it, one can make it dramatic. If the drama is not there in the actions of participants committing acts liturgical, you can, if you are adept with cinematic tools, put some drama there. You know—the way Ken Burns makes moving documentaries about the Civil War, baseball, jazz, and New York City, by constantly panning across or zooming into manuscripts and relics. Never mind that the historic actors are dead, or that the objects were never living—the camera and narrator are alive. By their shooting and zooming and talking they can dramatize the inert into the lively and engaging.

Of all the shooters of ritual, Leni Riefenstahl, unfortunately, was one of the most talented. She died recently in her nineties. Utilizing thirty cameras and one-hundred-twenty assistants, and pioneering documentary innovations that are remarkable even today, Riefenstahl, in *Triumph of the Will*, dramatized the 1934 Nuremberg Party Congress into a national coming-out ceremony.[9] Then in 1938, in the *Olympiad,* she transformed the 1936 Olympics into Greco-Germanic religion.[10] *Triumph of the Will* and *Olympiad* are masterpieces, studied not only by that rare obscurantist bird, the shooting-ritual scholar, but by documentary makers everywhere. The loop of ritualizing and dramatizing is so effective that each genre of action feeds the other. Consequently, the films continue to exert canonical force on their viewers, even those who dissent from Riefenstahl's ethics and politics.[11]

Shooting Violates

Tourist photos seem innocent enough until you are pulled up short, instructed by indignant locals that not all rites are fair game. Shooting a rite can disrupt it, or, if sustained, even transform it. Shooting rites causes trouble in situations where rites are held holy and cameras profane. You can understand the consternation of the locals. If *your* grandmother's funeral were disrupted by a bunch of handycam-carrying strangers, the expanding and contracting phallic lenses of their electronic gadgets trained upon *your* grieving uncle, profanation would seem to be the only possible outcome. Even scholars, dedicated to analysis, would protest the photographic rape of a memorial service.

Feminist scholars have launched the most thorough critiques of "the gaze" with its voyeuristic, objectivizing, violating possibilities.[12] On some occasions, shooting amounts to what

in the Spanish Southwest was called a "rite of reduction," an enactment formally imposing a hierarchy of clearly demarcated subordinate and superordinate positions.

Like women, indigenous people have become wary of the camera, since it has too often served as an instrument not only of sexism but also of racist colonialism. Late nineteenth century photographic projects like those of Edward R. Curtis not only rendered Indians iconic, but also functioned as a form of trophy-taking, the white man's peculiar form of head-hunting.[13] Shooting was a means of packaging the booty of conquest so it could be traded back East (you know, in New Haven and Cambridge). As a consequence of photographic and cinematic intrusion, many native groups now consider shooting an intercultural rip-off, so they forbid it during their ceremonies, or else make camera-toting white folks pay dearly for the privilege.

Shooting (Dis)embodies

What shooting seizes upon is bodilyness, and if ritual studies is about anything, it is about embodiment in social contexts. The study of ritual is not primarily the study of ideas in people's heads or feelings in their hearts; it is about meanings embodied in posturing and gesturing. Video, or film, is a methodological key to studying postures and gestures. Shooting the surfaces of things, bodies included, has analytical and not merely expressive or entertainment value. I will not labor the point since I have made it so repeatedly in the past.

Another side to photography's peculiar way of embodying exists. A while back my wife and I were studying Spanish, and boarding in a local home in Salamanca, Spain. One afternoon we noticed on the mantle several pictures of people, their mouths wide open. Something—we did not know what—was being deposited on their tongues. Later, when we inquired, we were instructed in a mixture of Spanish and English, "*Pan,*" they said, then, "*sagrado, sagrada*

…" They were trying to teach us the language we'd come to learn. Eventually, we pieced the meaning together. They were talking about bread, holy bread. Communicants had been photographically frozen in the act of consuming a communion wafer. Like a bloody sheet at a Moroccan wedding,[14] the framed photo was proof that the definitive act had been truly committed. Friends and relatives relished such photos. We saw them everywhere, so Spanish clergy had to have been complicit with the practice.

Such scenes give one pause. Many of the reigning theories of ritual, religion, and liturgy ill equip us to deal with such practices. The first impulse of many who study religious rites is to object to shooting rites; doing so is either in bad taste or a violation of sanctity. If we ask ourselves what reputable liturgical theologians might say about the act of shooting a host as it greets the tongue, the answer is not difficult to imagine.[15] What could be less dignified, or more crassly literalistic, than bared teeth and salivating tongues? The Spanish photos could be used in seminary liturgy courses as illustrations of the evils of popular religion and photographic imperialism. Why? Because shooting disembodies in the very moment that it creates a tactile or visual surface that the senses can grasp.

Shooting Complicates

The shooting mind can be a deeply contemplative one, but the shooting consciousness—that of the photojournalist, the film editor, the theater director, the camera operator—can also be a profoundly suspended, if not disbelieving, one.

Theologians and liturgists sometimes complain that the detachment attendant to the act of shooting is a prophylactic to faith. Several years ago I was shooting the Toronto Towneley Cycle of mystery plays. It was raining, and most of the audience, not up to the ordeal of redemptive suffering, had gone home for supper. A bedraggled, college-age Jesus was lugging a cross down the *via crucis*, which is to say, across the quadrangle of Victoria College. A few dogged photojournalists were still weathering the scene, so cameras were trained on the bedraggled savior. A photographer in a yellow poncho boldly approached the dripping Jesus on his way to Golgotha, which is to say, toward Bloor Street. The photographer drew surprisingly close to Jesus' face. A few non-journalists gasped. The shooter snapped a shot. Then, suddenly, he fell to one knee and began to weep as he clapped his hand over his mouth. At that moment I, having stepped back rather than in, shot him.

What is one to conclude from the photojournalist's actions? Certainly not that shooting obviates the possibility of faith. And certainly not that being deeply moved requires one to believe. Just as Huichol shamans can swallow hundreds of peyote buttons and still organize pilgrimages and know where baskets and bows should be placed, so one can simultaneously shoot and revere. Just as Hopi children learn to hold simultaneously the knowledge that kachinas are spirits as well as their relatives dressed up in masks and costumes, so one can ritualize in a fictive, or even ironic, mode. Clearly it is possible, simultaneously, to shoot and to revere, to embrace fictionality and to have faith. The only caveat is that you have to practice.

The social complexity of a feature film can be staggering. *Titanic*, for example, lists fourteen hundred names in its credits; the number of hands stirring the batter was enormous. Socially, cinema is the most complex of contemporary artistic acts. If for no other reason than this social complexity, cinematic art remains largely intractable to the few religious-studies scholars and theologians who try to analyze it. What I enjoy about field research and visual documentation is how they challenge assumptions about ritual and demand more nuanced theories of it.

Conceptually, the relationship between shooting and rites is not as simple as it may seem. We cannot, for example, merely equate the profane with what a culture shoots, or the sacred with what it will not shoot. Nor can we unequivocally claim, for instance, that shooting desecrates funerals but sanctifies weddings. The conceptual conundrum faced by students of ritual is not merely the result of machines, of digital cameras and such, but also of faulty theorizing. With only one or two exceptions, theories of ritual have not attended very fully to the seam between the subjunctive and the declarative, between fictive and ordinary reality. Too easily we have accepted a polarized cluster: on the one hand, we clump ritual with the sacred, believing, and not-acting; on the other, we cluster the profane, performance, acting, and shooting. But the fence that generates this easy methodological dualism is, in practice, breached coming and going, from both directions. Since both insiders and outsiders now have cameras, since ethnographic outsiders now participate, and since participating insiders quickly learn how to observe, the conceptual Berlin wall between ritualizing and dramatizing, two utterly constitutive kinds of human interaction, is crumbling.[16]

Even in contemporary Christianity, where the relationship between ritual and theater is fairly non-integral, the boundaries can bleed. The film *The Apostle* has two important behind-the-scenes out-takes.[17] In both of them we see how the insider/outsider, actor/non-actor boundary is breached. Not only are real preachers and a real congregation involved, but an actor and a technician, both members of the director Robert Duvall's crew, are caught undergoing conversion experiences during the making of the film. Duvall not only has to direct and act the part of Sonny, who is leaving his fictive congregation; he also has to negotiate with church members to keep the real congregation from dividing over the issue of being shot by "Hollywood." They worry that

"Hollywood" will reduce them to caricatures. Meanwhile, real pastors must not only preach and court the spirit, they must perform their preaching and spirit-courting for the cameras. So everyone, it seems, is crossing and re-crossing the seam between fictionality and ultimacy. Whereas Duvall, the director-actor, has to perform toward believing, the evangelists believe toward performing. In the last analysis perhaps the difference makes less difference than our theoretical postures would have led us to believe.

Whither?

I have now created a conceptual tangle. I have uttered a mouthful. However, one could write it as a single sentence: Shooting documents, reveals, validates, publicizes, mystifies, constructs, dramatizes, violates, (dis)embodies, and complicates. The sentence is probably a little dizzying, and this romp through shooting contexts may be too much like a roller coaster ride. But conducting field research and working among performing and media artists is like that, so if you feel disoriented, you have done a good job of stepping inside the zone that I sometimes inhabit as a field researcher and consultant. As if rites, by themselves, were not confounding enough, I have multiplied the complexity by considering rites as objects and contexts of photographic and cinematic activity. But to what end? With what implications?

I conclude with suggestions and provocations—the beginning, not the conclusion, of a conversation or debate:

1. Shooting, and all that it has come to represent here, is not going away. Not only religious rites, but virtually everything on the planet, has, or will have, a recording device pointed at it, for good and for ill.

2. As scholars and teachers we should learn to think and act not only *in* or *with* media and art but also *between* the media and *among* the arts.

3. This between-space is infested with a

thick knot of issues not neatly separable into ethics and aesthetics, economics and religion, or any of the other neat polarizations that usually give us comfort.

4. Because a neatly sectored model of culture is no longer viable, neither are curriculum models that over-value departmentalization.

5. Because shooting now regularly appears on both sides of the line that once separated practitioners and researchers, the models for research must necessarily be collaborative and interdisciplinary.

6. The false split between those who perform or participate, on the one hand, and those who think or theorize, on the other, is a major deterrent to good scholarship.

7. So let it be said: Scholars, rise up and seize the means of production. Forget television and shoot for the classroom. Learn to shoot and edit as you once, in the far-distant past, learned to use word-processors. As Martin Luther surely ought to have said, "Shoot bravely."

ENDNOTES

1. Ronald L. Grimes, *Symbol and Conquest: Public Ritual and Drama in Santa Fe, New Mexico* (Ithaca, N.Y.: Cornell University Press, 1976).

2. *Gathering up Again: Fiesta in Santa Fe*, directed by Jeanette DeBouzek and Diane Reyna. VHS. (Documentary, 1992).

3. See Walter Edwards, *Modern Japan Though Its Weddings: Gender, Person, and Society in Ritual Portrayal* (Stanford, Calif.: Stanford University Press, 1989).

4. Reported by Paul Adjin-Tetty.

5. See Ronald L. Grimes, "Consuming Ritual: A&E's *Sacred Rites and Rituals*," in *Contemporary Consumption Rituals: A Research Anthology*, ed. Cele Otnes et al. (Mahwah, N.J.: Lawrence Erlbaum, 2004).

6. James Van Der Zee et al., *The Harlem Book of the Dead* (Dobbs Ferry, N.Y.: Morgan & Morgan, 1978).

7. In the foreword of *The Harlem Book of the Dead*.

8. See *Dramas, Fields and Metaphors: Symbolic Action in Human Society* (Ithaca, N.Y.: Cornell University Press, 1974).

9. *Triumph of the Will*, dir. by Leni Riefenstahl (Documentary/propaganda, 1935).

10. *Olympiad Part 2: Festival of Beauty*, dir. by Leni Riefenstahl. (Documentary-art, 1938).

11. For an exploration of Riefenstahl's films and their behind-the-scenes dynamics, see *The Wonderful, Horrible Life of Leni Riefenstahl*, dir by Ray Muller. Documentary (New York, 1993).

12. See Marita Sturken and Lisa Cartwright, *Practices of Looking: An Introduction to Visual Culture* (Oxford: Oxford University Press, 2001).

13. Lucy R. Lippard, ed., *Partial Recall* (New York: New Press, 1992).

14. M. E. Combs-Schilling, *Sacred Performances: Islam, Sexuality, Sacrifice* (New York: Columbia University Press, 1989).

15. Since this lecture is named in his honor, one might, for example, try to imagine Aidan Kavanagh's response to such photos. See his *Elements of Rite: A Handbook of Liturgical Style* (New York: Pueblo, 1982).

16. See Ronald L Grimes, "Ritual and Performance," in *Encyclopedia of Religion and American Cultures*, ed. Gary Laderman et al. (Santa Barbara, Calif.: ABC Clio, 2003).

17. See chapters 2 and 4 in the "bonus materials" section called "The Journey of *The Apostle*" in *The Apostle*, dir. by Robert Duvall (Feature film, 1998).

RECOMMENDED READING

Banks, Marcus. "Representing the Bodies of the Jains," in *Rethinking Visual Anthropology*, ed. Howard Morphy et al. New Haven: Yale University Press, 1997.

Brown, Justine. *Hollywood Utopia*. Vancouver: New Star, 2002.

Martin, Joel W. "Redeeming America: *Rocky* as Ritual Racial Drama." in *Screening the Sacred: Religion, Myth, and Ideology in Popular American Film*, ed. Joel W. Martin et al., 125-33. Boulder: Westview Press, 1995.

Morgan, David, and Sally M. Promey, eds. *The Visual Culture of American Religions.* Berkeley: University of California Press, 1971.

Plate, S. Brent, ed. *Religion, Art, and Visual Culture: A Cross Cultural Reader.* New York: Palgrave, 2002.

Sekula, Allan. "On the Invention of Photographic Meaning," in *Thinking Photography*, edited by Victor Burgin, 84-109. London: Macmillan Education, 1987.

Ron Grimes is Professor of Religion and Culture at Wilfrid Laurier University in Waterloo, Canada, and holder of the Chair of Ritual Studies at Radboud University, Nijmegen (the Netherlands). One of the founding editors of the Journal of Ritual Studies, *he is the author of several books, including* Deeply into the Bone: Re-Inventing Rites of Passage *(University of California Press),* Readings in Ritual Studies *(Prentice Hall), and* Rite Out of Place: Ritual, Media, and the Arts *(forthcoming, spring 2006, Oxford University Press).*

The Concert Hall That Fell Asleep and Woke Up as a Car Radio

LIBBY LARSEN

I'VE BEEN LOOKING FORWARD TO WORKING with you today as I've been researching the topic of the concert hall in the United States of America. I knew I was going to give this talk, and I've taken the better part of four months working at the Library of Congress so that we could talk about some issues that I think affect all of us who have devoted part of our lives to communicating, communicating through musical language or communicating through the philosophical and spiritual epigrams of the day. All of us in this room are interested in communicating something of our spirit to the world in which we live. My particular interest is in communicating what it is like to be alive through the language of music, and to that end I have been a composer since I was about four years old. I want to tell you a little about myself so that you will know where I am coming from — I am going to talk about some things that I don't think we have talked about very often in the study of music in our culture.

People are just beginning to understand some of the implications of what it is like to live on such a large landmass, which we call the United States of America, with such a diverse population, which we insist on calling one. We are beginning to understand the implications of living on this large landmass, east to west, north to south: we wake up in the morning saying "Good morning, America," we say "America thinks this" and "America is that." My perspective is that of a composer who writes abstract music, sometimes with words, often without words, who makes an order of sound in time and space. My particular intent is to communicate something of what it is like to be alive in America — order, sound, time, space — to communicate something of what it is like to be alive in real time in our world.

Over the years I have studied many instruments. My principle instrument is piano; I took two years of voice, bel canto style voice; I sang in a rock band; I play harmonica. My seventh grade teacher, Sister Telupia, decided that the way she would discipline our class was that we would all have to own a Marine Band C Harmonica. We would keep them in our desks, and whenever we got a little out of control she would say "It's harmonica time" — an extraordinary teaching device — and we would get out our harmonicas. She taught us how to play harmonica, and we put on shows for our school in Minneapolis, Minnesota, playing harmonica and singing Irish songs. So I play harmonica. I also play electric bass, which I taught myself about seven years ago. I decided that I wanted to learn electric bass, so I bought all the Beatles' albums, got an electric bass, and played along with the Beatles from their earliest album to their latest album. You really can learn how to play bass that way.

I have a particular belief that colors everything that I would like to talk with you about today: cultures evolve the instruments and ensembles they need. Cultures evolve instruments and ensembles in order to study themselves through music in real time. That is my belief, and that is why I think I can stand up here and talk about "the concert hall that fell asleep and woke up as a car radio." I started thinking about the question of the concert hall when I was working on my doctorate at the University of Minnesota in the late 1970s. At that time I did a self-study because I was faced with the question: now that I have my doctorate, what next? Since I had been schooled in all the academic languages, and the formal rigor of a classical music education, I was asking myself, What have I got to say, and to whom can I say it, and who will listen to what I have to say?

I was faced with the quandary that I think is still central to all music education students. When I entered the University of Minnesota as a freshman I entered with an enormous repertoire of music. My repertoire included all of the Gregorian chants that I had sung for eight years in grade school, all of the rock and roll I had learned in high school, television jingles, all the music my parents had played on our record player (it was a record player then) at home—the big bands my mother loved, piano music my mother loved, Dixieland my father loved—I don't know why but we always had Shostakovich and Prokofiev in that stack. But my repertoire had a big hole in it, the classical canon that we study when we begin to study formally and academically. I spent nine years of my life, from freshman year of college through the end of my doctoral work, learning the canon.

When I received my doctorate it seemed that I had two choices, to take a faculty position at a university or college, or to see how I could use my skills to communicate something of what it was like to be alive in the concert halls existing then outside the academy. That would be orchestras and opera companies. (In 1978 we did not have a healthy chamber music ecology in the country, though we had a very healthy choir ecology, as we still do.) I noticed that living composers were not part of the concert world outside of the academy, and I decided that what I wanted to do was to work in the concert world as a living American composer trying to create pieces that spoke through that tradition, the tradition of the orchestra, the tradition of the opera company, the tradition of what was becoming the chamber music business, and certainly through the choral tradition. That's what I decided to do.

I wondered what I could write about, and I decided that I could write only about what I knew in a language that was technically educated but instinctually informed. I began to write pieces right away for the Minnesota Orchestra

and the Minnesota Opera. I would go in there and say, "Can I write you an opera?" (I was very young.) The answer always came back, "Yes," which was not unusual. That is actually part of the Midwestern ethic—you don't have to go through sixteen people to get to the conductor. In the Midwest you just call up the conductor and say, "I'd like to write a symphony. Can I write a symphony?" and the conductor will tell you yes or no. It's the Midwestern directness.

And so I began working with orchestras immediately. My first commission was from the Minnesota Orchestra to write a piece for their young people's concert. I was still working on my doctorate at that time. My second commission was from Garrison Keeler, and it was to write a piece for the Powder Milk Biscuit Band and the St. Paul Chamber Orchestra. Yeah! I wrote a concerto grosso. (I also wrote several country western songs under an assumed name.) This took me into the orchestral world, and in 1983 I became one of two composers-in-residence along with my great friend Steve Paulus. The two of us took on the job of composer-in-residence with the Minnesota Orchestra where we worked with Neville Marriner from 1983-1987. I have never worked with anyone who had more genius in the recording studio than Neville Marriner. He is also a cultural anthropologist. Not many people know that about him. To work with Neville Marriner you had to be able to smoke Swisher Sweets and drink champagne at any hour of the day, and you had to be able to pub (a verb, "to pub"). What that meant was that after concerts we would go to a local bar, order a bottle of wine for whoever was there, drink the wine, and play corks. Has anybody ever played corks? Its wonderful. You bounce the cork and see if you can get it to stand on its end. We could while away hours trying to get it to do that! Neville Marriner actually wasn't too good at corks. Steve Paulus was the best, but I wasn't bad.

In the bar we would talk about music, and Neville Marriner asked every single time, "Where are the young people in the audience for my concerts?" He would say, "Libby, Steve, I want you to find out where are the young people." I have been thinking about that ever since. I asked him, "OK, you ask me where the young people are. I'm asking you, Neville, where are my colleagues in your programming repertoire. I don't see my colleagues with any kind of regularity in your programming for the orchestra." We also asked, many, many times, "What is classical music in America?" I've been thinking about those three questions ever since. Where are the young people? Where are my colleagues? What is classical music in America?

Two more things happened. Right after I finished being composer-in-residence with the orchestra I joined the American Symphony and Orchestra board of directors. That is the oversight organization for all of the orchestras in the country, and in their wisdom they usually have two or three composers on the board of directors; it is a very interesting position. I began to understand "what is classical music in America." I began to understand where my colleagues were, which was not there, not in the orchestras. And I took part in a study (that I actually helped to engineer) with the symphony orchestra, a self-study, so that they could begin to answer "what is classical music in America?"

We assembled a very small group: Pauline Oliveros, Charles Wuorinen, Leonard Slatkin, Don Toleen (from the American Symphony Orchestra League), and me. We talked about all of the issues, except for Pauline, who is wont to be very quiet at meetings. She tends to be very quiet, very serene, and when she says something it is the only thing that needs to be said for the entire meeting. When she was ready to speak we all quieted down, and she said, "Well, there's only one thing that matters these days," and we were all, well, you know, "What could it be?" And she said, "Sound." That's it. That's all she said. And do you know, she was absolutely right. That was all that needed to be said at that meeting.

Here is why. There has been a revolution in sound. It's happened over the past one hundred fourteen years or so. It's happened thoroughly. It's happened worldwide, and it's the biggest thing to happen to music in two thousand years. Sound, the revolution in sound. She said "sound," and I said to myself, "And the classical music world hasn't got a clue about it, about what it means." The quality of sound has changed radically, ultra-radically, supernova-radically, in the past one hundred fourteen years or so, and it effects how we think of ourselves as classical musicians, how we think about classical music in the world in which we live, and it is terribly complicated. So I began to think about sound, where are the young people, where are my colleagues, what's going on here?

Two years ago I wrote an opera about P. T. Barnum's tour of Jenny Lind in America. I wrote the opera because I wanted to study the intersection between art and entertainment. I decided to blame the confusion between art and entertainment on P. T. Barnum, who was a marketing genius. He really was the first person in our culture to articulate that you could sell something to the mass of people. Barnum was the guy who defined the market place as an undefined mass of people and began to practice selling to the masses. We still use his model today. He's the person who thought up celebrity licensing, and he did it with Jenny Lind.

Jenny Lind was the biggest thing going in Europe at the time, but nobody in America knew who she was. And so he decided that he needed to sell her if he was going to recover his money from the tour. He licensed her name to everything—pin cushions, carriages, furniture, tongue depressors, anything he could think of. So well did he sell her name (without telling her, by the way) that he made seven times the amount of money from the tour that she did. He set up a model, a paradigm, for marketing art as entertainment.

At that same time I read a study by the McKnight Foundation, a study of arts in the suburbs (someone said today that that's an oxymoron). They asked who lives in the suburbs, how do they get there, do they appreciate the arts, what kinds of arts do they appreciate? One of the things they found out is that there is a great deal of artistic activity in the suburbs, and that, interestingly enough, a suburbanite's transportation habit gives that person thirteen car trips a day. A day! Those thirteen car trips do not follow the old model, to the center of the city, like the spokes in a wheel. Those thirteen car trips go in concentric circles, from suburb to suburb, and not to the center of the city.

What the McKnight Foundation is suggesting is that when we are trying to bring people into our concert halls we are really trying to lure them back into their cars for their fourteenth trip, at night or on a Sunday morning, to come to a centralized ritual hall, whether a concert hall, a large church, or an auditorium. The model of a centralized ritual place, and people who live around it and come to the ritual place for their ritual, is disintegrating if not already disintegrated. In fact the transportation habits of a culture are evolved by the culture as needed.

And so I thought, OK, I'm going to study transportation and classical music because I think the two of them are inextricably intertwined. I am going to spend my time, while I have all the resources at the Library of Congress, researching this to see whether it is true and what it means to my colleagues, to those of us who bring large groups of people together in congregations, whether to listen to music or for worship. If cultures evolve transportation habits and patterns in the ways that they need to, then those of us who spend our lives in congregational activities need to understand that, and realign the way we deliver our — I don't want to call it product, because it certainly is not a product — the way we speak to them.

And so I set off. I began to wonder if more people listen to music in cars or on personal sound systems than in concert halls. I began to wonder if we have enough places in our culture to practice abstract listening alone. Where can we practice just listening to music in our culture? I began to wonder if the concert itself can be looked at not as a single event but as a multi-venued modular experience. In fact, we may be talking about a whole different definition of concert. Let's say you are interested in a piece of music, or in a reading, or in a sermon. You could listen to the King's Singers live in an acoustically perfect hall, which is really just a big speaker you sit inside of. Then you could get into your car and put their CD in your sound system. That car is a wrap-around concert hall which gives you the best seat in the house. Is the car then part of a multi-venued concert experience? You could then listen to the King's Singers broadcast through the sound system of public radio, which can be a very different sound depending on who is on the mixing board and what their preference is for the mix of sound. Is it possible that we are now evolving a culture that allows us to listen to a single event in a multi-venued modular way? I think that the answer is yes.

I began to wonder if the definition of classical music has morphed, meaning that classical music now is more the sound of certain instruments than a particular repertoire. I wondered about it so much that I decided to put it to the test at Interlochen last summer. I was a composer-in-residence for a week, and I took myself over to the local public radio station and had lunch with Tom Paulson, who is their program director. I said, "What's classical music, Tom? What is your definition of classical music?" He really couldn't give me a definition. I said, "Well, is it Mozart?" and he said, "Yes." I said, "Is it Beethoven?" and he said "Yes." I said, "Is it Samuel Barber?" and he said "I don't know." I said, "Is it the Beatles?" and he said "That's not classical music, although the Beatles are classic."

There you have it. Now we have a teaching point. A point of learning. So I said, "May I ask you an experimental question?" and he said "Sure, go ahead." So I said, "OK, you have a programming slot, you have the Beatles performing 'Yesterday,' and you also have the Canadian Brass performing 'Yesterday.' Which do you play?" And without batting an eye he said "The Canadian Brass." And I said, "So you wouldn't program the Beatles playing their own music?" and he said, "No, I wouldn't, and I couldn't." So I said, "Why can you program the Canadian Brass and not the Beatles?" and he said "Because the Canadian brass are classical players." And I wanted to jump up on the table and say "See, I told you I told you!" But I didn't. I said, "Is it possible that the definition of classical music is changing from repertoire-based to sound-and-instrument based?" and he said, "Well, it could be possible." People like Glen Branca and Steve Mackie, who work with electric instruments, are not programmed on public radio because theirs is not classical music even though it is entirely classical in how the music is formed, and the thinking behind the notating, and the counterpoint, and the form, and the structure. It's the sound of the instruments. There are no electric instruments in classical music.

I also began to wonder if the development of electricity and portable sound over the past eighty years might signal the eclipse of a larger musical period and the beginning of another music period. Might we consider rethinking what we call the classical, and the romantic, and the early modern period of music? Might we take the classical, and the romantic, and the first thirty years of the 1900s, and think about that as an era in music, as a period in itself? It might make sense if we did. I began to think that maybe we are in a fudge period of time, between eras. There are always fudge periods between eras, when it seems to me that five things happen. The first of these things is that the instruments begin to change. Old ones are adapted and new ones are invented. Then the ensembles and the makeup of the ensembles change to reflect the sounds of the instruments combined. Then music changes, bringing secondary and tertiary parameters to the

foreground, and eclipsing parameters that have dominated the music of the previous period. Time signatures, key signatures, the dominants of beat, stress patterns, are eclipsed, and new parameters begin to take the foreground, timbre, flow, pulse. The notation system adapts to reflect the new instruments, the adapted old ones, and the evolving musical language. (We are also in the middle of a sea change in our notation system. I think that we are at the beginning of a tsunami, and that's digital notation. It may be that we will come to a point where digital notation replaces the Guidonian hand system. It may look like the Guidonian hand system, but if you are notating on a computer you are not notating the Guidonian hand system, you are notating a digital notation. It is translating what you are doing. And its actually quite rudimentary. So don't be fooled that you are actually notating for yourself when you are punching notation into a computer. It's not precise.)

Fifth and last, and this is what is essential to the rest of the talk, the performing venues change, and with them the essential and intensely private relationship of the listener to the music itself. It seems to me that in our efforts to feel one in our country we've given ourselves quite a dilemma, and that is, how do we feel one through music? How can I feel that I can communicate with you in a microsecond? We try to find ways for our culture to help us to feel one. We have franchise hotels, we've invented transportation systems, we have Burger Kings and McDonalds. Trying to feel our unity, trying to pull together as one, is actually beginning to cause severe cultural problems in the rest of the world as we translate our need to become one into other cultures that don't need our brand of oneness. It's posing some interesting problems.

To study waves of transportation I divided up the years from about 1750 to about 1956 into four major periods, and I went to the map division at the Library of Congress. (I had no idea how much fun maps are. Have you spent time with maps? Maps are emotional, they're just amazing!) I needed to find maps that gave me transportation and communication patterns. I constructed four time periods, and chose colored dots to represent the kinds of concert halls, performance venues, and gathering halls that were put in place during those time periods. The first map was drawn up in 1883. That was the year that the railroads gave us standardized time. Before 1883 we did not have the time zones that we have now; we had fifty different time zones in the United States, calculated by high noon. Because the railroads had become connected, and they needed to have a schedule, we have standardized times.

The first period that I worked on was the period 1750 to 1869 using that particular map. Working with a couple of assistants I researched the performance halls in America and we put red dots wherever we could find a documented performance hall. There were some red dots along the Ohio River, some in what would become Illinois, a couple up in what would become northern Illinois and Wisconsin. These performance venues were anything from small churches to mining tents, to large tents, to hurdy-gurdy houses—these I had never heard of before; they were dance halls in which you paid to dance with a female. These females were not prostitutes; their job was to dance with you in places where the proportion of male to female was low because these people were going out building the country. From 1750 up until 1869 we saw what the country looked like in terms of congregant spaces. We did not count small churches in each community. The red dots represented discrete gathering places other than churches.

1869 was when the transcontinental railroads were joined in Utah, and people began to be able to transport interesting things—lots of lumber, mud from Arizona, building supplies, people, and big instruments. After 1869 we saw an explosion of spaces. We used green dots to represent 1869-1903. (1903 represents the first

transcontinental car trip.) In areas around Denver, St. Louis, in Illinois, we had about five red dots. Between 1869 and 1903 it's just an explosion.

And then between 1903 and 1926 an explosion of blue dots. What happened to the green dots? They became movie houses. The blue dots represent discrete spaces, spaces that were built for the purposes of music, or theater, or dance, spaces that were built in the way that we build spaces now. The sound was appropriate for music but not for speech. And so we had a refinement in the kinds of halls that we built between 1869 and 1903.

At the end of the 1800s life became very interesting for classical music. Up until 1870 or so classical music in this country was not European. It was American classical music— camp songs, minstrel songs, the singing of psalms. Music began from the voice. After about 1860 a switch began, from voice to instruments. The opening of the conservatory at Leipzig had a tremendous effect on music in the United States. We began to send our potential music teachers not to singing schools but to Leipzig, to learn about music, how to teach it, what to teach. In the United States the music that was to be studied was the music that was brought back from Leipzig, played on those instruments, by the immigrant wave that began to arrive in the 1850s, 60s, and 70s.

At the same time people began to experiment with telegraphy and sound. Morse code was invented in 1844. People began to want to communicate by radio telegraphy. From about 1844 to 1900 was the big period of the formation of what would become radio and television. Gugliemo Marconi is extraordinarily important in what will happen in the next fifty years in classical music and the concert hall in America. He is the fellow who made telegraphy practical. He made radio possible. He made ship-to-ship experiments and ship-to-shore experiments, and he formed the Marconi Company that was one of the first radio companies. And the rest is history.

At this period — the 1890s to 1910 — there was an extraordinary convergence of personalities germane to this talk today. Four people's paths crossed. Marconi was one of them. Then there was Walter Damrosch. He was born in Berlin in 1862, came to the United States, and founded the Oratorio Society of New York, the New York Symphony Society. Damrosch was the conductor of the day. He conducted Bruckner, Tchaikovsky, Berlioz. He was really the first well-known conductor. Then there was Edward Krehbiel. Edward Krehbiel was the foremost arbiter of musical taste of his time. He wrote books about music, how to listen to music, and what to listen for. These two men knew each other. Edward Krehbiel wrote *How to Listen to Music: Hints and Suggestions to Untaught Lovers of the Art* (1897), and in that book he talked about the oratorio, the symphony, the opera, how to listen to a piano concert. He laid out what became the fundamental structure of how we approach music education and the definition of classical music in our country. He talked about choir, but choir was not so important. Whereas choral music had once been the vehicle for studying music it now became less important. He listed the instruments of the orchestra, told us about each instrument, and solidified the structure of the orchestra by saying "This is the symphony orchestra."

Who knows the name Francis Clarke Elliot? I didn't know the name either until I began my research. I stumbled across Francis Clarke Elliot, and I stumbled across the NBC Music Education Program.

These four people began to work not only with each other but with the Marconi Company, which bought out the Victor Company. Now the Victor Company is the fifth participant preparing the concert hall to become a car radio. The Victor Company, which had been developing ways of recording in the late 1890s, began seriously producing discs and records in the early 1900s. 1901 was when they began to record the voice, and they had an entire repertoire of records by 1910. The idea was that they would invent a portable gramophone, that they would sell a bazillion of them, and that people all over the country would be able to have music with them wherever they went. You took your gramophone with you, and you also had to take the music with you. You took music with you because Victor had sold you a set of records, and those records were repertoire, and that repertoire was set by Damrosch and Krehbiel and Elliot and those who were forming what was the basis of a contemporary music education at the time.

Now comes the car. This car is a Winton. In 1903 the first transcontinental car trip was made by Dr. Horatio Nelson Jackson who made a bet of $50 that he could drive from San Francisco to New York. At that time there were only one hundred fifty miles of paved road in the country — everything else was dirt and mud. Dr. Jackson got in his car and made it to New York — it took him a long time. I tried to see if he could take a Gramophone in this car, and he couldn't.

In 1910 Francis Clarke Elliot joined the Victor and Marconi companies, and was developing the Victor Redseal record music curriculum, which was used over the radio until 1943. I went through the Victor Redseal catalog index just to see what I could see, and I saw in the index 1638 separate subject headings. It is comprehensive. There are 704 pages. It is biased toward instrumental, German, French, European, and folk music. Four people in the book are mentioned by last name only, Beethoven, Charlemagne, Napoleon, and Shakespeare. Everybody else gets a first name. I don't know what that means but I think it is kind of interesting.

Then I laboriously went through and listed the number of references given for each of the subject headings. The group with between thirteen and sixty references — forty-two entries, twelve composers, no Americans. So I thought, OK, I'll trudge on and keep counting. Headings mentioned eight to twelve times (remember this was used until 1943)—seventy-two entries, fifteen composers, no Americans. I thought, well, I'm still looking for my colleagues. Subject headings with four to seven references—we are doing better here—six Americans referenced. Edward McDowell had the most references, and that's interesting because we don't hear much McDowell; he's not studied very much now. The rest of the references were mentioned one to three times, and there were a few more Americans.

I did a little checking to see if the way we were studying music was reflected here, and so I looked for jazz. You know that jazz has had a hard time making its way into the academy. There were three references to jazz. I looked up the woman composers, and in fact women composers are listed in this book, all in one paragraph on page 196 as a list. About fourteen woman composers are mentioned, but only four examples of their music were recorded. I looked under African American composers—nothing. I looked under "black," nothing. I looked under "negro," and there were nine references to negro. In the index there are tree types of negro music: the work song, the spiritual, and sorry, senior moment, one other. I looked for William Grant Still, not mentioned. I looked for Florence L. Price, not mentioned. I looked for Henry Burleigh, who was mentioned as an arranger of spirituals. George Gershwin was mentioned under "negro" because of Rhapsody in Blue. And folk music—many references, and the way folk music was approached was by country, so Irish music, Spanish music, everything except German and French and English music. And usually under a sign like an emotion, so happy Irish music.

What's so astounding to me is that such a boxed set of music was used until 1943 in the schools. It formed music education. From it we derived our approach to the elements of music, beat, rhythm, harmonic function; they are all derived from this core repertoire, which went along with the gramophone. Eventually because of transcontinental road races, after Horatio Nelson Jackson made it across the country, all the car companies got interested, because they wanted everybody to buy cars. In 1903 one in eight thousand Americans owned a car. The population was something like eighty million. They wanted a car in every garage. Now we have two plus cars for every family in America.

Between 1903-1913 amateur radio stations increased megafold. In 1901 there were five hundred amateur radio stations, by 1908 there were ten thousand stations, with lots of patents being registered. By World War I radio telegraphy was a very important means of communication. When the war began the Navy took over all the radio stations; all the amateur radio stations were put out of business so that the Navy could control the war communications. At the end of World War I the Navy would not give up control of the radio stations; the government and the Navy decided that they would run the radio stations, and that's what happened. They schemed to create what would become NBC in 1926. The National Broadcasting Corporation was a combination of Westinghouse, AT&T, RCA, and the United Fruit Company, a radio company created so that we could communicate from South America, even from a banana tree. These companies combined to create NBC, and NBC was a government controlled network of radio stations.

What happened to radio sales is quite amazing. The Marconi Company predicted in 1916 that by 1922 they would be able to sell one hundred thousand radio music boxes, basically radios that you could plug into your wall, and in 1922 they sold eleven million; in 1923 twenty-two million; in 1924 fifty million. People just bought radios. And what was being broadcast over those radios? They broadcast sports, and they found that they could broadcast music. KDKA in Pittsburg put a gramophone in front of the transmitter and transmitted music out of the air; people received it, and liked it, and so music began to be transmitted over the air, first through records, and then live music began to be broadcast over the air. And eventually opera. People wanted to take the music with them, and so they began to put radios in their cars. You basically just bolted your receiver to your car and set up your own antenna. People began to listen to radio all over the world. And then politicians got interested. Once politicians got involved the government and radio came together, NBC was formed, the whole canon that was developed by the Victor Record became the education canon for NBC, the canon that then informed the way we developed our music education system, and the way that we developed our concert system in the country.

Where are my colleagues? They were never there. All of my work on behalf of American composers in the orchestral world is pioneering work. All of us who worked so long to place the American composer in an American orchestra now know what it is. We thought we were there and then we got thrown out. We were never part of the canon.

Where are the young people? In their cars. I'm in my car. I listen to music in my car. It's one of the only quiet private spaces for listening to music. Can I listen in the same span of time that I would listen in a concert hall? Only if I pull off to the side of the road. Does that affect the way that I listen to classical music? Yes, it does. Does the sound of produce music, music that is mixed on a sound board, affect how we think of classical music? Yes, it does. Are orchestra halls building sound systems to remix the music? Yes, they are. They won't tell you, but they are. Is there a difference in the way we perceive classical music because of sound and transportation? Yes, there is. And that is the end of this speech.

Libby Larsen is one of America's most performed living composers. She has created a catalogue of over 220 works spanning virtually every genre from intimate vocal and chamber music to massive orchestral and choral scores. Grammy Award winning and widely recorded, including over 50 CDs of her work, she is constantly sought after for commissions and premieres by major artists, ensembles, and orchestras around the world, and has established a permanent place for her works in the concert repertory. She is currently completing a book, The Concert Hall That Fell Asleep and Woke Up as a Car Radio *and her next major opera work,* Every Man Jack.

Stories of Resurrection: Traces of God in New Community

CAROL WADE

THE UNITED STATES HAS BEEN ONE OF THE most religiously observant countries in the contemporary world, but of the seventy million people born between 1946 and 1964 almost fifty million left the church, rejecting not God, but rather "lifeless religion and "stale churches."[1] With two to three generations of unchurched people in America, the United States along with most of the Western world has re-entered a rank once typically reserved for Third World countries, that of "mission." Exploring new ways to speak of God in a post-Christian world is imperative.

Robert D. Putnam reports in his best-selling work *Bowling Alone* that in America between 1986 and 1998, while museum attendance was up ten percent and movie-going was up by twenty-five percent, church attendance in the United States was down ten percent.[2] Contemporary urbanites hungering for an inchoate spiritual experience stand in line for hours waiting to see the latest Picasso or Matisse exhibit, or one of the film installments in the Tolkein trilogy, but such spiritual seekers scarcely consider the church as an option in their quest. Why museums or films but not the church?

Cultural studies and everyday experience show that as we oscillate between late- and post-modernity we are moving into a post-literate age, with thought forms shifting from linear to non-linear as intuition and imagination counter rational discovery made solely through scientific method. Beginning roughly with people born in the late 1940s, and continuing in every subsequent generation with ever-increasing speed, visual images are supplanting print as the metaphor of choice, with story and symbol as our chief means to receive and process information, to experience and construct

meaning, to convey emotion and communicate. The prescient dictum of Marshall McLuhan, "the medium is the message," still holds, as Pierre Babin writes a quarter-century later: "The medium is not just a limited technical prop, but the totality of the infrastructures and conditions necessary for a medium to function."[3]

If mainline churches with liturgies of printed texts rooted in the Enlightenment and modern linear thought forms, who lament the loss of the post-baby-boom generations, believe that such people must be converted from the effects of digital age alienation and passivity if they are to return to the church, then the church is not properly reading its context. "Electronic culture," writes Leonard Sweet, "creates *interactive*, not passive people."[4]

Interactive people of the digital age who seek a transcendent experience of God and authentic encounter with neighbor are bypassing the mainline churches in favor of creating their own "do-it-yourself religion" characterized by non-linear thought forms situated within a social model of interconnectivity.[5] Finding new ways to speak of God in worship, ways that preserve the historic witness of a church secured in faith, entails not simply finding new ways to *speak about* God, but rather finding imaginative ways to *experience* God through story, image, and symbol—the language of the digital age.

To this end I created "Stories of Resurrection: Traces of God in New Community," an experimental liturgical event drawn from religious dramatic forms, both contemporary and medieval, which celebrates the faith stories of newly baptized Christian adults. Striving to integrate worship, teaching, and evangelism, the project seeks to connect mainline worship that adheres to set liturgical forms and texts with digital image, symbol, and dramatic storytelling as a form of alternate proclamation of the Gospel. Bridging theory and practice, the project tackles the serious challenge facing the twenty-first century church: how to uphold tradition and yet remain open to innovation, how to be seeker-sensitive within the renewed missional context of secular Western culture and deeply rooted in the historic witness of the church.

The Church Setting

The use of drama, image, and electronic media as conversation partners for proclamation of the Gospel is a prominent feature of the contemporary worship genre, by which I mean Protestant North American megachurch worship, not typically part of the mainline worship tradition. My first challenge then was to determine in what type of parish, and in what context within parish life, I might introduce

such a venture to an assembly accustomed to a long history of mostly fixed liturgies following set texts and rubrics. I chose to work within the context of a large urban Episcopal parish with highly intentional, well-planned traditional worship, accompanied by a large music program, along with strong preaching and catechetical programs. This type of parish draws many seekers and converts roughly aged twenty to forty. This type of parish is, however, open to pushing the limits of traditional rubrics through the use of innovative ceremonial and symbol in an effort to create liturgical variety while marking sacred time; as such it might be more closely aligned with the postmodern, non-linear intuitional approach than one might at first suspect. Therefore, we can see some similarities with mostly suburban Protestant megachurches in terms of mission, and yet we know there are also discontinuities in terms of worship style, traditions, theologies, and urban setting.

I determined that working in the

FIG. 1 *"White"*: Jennifer Muller Dance Company. Photo ©Johan Elbers 2005.

context of the post-baptismal phase of the catechumenate, the period following the Easter Vigil, could be advantageous for liturgical experimentation. The catechumenate is a process of preparing adult converts for baptism; it finds its inspiration in the historic catechumenate of the fourth century with the sermons and teachings of Cyril, Ambrose, Chrysostom, and Theodore. The contemporary catechumenate is a process of spiritual journey involving staged rites and regular gatherings in small groups to study and reflect on Scripture. The catechumens make vivid connections with Scripture by developing and sharing stories in the form of spiritual autobiographies. The catechumenate, which can typically span the course of a year, was reclaimed following Vatican II, and has been adapted in various ways by most mainline denominations. Its final stage, known as post-baptismal catechesis, or mystagogy, begins in the Easter Octave and continues through Pentecost. The mystagogical phase is a time of continued conversion, spiritual growth, meditation on the meaning of the sacraments of baptism and Eucharist, and incorporation into community and discernment of ministries. My liturgy is intended to take place at a midweek Easter service following the Easter Vigil.

In seeking to explore the challenge of incorporating newly baptized adult converts into community in the days following the Easter Vigil, I believe I found both a pastorally and strategically appropriate time to introduce a new form of worship, an alternate proclamation of the Gospel within a multi-media context. Introducing this in the context of a one-off celebratory event seemed to be less confrontational, and a good pastoral solution. The post-baptismal phase of the catechumenate has typically been problematic: neophytes often experience a marked emotional letdown following the intense preparation culminating in the Vigil, and difficulty in integrating into normal parish life.

Another way to view the setting is to employ a set of classifying labels for North American Worship developed by Lester Ruth.[6] This is based upon James F. White's assessment of the ethos of a tradition. Ruth believes that the way in which a community plans its liturgies may be classified as "congregational," operating as an independent congregation, or "connectional," using resources common to its tradition. When churches face the issue of inculturation, Ruth believes they respond in one of these two ways.

My project is situated within the context of a church that is connectional. To contend with the issue of inculturation, that of culture and media savvy urbanites within a postmodern context, I loosely use two resources common to the tradition of my parish setting. First, the liturgical event follows the Prayer Book structure as interpreted in the parish's weekly eucharistic worship — gathering, word, table, and sending. Secondly, the parish traditionally draws from and interprets certain medieval ceremonial and liturgical enactments in its worship

Seeking to preserve the historic witness of the faith and yet be open to innovation, I have drawn upon some existing Anglican traditions. In so completely recasting them in a contemporary context, however, and working in media forms more akin to the North American Protestant megachurch, I believe I have ultimately worked within a third category that Ruth employs, that of being officially connectional but working in an autonomous congregational model for purposes of inculturation.

Drama in Contemporary Worship

"Worship," writes Kenda Creasy Dean, "constitutes one of the oldest forms of play known to human society. Human beings have always engaged in 'sacred games' that dramatize the values of their cultic communities."[7] Drawing on her research on the culturally contextual worship of adolescents and their need for a playful and imaginative style of worship, Dean advocates considering such qualities in worship for all ages. Worship that is relational and interactive, she writes, "invites our participation in an expanded view of reality." Quoting Wolfhart Pannenberg, she observes, "Play points to a larger reality, a 'true order' of things intuited but not fully grasped intellectually." Finally, she notes:

> The act of playing has a "back and forth" quality to it; it is always relational, always involves an "other"—an imaginative object, a playmate, a conversation partner, a community. Play's reward comes from the deep satisfaction of losing ourselves in the play, the moment of self-abandonment in which the reality we glimpse but cannot grasp somehow grasps us. In this surrender, "something happens" indeed: the self is re-created, infused with intrinsic worth and meaning as we give ourselves over to an Other—an Other that has already given itself over to us (137-38).

Drama performed by adults is indeed a kind of childlike play that seeks to be transformational. When audiences are drawn into a drama, they too can experience a form of imaginative play.

Robert Webber's observation on the arts in general can be applied to an effective implementation of drama in worship: "The arts are important not only because of the Incarnation, but also because they communicate. The arts are the language of intuition, a poetic, imaginative way of supporting and enhancing the text of worship, the Gospel."[8]

Using drama in worship can be a playful means of transformational communication. However, this notion of playfulness should not make us think that drama, in general or as used in worship, is by any means trivial. The classic definition of drama as a representation of life comes to us from Aristotle's *Poetics,* in which he writes that drama is "an imitation of an action that is serious and ... complete in itself."[9] It consists of a reversal, or *peripeteia*, which, according to Aristotle, causes the action "to veer around in the other direction," thus dramatically aiding us to experience transformation.

I designed my project to be in conversation with two dramatic forms. The first is found in the contemporary North American Protestant megachurch tradition, perhaps best known through the Seeker Services at Willow Creek Community Church in South Barrington, Illinois; the second is medieval liturgical drama. From the dramatic liturgy of Anglo-Saxon England I chose the tenth-century Easter play, *Visitatio Sepulchri*, from Winchester Cathedral.

The Seeker Services. "Few topics can polarize a conversation within Christian circles the way the subject of Willow Creek Community Church can," writes Todd E. Johnson. "Regardless of how favorably one views Willow Creek, most believe it is a unique phenomenon in the Church."[10] Willow Creek's mission to those outside the church surpasses most efforts in today's church. In its mission to reach its target audience, identified by Willow Creek as "unchurched Harry or Mary," drama serves as a key element.

As the paradigmatic church of the seeker movement, Willow Creek has changed the way many worship. Founded in 1975 with the express purpose of reaching those outside the church, it now attracts upwards of fifteen thousand people to its weekend Seeker Service. The church campus, which resembles a community college or corporate training center, is designed to reduce the cognitive dissonance between the religious realm and the working and shopping worlds of middle-class suburban America. Typically, no crosses or other religious symbols are on display.

I first observed a Willow Creek drama as a participant-observer at its annual Leadership Summit conference via satellite downlink at

Fuller Seminary in Pasadena, California, during the summer of 2002—this was broadcast to over twenty-five thousand church leaders around the world. The professionally produced and polished drama was acted in its forty-five-thousand-seat auditorium equipped with movie-theatre-style seats, proscenium curtained stage, and state-of-the-art technical equipment.

Other Protestant churches widely emulate the style and format of drama employed by Willow Creek, although they adapt it in some settings to reach both seeker and believer. I will limit my focus to the Willow Creek model, as it offers the greatest contrast with the historical model of sacred drama, the *Visitatio Sepulchri*.

At Willow Creek a need is first identified, and a short skit is developed to present the problem in a way that can be experienced emotionally by the assembly. G. A. Pritchard, in *Willow Creek Seeker Service*, describes the dramas as follows: "They [the skits] involve revealing common human problems, enabling Creekers to identify with unchurched Harry, providing self-understanding for Harry, and lowering Harry's defenses."[11] Each skit is typically five to eight minutes in duration. It illustrates a problem that will be addressed in the message spoken by a pastor. Pritchard quotes one Willow Creek staff member as saying: "Drama is the best way we know of to really portray the problem of whatever we're going to talk about. In other words, every service has a theme or a main point. And drama is the way that we can connect people with the problem, not the solution" (92).

Willow Creek's use of sketch-style drama and overall programming reflects the shift from word- to image-based communication. Creekers believe that if they are to reach "unchurched Harry" they must speak his language, the language of the media. Pritchard points out that the prevailing opinion of the staff at Willow Creek is that as a result of the communication revolution "individuals are increasingly unable to follow an argument, think critically, and process information from a single source

without visual and auditory stimulation" (91).

The method of inculturation then, to use Lester Ruth's categories, is that of the congregational model. There are no real referents to the historical tradition, and there are no set liturgical texts to be considered. Willow Creek uses popular culture as its referent. The short television skit, a simple, uncomplicated version of a *Saturday Night Live* sketch, is the model. Not all, however, are of a humorous nature. One drama, entitled "Great Expectations," involved a couple having trouble conceiving a child. They tried to adopt, but at the last minute the adoption fell through. The wife erupted in rage at God, and the husband tried to comfort her—the skit ended there. A skit is never fully developed into a drama per se, one with a reversal or transformational moment.

Pritchard reports the following: "When Willow Creek has attempted to use drama to teach answers to unchurched Harry, the results have been less than satisfying" (93). We see here that the drama is used to set up a pedagogic moment, servant to the pastor's message; it is not intended to function pedagogically on its own, nor is it intended in any way to function in a sacramental mode. Drama is not considered a suitable way to preach the Gospel when the goal is to raise a question and provide an answer that gives clear assurance and a "how-to" application; the drama sets up the problem, the message offers the solution.

Pritchard offers the following critique, "Creekers generally seek to avoid complexity and they believe that nuances are dispensable. Creekers often use visual stimulation as a substitute for thought and do not value verbal precision." He also points out that in Willow Creek's overall use of the arts there is "a potential lack of willingness to upset or confront Harry" and thus a high priority is placed on providing entertainment, with the result a "cheerful Christianity" (93).

Willow Creek and most other communities offering contemporary worship do not follow a lectionary or liturgical year. Thus, without the progression through the liturgical year—especially entering into the darker aspects of Lent and the cross—and without the use of deep symbols, the move into a more mature faith and response to discipleship is at risk. I believe that the dramas set within the overall programmatic goals of Willow Creek run amiss by offering a therapeutic message rather than the Gospel message in all its complexity. This has inspired me to rethink the model through the lens of medieval liturgical drama.

Visitatio Sepulcri. The tenth-century liturgical drama of Anglo-Saxon England arose in the era of Benedictine Reform, a time of church revitalization amidst cultural transition, not entirely dissimilar to our contemporary situation. Tracing the earlier roots of the reform in Anglo-Saxon England, M. Bradford Bedingfield writes:

> When Augustine arrived in Canterbury in 597, in an attempt to revive a Christian church in the British Isles that had been largely smothered by Anglo-Saxon migrations, he was given a mandate by Pope Gregory to marry the best of local traditions with the practice of Rome, and this approach remained a dynamic in subsequent reforms. This sort of philosophy surely encouraged a diverse liturgy, but the paucity of surviving manuscripts from before the tenth century stunts our appreciation of it…. We can develop a much clearer picture, however, of the liturgical activities of the later Anglo-Saxon church as the Benedictine Reform spurred the production of a plethora of liturgical books and other documentary witnesses to what has recently been referred to as a "period of national liturgical experiment and innovation."[12]

In the tenth century, Ethelwold, Bishop of Winchester, drew up what is considered the earliest extant playlet of the *Visitatio Sepulchri.* Complete with stage directions for its performance at Easter Matins, the scriptural core of the story—the visitation of the women at the tomb seen through the lens of the Roman Liturgy—can be said to represent the birth of medieval drama. The *Regularis Concordia* contains the written text of the *Visitatio Sepulchri,* along with staging directions. It appears to be a combination of two versions of the *Quem quaertis* ("Whom do you seek?"), a familiar medieval trope crafted into two episodes or scenes. This is accomplished by the introduction of two newly composed antiphons, *Venite et videte locum* ("Come and see the place") and *Cito euntes* ("Going quickly, tell the disciples") which can be found in The Winchester Troper, another tenth century document containing the text with music for the *Visitatio Sepulchri* at Winchester.

Three texts from the Vulgate serve as the source of the *Quem quaertis* dialogue used by Ethelwold and his associates: Matthew 28:1-8, Mark 16:1-8, and Luke 24:1-12. These tell the story of the "Marys" being met at the tomb by an Angel. According to the *Regularis Concordia* the Angel, wearing a simple white alb, "stealthily" makes his way during the third lesson of Matins to the area of the main altar, which in the Old Minster would have been oriented to the east. We have no description of the set piece representing the sepulcher, but it was most likely some sort of veiled receptacle located on or at the high altar; probably with a hollowed-out section for the placement of relics, thus already suggesting the idea of a tomb.

The Angel, poised at the tomb during the lesson, quietly sits watch over this liturgical "Jerusalem." This was evocatively rendered at the service of None on Good Friday, when "Golgotha" was poignantly recreated as all, bishop and novice alike, crept to the altar area for the adoration of the cross prior to the

Depositio; then the cross and/or host wrapped in linen, symbolic of Christ's lifeless body, was placed at rest, thus creating the "Holy Sepulcher." The Angel awaits the women with a palm branch in hand; this acts as a polyvalent symbol, harkening not only the triumphal entry of Jesus into Jerusalem celebrated in the Palm Sunday liturgy, but also the imagery found in the book of Revelation (7:9) where the worshipping throngs gathered around the throne in heaven arrayed with crowns and holding palm fronds; finally, the palm could also be read as a hopeful "green" sign of new birth and new life.

Meanwhile, during the singing of the third responsory (*Dum transisset sabbatum*), the three women, traditionally called the "Marys" (who were actually men vested in copes, with thuribles in hand to represent the aromatic spices for the anointing) approach the sepulcher. Perhaps they enter north of the altar, where the worshipping community (composed of at least clergy, monks, novices, and boy singers, seated in two banks of stalls along the north and south sides near the high altar) catch sight of them as they wend their way around to the nave, and thus begin their doleful pilgrimage to the tomb. If seculars were present, the sight lines would have been quite good given the open basilica-style structure of the Old Minster. When the women draw near the sepulcher, "step by step," according to the rubrics, "as if searching for something," the Angel "sweetly" and "softly" intones the question that begins the traditional dialogue of the *Quem quaertis*: "Whom do you seek?" The Marys answer, "Jesus of Nazareth." This is followed by the angelic pronouncement, *Non est hic*, "He is not here, he is risen!"

The women make their way back to the two banks of stalls to tell the news of the resurrection, replete with the joyful alleluias that had been "put away" for the duration of Lent. The Angel then summons the women back to "come and see" the place inside of the tomb. The women lay down their thuribles and lift up the linen, now empty of cross and host, while the Angel exhorts the women to "go quickly and tell." Once the linen has been lifted for all to see, it is placed on the altar by Mary Magdalene in a gesture resembling the preparation for the Mass: here, in medieval sacramental thought most notably, Jesus is to be found. This is true not only for a novice being newly educated in the events of the paschal mystery, but also for seasoned monks, and seculars, if present, as well. The whole of the drama is brought to its conclusion, along with the Office of Easter Matins, with the singing of the *Te Deum laudamus*, while the bells ring out again after their silence, announcing the great joy of the resurrection.

The juxtaposition of Ethelwold's newly composed material for his *Visitatio Sepulchri*, along with well-known liturgical texts and canticles such as the *Te Deum*, dramatically enacted within the context of worship, make the holy dramatic and the dramatic holy. Players dressed in the common liturgical garb of worship while at the same time suggesting specific characters from Scripture; familiar space sculpted into a "liturgical Jerusalem"; newly composed chants along with traditional readings, music, and gestures allow the entire event to create a sense of time and space condensed and yet unhinged — heaven and earth intersecting in a historical yet timeless moment — a first century Jerusalem/tenth century Winchester dichotomy revealing and yet hiding the supreme mystery of the Christian faith. As Umberto Eco writes, "The formation of symbols was artistic. To decipher them was to experience them aesthetically. It was a type of aesthetic expression in which the Medievals took great pleasure in deciphering puzzles, in spotting the daring analogy, in feeling that they were involved in adventure and discovery."[13]

The medieval use and appreciation of story, drama, and symbol in general, but specifically as employed in the Easter play, is in stark contrast with the theory and practice of drama in much of contemporary worship. The density and depth of the symbolic world employed by medieval people is profound, highly engaging, and participatory; it possesses not only a pedagogical goal, but, more pointedly, a participatory or sacramental purpose. The drama endeavors to create what postmodern seekers so desire—an encounter or an experience of the risen Christ.

Issues of Postmodern Inculturation

Lester Ruth, by combining the taxonomies of James F. White and Robert Webber, defines two categories, "personal story churches" and "cosmic story churches," representing a continuum rather than distinct categories.[14] The catechumenate is intended largely to incorporate catechumens into the "cosmic story." Although it is a spiritual journey, the formalized rites culminating in initiation at the Easter Vigil focus predominately upon the cosmic story and incorporation into the mystical body of Christ. The postmodernist, in a shift away from the modernist's formalism and highly individualized spiritual experience in a corporate setting, wants an experiential encounter, but one that allows for connectedness. The postmodernist deeply desires participation in community.

My project aimed to model this connectedness. The catechumens, having been incorporated into God's story at the Vigil through their baptism, would, as an interconnected group, not only place their stories next to God's story, but also make themselves known within the larger community. This liturgical celebration, following on the heels of the Vigil, would allow for worship that incorporates "personal story" into an otherwise "cosmic story" church.

Focusing on the personal story told in fragmentary pieces, juxtaposed with a confident Christian story, is another way to respond to postmodern resistance to the totalizing claims of master narratives. As suggested in the writings of Lieven Boeve, it allows for an approach that respects particularities and otherness, juxtaposed with the importance of the Christian narrative for the Christian, and holding open the possibility of recognizing mutuality and the fragmentary nature of all narratives.[15]

Cultural particularity. Following John Witvliet's concern that liturgical expression ought to reflect the particular cultural context of the local congregation, I aimed to create what he calls a "sufficiently complex understanding" of how worship is at once transcultural, contextual, countercultural, and cross-cultural.[16] The juxtaposition of biblical text, personal story, and image aimed to work on a transcultural level in speaking of the catholic faith, especially through symbols of the Easter story—but symbols constructed by using images and stories from the culture juxtaposed with stories from Scripture. Secondly, the liturgy certainly aimed at incorporating some cross-cultural elements through a choice of music and story that included elements from the African American tradition (the use of Alvin Ailey's *Revelations* in the gathering video, its integral place within the story of the drama, and the singing of gospel music used by Ailey in his work), as well as a story of death and rebirth as recounted in the tale of an Argentinean rite of infant baptism. Thirdly, the authenticity of the presentation, the openness in which participants shared their stories, was somewhat countercultural for typically more emotionally guarded urbanites, but not completely at odds, given postmodern desire for community and intimacy. Finally, with concern for postmodern cultural particularity, I aimed to work primarily in a contextual manner—what Wivliet describes as, "reflecting the unique genius of the culture in which it [worship] is placed." Engaging the dramatic and visual arts in a community that defines itself to a large extent within the context of a creative and artistic milieu was of first importance in my liturgical task. I aimed to speak the language of the culture defined by art, but not without heeding the admonition of Bryan Spinks and John Fenwick to the church as it responds to Western secular values: " challenge individualism, and selfish materialism, and dare to speak the mystery of God and transcendent."[17]

Engaging the culture and working in a contemporary mode was an important part of the task, given that the denomination is, in general, resistant to contemporary paradigms, and its ceremonial practice seems to prefer and even idealize what Gordon Lathrop describes as "*an archaic, imagination-bearing event.*"[18] Lathrop cites processions, archaic vesture, and hierarchically organized candlelit space as examples, and all were present at the Easter Vigil.

Ruth Meyers emblematizes the difficulty in integrating contemporary paradigms into historical worship; speaking to a totalizing view concerning the church's practices in the contemporary catechumenate she offers a trenchant but apt critique: "[T]o the extent that the catechumenate attempts to reproduce practices from the fourth and fifth centuries, it is little more than an exercise in historical romanticism."[19]

Faced in my project with the age-old challenge of recontextualizing the presentation of the Christian message, I charted my course by words delivered in Bryan Spinks's Pitt Lecture at Yale Divinity School's Tercentennial Convocation in 2001:

> The church in a post Christian society may not be in the same situation as it was in the era of Christendom, but neither can it do backward somersaults and land in the third century... there can be no liturgical meta-narratives and no golden ages. The whole tradition is a possible source of inspiration, but never replication. It may be that the creativity of the medieval period could be a more helpful inspiration than has been hitherto thought.[20]

Embodiment. A harbinger of the intense postmodern turn to the body, the choreographer Martha Graham, heralded for creating an entirely new art form that speaks profoundly of the redemption or freedom of the body, firmly maintained that she had simply rediscovered what the body already knew.[21] Today, cognitive science is coming to similar conclusions: the mind is intrinsically embodied. Scott Holland, in his work "Even the Postmodern Story Has a Body,"[22] offers the following summation of George Lakoff and Mark Johnson's empirical research as presented in *Philosophy in the Flesh: The Embodied Mind and Its Challenge to Western Thought:*

> −Reason is not disembodied as the tradition has largely held, but arises from the nature of our brains, bodies, and bodily experience. This is not just the innocuous and obvious claim that we need a body to reason; rather, it is the striking claim that the very structure of reason itself comes from the details of our embodiment. ...− Reason is not purely literal, but largely metaphorical and imaginative. −Reason is not dispassionate, but emotionally engaged.[23]

For Christians, both modern and postmodern, who find our hope in a resurrected Christ, to reflect upon our embodied nature seems good. Bruce Morrill reminds us of a theological principle:

> God saves our humanity right in our very material actions and circumstances. This is a necessary consequence of the theological commitment to the embodied character of our sanctification, for there is no disembodied realm where we are being saved.[24]

Since the beginning of modernity we have been progressively disembodied.. The reclamation of the body, not only for wholeness in life but in worship as well, ought to be considered. Don Saliers writes of the importance of our remembering our bodies in worship:

> In some respects, our bodily movements … may be the most deeply theological aspects of our communal worship. For the human body is itself a primary symbol of God's glory … it is the fundamental conception of God incarnate in a human being that gives such theological significance to bodily action.[25]

That I endeavored in my project to reclaim the story of Mary Magdalene, the first witness, juxtaposed to the story of a new witness named Peyton (a student at Yale Divinity School), largely through images of the choreography of Martha Graham, seemed important for expressing some aspect of the indwelling of the sacred in our lives. Nicholas Wolterstorff writes: "We stand in these intimate relations because we have bodies…to denigrate dance, for example because it so intimately involves the body is to denigrate a whole dimension of oneself."[26] The stark and powerful bodily images were intended to function in a manner similar to Louis-Marie Chauvet's understanding of sacrament: "The sacraments serve as a *buffer* which repels every temptation Christians might have to ignore the body, history and society…the sacraments state that the word of God wants to enter our bodies, that is our lives…"[27]

As director, I worked with two images. Peyton, as she moves through her story of conversion, transforms herself from a disembodied person to an embodied one. Each time she steps into the light a healing leads to wholeness through faith. The second image was of the juxtaposition of stational and processional liturgies in medieval drama, a directing technique I learned from Margot Fassler. In medieval drama the processions

moved the crowd from one *sedes*, or playing area, to another—from one scene to another—while the stational liturgy alerted the crowd that something important was happening, and as such expressed a need to stop, speak words, or say prayer. Peyton's story functioned as the stational liturgy while the interconnecting stories of the other actors functioned for the most part as the processional liturgy.

The use of photographic images in the project, specifically images of dance, is intended to function in a pedagogical, pastoral, and theological mode—a meditation on the goodness of the human body as that which connects to bodily resurrection, but my hope is that the use of art will also function sacramentally. The images are stark and iconic, symbolic rather than purely realistic, like the thurible in the medieval drama that represented a container of myrrh. Robert K. Johnson writes: "The visual reinforcement allows for a liturgy of enactment that is transformative. The pedagogical has become the sacramental through the gracious presence of the Spirit of Christ, who fills it with his divine presence."[28]

Reading the Images. I will now briefly and selectively describe some of the larger movements of the piece through my discussion of a few of the images that embody key themes.

Artists such as Frantisek Kupka (1871-1957) believed that using pure pigment created a direct experience of light, and his premise raised two questions for me. I wondered whether we do indeed have direct encounters with God, and if so, how these are manifest. More specifically, in what way do the visual cues around us, namely the interplay between light and darkness, bespeak or become a vestige of God.

"Dance," observes the photographer Barbara Morgan, "is experienced continuously in time and space, but it is remembered in moments of combustion … that haunt and stir the memory."[29] In the words of my subtitle, "Traces of God" speaks of our transient

FIG. 2 *Cross Fade* by Alwin Nikolais, 1974. Photo courtesy the Nikolais–Louis Foundation for Dance.

FIG. 3 "A Letter to Queen Victoria" in *Dance: Rituals of Experience* by Jamake Highwater. Photo ©Lois Greenfield

knowledge of the divine, which even when experienced as disclosure is somehow set against the backdrop of mystery and incomprehension. This is articulated later in a story of watching a Balanchine ballet when a woman is lifted up and vanishes into both darkness behind the curtain and into light—the space she once occupied is now filled with color and light. As Don Saliers writes:

> The visible reveals the invisible world—
> that which the natural eye cannot see.
> In those instances we might think of the
> primary eschatological sense being sight.
> Hence the prominent metaphor of "seeing
> God" and "beholding the mystery." The
> visual dimension of liturgy is a means of
> communication and a sign itself of the
> incarnation.[30]

With regard to the idea of God in both light and darkness, Delores Williams and others have called for a rethinking of images of light and dark, black and white.[31] I used color images bracketing black and white images to portray something of the idea that color and darkness both reveal God. Culturally we are conditioned to think of God in the category of light, but when Peyton first begins to yearn for God, to feel the tug of the divine in her heart—and until she articulates a coming to faith—I use black and white photography. Richard Davey writes about the use of black in art: "It can declare the absence of God … but black is created through the mixing of all colors, and so the apparent absence could in reality be the absolute presence of the Divine light."[32] I draw on the apophatic mystical tradition of God dwelling in the darkness, along with the idea that perhaps it is the time when we are coming to faith, when we are simply not sure of God's presence, that God is most present. As Peyton says in her story of Ailey's "Fix me Jesus," from *Revelations*, "Just when the woman looks as if she will fall, the man catches her—God is always there, always present."

Another aspect of Kupka's artistic philosophy also influenced my theological project. Kupka makes use of many circular forms in his work, which he interconnects like a Venn diagram. Such imagery speaks to me of the coinherence of the Godhead, a dance-like social model of the Trinity. Not only does it suggest a sense that the Triune God is on the move in the story/stories of resurrection, but it models an understanding of community as well, an ecclesiology of circular and overlapping intersubjectivity.

Feminist theologians have taught us much about circular community. Leaders certainly must exist in an ecclesial structure, as in any social structure, but leadership can be fluid and intercommunicative. Those that are officially called out by community to lead can do so by empowering others; their leadership can function as a focal point rather than a hierarchical point. Mary Collins writes, "In feminist liturgies dualisms regularly are transformed to circles and spirals and spheres and squares, symbols that embrace multiple energies in tension."[33]

Using James Joyce's evocative phrase, "In the beginning … was the sounddance," announces a movement away from dichotomies such as mind/body that have led to our progressive disembodiment, or the audible/visible split found in the theology of God's presence vs. God's word in the Hebrew Scriptures (e.g. Isaiah vs. Deuteronomy) that has, to some extent, been used to fuel the polemical Catholic/Protestant divide. Another way to think about this is, as the theater artist Robert Wilson reminds us, that the visual book need not be subservient to what you hear (Fig. 3 [Imago]).[34] The "Word" that in the beginning was with God and was God (John's prologue) is not the Greek abstract notion of *logos*. The Incarnation tells us otherwise, for the Word becomes embodied—the mode necessary for our salvation from disembodiment. Thus I began our story by assigning the text from the Fourth Gospel's account of Mary Magdalene, "Now Mary was at the tomb, weeping …" as a "sounddance" to be spoken by all; each member takes some part of the words, and thus it takes the entire body to make the "sounddance" that reintroduces Mary/Peyton into the Easter story.

The process of seeking out images for this liturgy was something akin to using homemade bread rather than thin wafer crackers for the Eucharist. The images chosen were meant to resonate, to be real and full, not thin and irrelevant symbols—hand chosen, hand crafted, as a gift to the storyteller and to the assembly. Individual members of the assembly may not be able to articulate explicitly how the texture and detail of symbols affect them, but on some level they intuit and experienced as it a deep and authentic source of mediation.

Susan Ross, drawing on Paul Ricoeur's famous dictum, "The symbol gives rise to thought," suggests that symbols provoke reflection, kindle the imagination.[35] This is indeed what happened in my study of the medieval Easter play, *Visitatio Sepulchri.* The use of symbol was thrilling.

The use of the linen to bury the cross on Good Friday, and its subsequent showing as a sign of the resurrection, caught my sense of adventure and discovery. When Mary Magdalene held up the cloth at the climactic moment of the play, and then placed it on the altar as the place where the assembly would now find Christ in the Mass, my imagination was kindled. A white cloth marking the playing area in figure 1, *Primitive Mysteries,* spoke to me of Mary Magdalene, the linen in the *Visitatio Sepulchri,* women and the priesthood, and sacramental theology in general.

Conclusion

My liturgy was intended to function as the "liturgy of the word" portion of a service that would include gathering, collects, readings from the texts included in the drama, and, following the drama, the liturgy of the table and sending.·

I look forward to working this out in a real context so that I may see what changes need to be implemented to balance the power of the technological enhancements.

The technology of media is one the most powerful tools for post-modern storytelling. Speaking of electronically produced images, James White cautions:

> We must be careful that they do not submerge the rest of the service…. The power of the electronically produced visual images is so strong that we must know what we are doing. These media can dominate everything else so easily that the rest of the service seems overwhelmed. If we try to illustrate the sermon, we may find we have to stop preaching.[36]·

This clearly became a consideration in my project. Once the images were juxtaposed with the stories, it became clear that the actors would have to sit *schola* style and refer to the screen—the images were simply too powerful.

Robert Webber believes that churches that are renewing themselves are paying more attention to the arts in recognition that worship itself is an art, and that they are also integrating the arts in worship. "The churches most sensitive to the arts are churches that give the arts a servant role in worship." He continues, "While it is possible to worship without the arts, modern worshippers are acutely aware of how important the arts are to worship."[37] It is to this end that I created this project in conversation with both historical and contemporary voices.

In this project I have looked at the use of drama in the Seeker Service at Willow Creek and the medieval use of drama at tenth-century Winchester. In the process I have criticized the Willow Creek model as off-loading tradition and historical references, while I also offered a critique of my own tradition, which is resistant to contemporary paradigms and at times engages in exercises of historical romanticism.

To the seeker movement at Willow Creek, T. S. Eliot's concluding section of *Little Gidding* seems fitting:

> A people without history
> is not redeemed from time, for history is
>   a pattern
> Of timeless moments....

And to my tradition, with its tendency to historical romanticism and to favoring golden ages, an aphorism of Cyprian of Carthage in his Epistle to Pompey is instructive: "Custom without truth is just old error."

ILLUSTRATIONS

1. *Primitive Mysteries* by Martha Graham, 1935 (photographer: Barbara Morgan) in Barbara Morgan, *Martha Graham: Sixteen Dances in Photographs* (Dobbs Ferry, N.Y.: Morgan & Morgan, 1980), 45.

2. *Cross Fade* by Alwin Nikolais, 1974 (photographer: Nikolais Dance Theatre, uncredited) in Highwater, *Dance*, 184.

3. *Imago* by Alwin Nikolais, 1963 (photographer: uncredited) in Francesca Pedroni, *Alwin Nikolais* (Palermo: L'EPOS, 2000), vi.

ENDNOTES

1. See Timothy J. Wright, *A Community of Joy: How to Create Contemporary Worship*, ed. by Herbert Miller (Nashville: Abingdon, 1994), 60.

2. *Bowling Alone: The Collapse and Revival of American Community* (New York: Simon & Schuster, 2000), 114.

3. *The New Era in Religious Communication* (Minneapolis: Fortress, 1991), 29. See also Constance M. Cherry's essay "Merging Tradition and Innovation in the Life of the Church," in *The Conviction of Things Not Seen: Worship and Ministry in the 21st Century*, ed. Todd Johnson, 19-32. (Grand Rapids: Brazos, 2002).

4. In the Preface to Len Wilson's, *The Wired Church: Making Media Ministry* (Nashville: Abingdon, 1999), 11.

5. For recent articles on "emerging" or "post-modern" churches see Elisabeth Bernstein, "Do-It-Yourself Religion," *The Wall Street Journal*, 11 June 2004, W:1; and John Leland, "Hip New Churches Pray to a Different Drummer," *The New York Times*, 18 February 2004, 1.

6. Lester Ruth, "A Rose by Any Other Name: Attempts at Classifying North American Protestant Worship," in *The Conviction of Things Not Seen*, ed. Todd E. Johnson (Grand Rapids: Brazos, 2002), 52.

7. "Moshing for Jesus: Adolescence as a Cultural Context for Worship," in *Making Room at the Table: An Invitation to Multicultural Worship*, ed. Brian K. Blount and Leonora Tubbs Tisdale (Louisville: Westminster John Knox, 2001), 137.

8. *Blended Worship: Achieving Substance and Relevance in Worship* (Peabody, Mass.: Hendrickson, 1994), 105.

9. Aristotle, "Poetics," in *The Pocket Aristotle*, ed. Justin D. Kaplan (New York: Washington Square, 1958), 348.

10. "Disconnected Rituals: The Origins of the Seeker Service Movement," in *The Conviction of Things Not Seen*, edited by Todd E. Johnson (Grand Rapids: Brazos, 2002), 53.

11. *Willow Creek Seeker Service: Evaluating a New Way of Doing Church* (Grand Rapids: Baker Books, 1996), 92.

12. *The Dramatic Liturgy of Anglo-Saxon England* (Woodbridge, Suffolk: Boydell, 2002), 1, citing Christopher Jones, "The Book of Liturgy," *Speculum* 73 (1998), 685.

13. *Art and Beauty in the Middle Ages* (New Haven, Yale University Press, 1986), 55.

14. "A Rose" (note 6), 47.

15. See Lieven Boeve, *Interrupting Tradition: An Essay on Christian Faith in a Postmodern Context* (Louvain: Peeters, 2003)

16. "Beyond Style," in *The Conviction of Things Not Seen* (Grand Rapids: Brazos, 2002), 78-79.

17. Bryan Spinks and John Fenwick, *Worship in Transition: The Liturgical Movement in the Twentieth Century* (New York: Continuum, 1995), 166.

18. *Holy People: A Liturgical Ecclesiology* (Minneapolis: Fortress, 1999), 28 (Lathrop's italics).

19. "Journeys of Faith: Current Practices of Christian Initiation," in *The Conviction of Things Not Seen*, ed. Todd E. Johnson (Grand Rapids: Brazos, 2002), 97.

20. "Berkeley, Liturgical Scholars and the Liturgical Movement." This lecture was published in *Berkeley at*

Yale 20 (2002):8-13. The quotation is taken from pp. 12-13.

21. See Marian Horosko, *Martha Graham: The Evolution of Her Dance Theory and Training*, rev. ed. (Gainsville: University of Florida Press, 2002), IX.

22. In *The Presence of Transcendence*, ed. by Lieven Boeve and John C. Ries (Leuven: Peeters, 2001), 239-50.

23. Lakoff and Johnson, *Philosophy in the Flesh*, 4, quoted by Holland, "Even the Postmodern," 243.

24. "Initial Consideration: Theory and Practice of the Body in Liturgy Today," in *Bodies of Worship* (Collegeville: Liturgical Press, 1999), 3.

25. *Worship as Theology: Foretaste of Glory Divine* (Nashville: Abingdon, 1994), 163-64.

26. *Art in Action* (Grand Rapids: Eerdmans, 1980), 71-72.

27. *The Sacraments: The Word of God at the Mercy of the Body*, (Collegeville: Liturgical Press, 2001), 114.

28. "Visual Christianity," in *The Conviction of Things Not Seen*, ed. Todd E. Johnson (Grand Rapids: Brazos, 2002), 182.

29. Barbara Morgan, *Martha Graham: Sixteen Dances in Photographs*, rev. ed. (New York: Morgan & Morgan, 1980), 149.

30. *Worship as Theology*, 193.

31. See Linda Moody, "Women's Theologies in Dialogue," in *Women Encounter God* (Maryknoll, N.Y.: Orbis Books, 1996), 127.

32. "Sacred Light: The Art of Richard Kenton Webb, *Image* 22 (Winter/Spring, 1999), 98-109.

33. "Principals of Feminist Liturgy," in *Women at Worship: Interpretations of North American Diversity*, ed. Marjorie Procter-Smith and Janet R. Walton (Louisville: Westminster / John Knox, 1993), 14-15.

34. See *The A.R.T. News*, 6 (March 1986): 3.

35. Paul Ricoeur, *The Symbolism of Evil*, trans. Emerson Buchanan (Boston: Beacon Press, 1967): 347ff, quoted in Ross, *Extravagant Affections*: A Feminist Sacramental Theology (New York: Continuum, 1998), 78.

36. *New Forms of Worship* (Nashville: Abingdon, 1971), 146-47.

37. Webber, *Blended Worship* (note 8), 115.

ADDITIONAL READING

Bauman, Zygmunt. *Postmodernity and its Discontents.* New York: New York University Press, 1997.

Borgmann, Albert. *Crossing the Postmodern Divide.* Chicago: University of Chicago Press, 1992.

Borsch, Frederick Houk. *Many Things in Parable: Extravagant Stories of New Community.* Philadelphia: Fortress, 1988.

Bynum, Caroline Walker. "Women's Stories, Women's Symbols: A Critique of Victor Turner's Theory of Liminality." In *Anthropology and the Study of Religion*, ed. Robert L. Moore and Frank E. Reynolds. Chicago: Center for the Scientific Study of Religion, 1984.

Campbell, Thomas, and Clifford Davidson, ed. *The Fleury Playbook: Essays and Studies.* Kalamazoo: Medieval Institute Publications, WMU, 1985.

Chapungco, Anscar J., O.S.B. *Cultural Adaptation of the Liturgy.* New York: Paulist Press, 1982.

Chauvet, Louis-Marie. *Symbol and Sacrament: A Sacramental Reinterpretation of Christian Existence*, trans. Patrick Madigan and Madeline Beaumont. Collegeville: Liturgical Press, 1995.

Edwards, Kathleen. *The English Secular Cathedrals in the Middle Ages.* Manchester: Manchester University Press, 1967.

Fassler, Margot E., and Rebecca A. Baltzer, eds. *The Divine Office in the Latin Middle Ages: Methodology and Source Studies, Regional developments, Hagiography.* New York: Oxford University Press, 2000.

Gennep, Arnold van. *The Rites of Passage*, trans. Monika Vizedom and Gavrielle L. Caffee. Chicago: University of Chicago Press, 1960.

Hardison, O. B. *Christian Rite and Christian Drama in the Middle Ages: Essays in the Origin and Early History of Modern Drama.* Baltimore: Johns Hopkins Press, 1965.

Irvine, Christopher, and Anne Dawtry. *Art and Worship.* Collegeville: Liturgical Press, 2002.

Jenson, Robert W. *Visible Words: The Interpretation and Practice of Christian Sacraments.* Philadelphia, Fortress, 1978.

Kavanagh, Aidan. *The Shape of Baptism: The Rite of Christian Initiation.* Collegeville: Liturgical Press, 1978.

Lakoff, George, and Mark Johnson. *Philosophy in the Flesh: The Embodied Mind.* New York: Basic Books, 1999.

Lara, Jaime. "Conversion by Theatre: The Drama of the Church in Colonial Latin America." *Yale Latin America Review* (1999): 48-52.

Miller, Kim, and the Ginghamsburg Church Worship Team. *Handbook for Multi-Sensory Worship,* 1. Nashville: Abingdon Press, 1999.

Mitchell, Nathan. *Liturgy and the Social Sciences.* Collegeville: Liturgical Press, 1999.

Mittelberg, Mark. *Building a Contagious Church: Revolutionizing the Way We View and Do Evangelism.* Grand Rapids: Zondervan, 2001.

Morgan, David. *Visual Piety: A History and Theory of Popular Religious Images.* Berkeley: University of California Press, 1998.

Morgenthaler, Sally. *Worship Evangelism: Inviting Unbelievers into the Presence of God.* Grand Rapids: Zondervan, 1995.

Osborne, Kenan. *Christian Sacraments in a Postmodern World*: *A Theology for the Third Millennium.* New York: Paulist, 1999.

Rite of Christian Initiation of Adults. (R.C.I.A.) Chicago: Liturgy Training Publications, 1988

Ross, Susan A. *Extravagant Affections: A Feminist Sacramental Theology.* New York: Continuum Publishing Company, 1998.

Saracino, Michele. "Writing the Body in Postmodern Theology." In *The Presence of Transcendence: Thinking 'Sacrament' in a Postmodern Age,* ed. Lieven Boeve and John C. Ries. Lueven: Peeters, 2001.

Sargeant, Kimon Howland. *Seeker Churches: Promoting Traditional Religion in a Nontraditional Way.* New Brunswick: Rutgers University Press, 2000.

Schragg, Calvin O. *The Self after Post-modernity.* New Haven: Yale University Press, 1997.

Spinks, Bryan. "Vivid Signs of the Gift of the Spirit? The Lima Text on Baptism and Some Recent English Language Baptismal Liturgies." In *Living Water, Sealing Spirit: Readings on Christian Initiation,* ed. Maxwell Johnson. Collegeville: Liturgical Press, 1995.

Tilley, Maureen A,. and Susan A. Ross. *Broken and Whole: Essays on Religion and the Body.* Lanham, Maryland: University Press of America, 1995.

Torevell, David. *Losing the Sacred: Ritual, Modernity, and Liturgical Reform.* Edinburgh: T&T Clark, 2000.

Turner, Victor. *Dramas, Fields and Metaphors.* Ithaca: Cornell University Press, 1974.

The Ritual Process. Chicago: Aldine Press, 1969.

Walton, Janet R. *Art and Worship: A Vital Connection.* Collegeville: Liturgical Press, 1988.

White, Susan. *Christian Worship and Technological Change.* Nashville: Abingdon, 1994.

Witvliet, John. "The Blessing and Bane of the North American Evangelical Megachurch." In *Worship Seeking Understanding.* Grand Rapids: Baker, 2003

Yarnold, Edward. *The Awe-Inspiring Rites of Initiation: Origins of the R.C.I.A.* 2[d] ed. Collegeville: Liturgical Press, 1994.

Young, Karl. *The Drama of the Medieval Church.* 2 vols. Oxford: Clarendon Press, 1933.

Carol Wade is the Canon Liturgist at the Washington National Cathedral where she oversees the worship life of that community. She holds masters degrees in Divinity and Sacred Theology from Yale University, and teaches at liturgical conferences and works as a retreat leader. This article is her Colloquium presentation while a student at the Institute in 2003; she received the Director's Prize for best Colloquium presentation that year.

The Power of Ritual: San Fernando Cathedral

VIRGILIO ELIZONDO

IT IS A GREAT PLEASURE TO BE WITH YOU, AND to share the experience of a grass-roots priest. I've served many different types of communities, sometimes bilingual communities, and now San Antonio, Texas, which has three languages, Polish, German, and Spanish. I very quickly became the most popular Polish-speaking priest in the community, for they can say whatever they want to, and I can not ask questions.

Let us look at the background of ritual. I grew up on the Mexican side of San Antonio, speaking Spanish. I did not know that there was any other language in this country besides Spanish; I grew up in a very Mexican neighborhood, eating Mexican food, as my father owned a grocery store. When I went to the first grade I found out something quite shocking: I wondered who all of the foreigners in the classroom were, foreigners speaking English. Well, I flunked the first grade. I hated school, but I had a very strict mother or I would have been a school dropout. Then my dad would have said, "If you want to work, then work." But thanks to my mother, and a great teacher I had sometime in grade school, a German-American who took an interest in me, I got excited about learning.

Originally I wanted to be a scientist, and my first degrees were in chemistry and math. Then I noticed that I wanted to be a priest. When I studied for the priesthood I found that all my studies were different from the religion that I had grown up in, the religion that I loved. The religion I grew up in embodied my whole being; the whole neighborhood was centered around the parish church. I always tell people that there was a little bit of a "circus" in our parish church, in the best sense of the word. Everything took place there. It was a great place, a place you wanted to go. We didn't need rules to tell us we had to go to church, we wanted

to go. I had a great religious experience as a kid. In the seminary I learned all the negative words that you can imagine — that we were superstitious, somewhat pagan, uninformed, underdeveloped — and that's not right.

I was ordained in a time when there were many movements, and one of these was the Chicano movement that claimed the fundamental right for Mexican-Americans to be ourselves, especially in the Southwest. We started to think that many of our people had never crossed into the United States, but that the United States had crossed to us; fifty per cent of Mexico had become part of the United States. Many people had never migrated; they were foreigners in their own home country. In fact, the Treaty of Hidalgo had guaranteed that Texas would be in perpetuity a bilingual state. The treaty was never respected. The whole Southwest was in many ways a land of colonized people. We claimed the right to be a political movement, an educational movement. Students struggled for the right to be, the right to study who and where we were. We never studied our history in school; neither church history nor our civic history was ever presented. We never knew our heroes, our background — and what is a people without a background? Our education became very important. We wanted to be part of the whole.

As a priest I got asked many questions. I remember a man who asked beautifully that the local church pursue the heritage, the language, the traditions, the customs of the people it was serving. He said that the church was not a foreigner, that there was a theology of the civil movements. And we said: "What does that have to do with the church?" Was this from a sense of shame? Was it an apology? No! Ours were beautiful, profound, deep experiences of God.

So we started exploring our faith tradition.

The Mexican American Cultural Center in San Antonio, Texas, started exploring our missionary history, how we became Christians — and that means Catholics, because Catholicism was the only religion in Latin America. We started to see how our origins were totally different from the origins of the religions of the United States, from Reformation and Counter-Reformation religions, and how our medieval religion mingled beautifully with the indigenous religions. We started to trace our origins, how our faith had been born. We found this fascinating, more and more exciting. We found how our traditions were deeply biblically-based, because the printing press wasn't running yet, and people didn't have bibles, but the missionaries were very biblically based. But we also learned that even though they fought many of our traditions, they learned to combine them to make expressions of God that were very profound; even though they were labeled as pagan, heathen, backwards, they were profound expressions of God, the Deity, spirituality.

We started to retrieve our Spanish traditions, and also our Native American traditions, in Mestizo Christianity. This is a beautiful blend of the medieval Christianity of Spain, which is very different from the Christianity of Western Europe. Don't forget that Spain was a country where three great religions — Islam, Judaism, Christianity — co-existed for eight hundred years, enriching one another. Don't forget that when you go to a Latin-American wedding you have a fully Hispanic bridal series, you have an exchange of the coins and the pineapple, the lasso, the ring. That came from the Spanish tradition. In Spain we are very ecumenical. When we pray to God, we pray to Allah; we express "I hope" by *ojala*, "May Allah's will be done." We started to promote all this, we started to do workshops, and people started to learn about *pasados, apastonelas*, all that kind of thing. I've been working at that for a good while, trying to recreate this traditional religion, give it new meaning, talk about how to promote it.

When our Bishop Flores came to San Antonio he needed a new rector for the cathedral, for San Fernando Cathedral. He called me and said, "Look, you can talk about this stuff, about how it's important, how artful it is, to give people a deeper sense of identity, of existence. This is a place where you can be yourself, and practice your religion." So I became rector of San Fernando Cathedral. That was about 1983. I couldn't believe the challenge. I knew the cathedral well — as a boy I used to play around there. People knew me before I knew them. I remember the cathedral in its heyday, when it was the most popular church in town. Some of the people, the parishioners there, liked to say, "Our family founded this church, and therefore we were here when this was New Spain, we were still here when it became Mexico, and we were here when it became the Republic of Texas, we were here when it became the United States, we were here when it became the Confederacy of the South, and we're still here now. We don't know what country will come through next, but we'll still be here." That's the parish I went to.

The parish had very deep roots, but was also a parish that immigrants were attracted to. But it was a parish where the air conditioning wasn't working in the heat of San Antonio, where the kneelers were totally worn out, with no parking whatsoever in this downtown place. It seemed to be dying; few people were coming to church.

So I went there, and I started asking people, "What are the religions practices that people are practicing here?" And they started to tell me, "What is important, Father, is that we really experience God, and togetherness, and a connection to those who came before us, so that we know that we're not alone." So we started to water the plant that had been there, that was kind of dying. We breathed new life and identity into those people, and empowered a people that remained a people in the midst of anything that threatened to destroy their identity. Don't forget that San Antonio was a very racist city, like many other cities in this country. I can still remember signs, ugly little signs that said: "Niggers, Messians, and Dogs Not Allowed." I can remember that, and it's painful. So be clear: It was a very segregated society, where the Mexicans were being put down.

Texas had a policy of "pass without learning" in most of the schools. They would pass Mexican kids from one grade to the other with no concern about their learning. Therefore they would graduate from high school with no more than a second-grade reading level, and would become cheap labor. When slavery came to an end people found that hired cheap labor was more profitable than slavery because they didn't own the laborers. So Texas was an internal colony in the United States.

But San Fernando had its dignity. It was a church where people were someone. It was very similar to the Black churches in this country, where people could be themselves. San Fernando at one time had been one of those places, but it was dying. So I came in, and started to recreate the rituals. How would people like to do it? I didn't tell them how to do it, I stimulated their ritual imagination.

So we started creating rituals. We started with a whole year based on popular rituals. I can say that we had four things: popular rituals; art, where we invited artists to come and paint different scenes the way they would see them today; traditional music that people remembered and wanted to maintain; and new music. This was a combination of the traditional and the new, of continuity and transformation. And we had very good biblical preaching. I find it very important to correlate the good biblical preaching with different aspects of people.

Believe me, the response was phenomenal. Pretty soon the church started to be filled. We started televising the local Mass, which became so popular that it was picked up by the networks. — So we're coming to your area! — At one time we had a bigger Sunday audience

than the pope. People thought of it as a very festive service, very Latino, with a lot of singing, and decorations, and special events, special celebrations. For example, on the feast of the Presentation of the child Jesus, February 2, we invited all the families with babies one year and younger to the television Mass, and we had a prayer offering to God the gift God had lost. It was really moving, really beautiful. At another time a famous singer died, and we had a special memorial television Mass for Celina. The Mass celebrated the events of the community, whether sorrow, joy, or success.

One of the things that we started was around the events of Holy Week. We were doing this just around our neighborhood when I realized that earlier those processions had been done right in central San Antonio. Those streets are part of our history. The street with the park is named Della Rosa. The street in front of the cathedral is called La Soledad, Our Lady of Solitude. But they wouldn't let us take over the city "because it was a religions event." I said, "No, look, this is not a religious event, it's just a cultural event. You won't find this in any official ritual book in Roman Catholicism, and so it's not an official ritual of Catholicism." And they said, "Oh, O.K." I said, "It's an event for tourism." And they said, "Oh, that's great."

The first time we did it we were scared of how people would react. Six thousand people turned out. Last year over thirty thousand people came at ten on Good Friday morning, of all denominations and all backgrounds. In fact one of the leading Baptist churches, Emmanuel Baptist Church, canceled their Good Friday service and joined us in the procession. After we finished our official liturgical service, they had their service right there also. It was a beautiful unity in the cross.

The most moving event we had during my tenure there was at the beginning of the First Gulf War, when these two or three guys came to me and said, "Father, we're going to the Gulf War, give us a blessing." I said I'd be happy to give them a blessing, even though I did not approve of the war; I'd give them a blessing. And I said, "Let me give the blessing on Sunday, on television, when the three of you will pray for everyone who's going to the Gulf War." They got permission, then called back later and asked, "Can a few of our friends come with us?" By that evening the whole battalion was coming! We called the press, and we asked the people if we could have the service outside because the whole battalion was coming. Well, they came in their fatigues, and they all came, Jews and Catholics and non-believers, blacks, whites, browns, everyone came, and at the end everyone prayed over the men that God would protect them and guide them. It was a very moving moment. We even had mariachi bands in the plaza. At the end the buses came and took them to the airport. In that way the church celebrated things in the community.

We weren't afraid to challenge people. For example, in the Latino community one of two big problems is the high school dropout rate, which is very scary to us. The other is that we don't vote. That's part of our social responsibility. Yes, we feel grateful to God, but praise and privilege have responsibilities.

I got two letters that I'll never forget. One was from an English-speaking lady who watched Irish television. She wrote, "I'm an elderly Irish person, and if heaven is going to be anything like your liturgies, then I can't wait to get there." The other one was from a fellow who said he was an atheist. "I was flipping channels one Sunday morning and ran into the program. And I found it so human, so unplastic, so real, that I fell in love with it, and I watch it every Sunday. Here's $1000 to keep it going, from a self-proclaimed atheist."

Most of this came from the heart. Latino worship is from the deep heart: it's festive, communicative, incarnational. So that's the way we got the cathedral going; it was all through ritual, dance, music, art, good preaching, and trusting the people. We said "How would you like to do it?" They tried some things that I didn't care too much about, but they worked out. We did well.

Then the Lilly Foundation got very interested in what we were doing, and commissioned a study. They were able to bring in scholars of different disciplines, anthropologists, religious scholars, artists, news directors, business people, so that they could experience one of the great religious celebrations, the feast of Our Lady of Guadelupe or Holy Week. We paid their way, gave them a stipend; they didn't have to pay for anything. They lived with the people; then afterwards we did a debriefing with them, and it helped us reflect on what they were seeing, feeling, experiencing. We had several of those, and then we put together a theological study of our parish. It was a theological reflection on how a dying parish was transformed into a vital community.

So that's the story of San Fernando Cathedral.

———————————

Virgilio Elizondo is a diocesan priest of the archdiocese of San Antonio. He holds a PhD/STD from the Institut Catholique de Paris. He is the founder of the Mexican American Cultural Center, and Professor of Pastoral and Hispanic Theology at Notre Dame. Among his honors are the Catholic University of America award for creative contribution to theology, and the University of Notre Dame's "Latarae Medal" — the University's highest honor. He is the author of Galilean Journey: The Mexican American Promise; Gudalupe: Mother of the New Creation; *and* A God of Incredible Surprises: Jesus of Galilee, *as well as several other books, and has edited 20 issues of* Concilium.

Advent and Christmas at the Farm

GRACE LEE BILLINGS

Far Fields Farm is a hundred-acre family farm on a hilltop in Washington, Connecticut. It is secluded, at the end of a long dirt road, and seems barely touched by the world. It is there that Grace Lee Billings and her husband Jack Johnson raised their three sons.

LIKE MANY YOUNG FAMILIES, JACK AND I stumbled into celebrating the holiday season—the Christmas tree, opening presents, and then crossing the road to Grandma and Grandpa's house to join the rest of the family for a festive turkey dinner. Between family living near by, and the "selling of the holidays," the religious meaning of our Christmas deteriorated in direct proportion to the increase in the number of our children. What had been ten presents under the tree for Alex burgeoned to thirty or more presents after the twins were born. On Christmas morning two exhausted and grumpy parents watched the children thoughtlessly rip through the pile of presents. The culmination of a year had descended into a spectacle of hollow commercialism.

Then came the "darkest Christmas of them all." The boys, tiny as they were, sat in their jammies Christmas morning surrounded by their loot—trucks, hamsters, tricycles, books, games, clothes, candy, stuffed animals—when one of them said, "Is that all there is?" The question was probably an innocent request for information, but Jack heard it differently. He was furious, a rare happening indeed. Jack erupted in a tirade on their ingratitude, and called them spoilt brats. At the end of this colorful explosion the boys were convinced that this was their last Christmas. They told us a few years later, remembering the famous diatribe, that even one package under the following year's Christmas tree would have seemed lavish. In reflective hindsight, Jack and I saw Christmas as a disaster of our own making. But was there an alternative?

The next November our friend Seton suggested that we celebrate Advent. For four years he had lived as a Benedictine monk at Mount Saviour Monastery in upstate New York. There he was known as Brother Aelred, but I preferred to call him by his baptismal name. When he left Mount Saviour he settled for a time in a house known as Sheepfold, near the Abbey of Regina Laudis in Bethlehem, Connecticut, and later he established a small non-canonical monastery in a house called Dayspring, also in Bethlehem. A number of people in our area of Connecticut—the Farm is in Washington—liked to join him and his confrères for worship. Some of us were regular church-goers, some not; I was raised an evangelical, Jack and the boys were members of no church.

Seton and Mark, who had also been at Mount Saviour, had always observed this season in their years in the monastery. They wanted to add it to the Dayspring celebrations, but they felt it needed to be done outside of "the Sunday Mass." Most of the regulars in the Dayspring gathering said that they couldn't participate in four Sunday evenings, but a small group—our family, Nancy and Tom Ware, their three sons, the McDermott family, Seton and Mark—made the commitment. As our twins, Eliot and Nicholas, were still little, and might need to be in bed early, we decided to have Advent at the Farm rather than at Dayspring. The change of venue focused Advent on family rather than on church. From this small start we found our way.

In preparation, Seton, Mark, Nancy, Maureen McDermott, and I met at the Farm. We knew each other well, knew the Dayspring style, and enjoyed singing together. Now we needed to flesh out a program that was simple enough for the children but meaningful enough for the adults. We decided to follow the same format each of the four Sunday nights, establishing a rhythm. The first Advent program that we devised worked so well that we kept it for the seven years that we celebrated together. Four adults were chosen to prepare a "homily," one for each Advent Sunday, keeping a single theme through the season. Our first Advent theme was the nativity scene. Each Sunday was to focus on a different part of the story: the angel's part; the shepherds' part, Mary's part, and finally the three kings' part. After planning some Advent music, and promising to meet to practice, we ended our meeting. As Seton went out the door that night he said, "Oh by the way, don't forget the feast of St. Nicholas."

In Switzerland, where I grew up, the sixth of December was a special day. All of the bakery shops were filled with gingerbread cookies covered with a bright paper picture of St. Nicholas dressed as a bishop. My friends put their empty shoes at the foot of their beds on December fifth, and prayed that St. Nicholas would fill them during the night with candy. Rather than candy, disobedient children were given a bundle of twigs (called *une verge*) to be used for disciplining them during the year. Parents warned their misbehaving children, "If you are not good, Père Noël will bring you a *verge*." The Swiss tradition celebrated December sixth as a feast day, while Christmas was more somber, a religious day, with a few presents.

I decided to celebrate December sixth with a high English tea. Eliot asked if there was a feast of St. Eliot so that he too could have a celebration, but we couldn't find one. In truth, we always celebrated December sixth as the feast of St. Eliot and St. Nicholas. By celebrating Advent and the feast of St. Nicholas, all of December became a very special month.

At the end of the tea, the boys wrote to Santa asking for only a few things. A French friend explained to her children, "Christmas is not *your* birthday. On *your* birthday you can ask for all that you want, but on Jesus' birthday you should think of others." Somehow our children understood this message. After some discussion

and comparing of notes, Alex wrote out the short letter, usually beginning, "Dear Santa, How are you? We are fine. We would like …" He addressed the envelope to the North Pole, and the boys ran it out to the mailbox. Jack and I made a point of retrieving this valuable letter before the mailman took it away the next day. This simplified the Christmas shopping, as Jack's parents and my mother each gave an item from the list of three or four things, while we gave the most important items (new skates, a radio). With the joyous and fancy St. Nicholas tea, Christmas was now both launched and limited.

Sometimes the boys and I went to the Abbey of Regina Laudis to see their Neapolitan crèche. To get to the barn where the nuns permanently displayed this Renaissance treasure, we had to walk through snowy woods. Inside the gray barn, and behind a huge plate glass window, we saw a miniature Italian village displayed on a hillside. Before us, in the most beautiful detail, were cottages, doves in cages, peasants sitting at tables with tiny tankards and plates, ox carts on the road, woodsmen cutting logs, children at play, all against a background of distant hills and valleys. In one corner, inside a half-open barn, was the Virgin — resplendent in pale blue and pink satin — showing her newborn son to the kneeling shepherds. Outside, under a magnificent Star of Bethlehem, the three kings approached with their camels and horses following behind. Every detail enchanted us. How we wished we too could have such a diorama in our barn!

But our barn told a different story. The boys and I rarely visited the cold and forlorn hayloft in winter. We did go up to collect hay to put around our own small crèche, displayed on a table in the living room. The loft, with its sweet smell of summer, was caught in the icy cold of December. In our plain cold barn we imagined the original manger scene with the Christ child lying in his swaddling clothes in a humble shed, with the holy family gathered in awe around him. In our hayloft there was no place for the satin, gold, and velvet of the Regina Laudis manger, but the hay bales had tiny field flowers caught in them, and this seemed very festive to us.

However, the real heart of our Christmas celebration became the four Sundays of Advent. They made us understand and share the spirit of the season as no presents could ever possibly do. Our friends came to the Farm on those dark December nights, passing through unlit countryside, then coming down our long isolated road, and finally arriving at our house. Only the most necessary lights were turned on in the driveway and on the way to the front door. Inside the front hall, only dimly lit by a lantern, they left their coats and hats on the settle, then came quietly into the living room. There a huge fragrant evergreen wreath was placed on the floor, with a candle in the middle to light the room. The children sat around the wreath, while the adults sat on the couch and chairs in a circle around the room. On that first Sunday of Advent, as we waited for the last guests to arrive, even the children were taken by the darkness of the big living room, lit by the flickering candle. For us the darkness was directly from Isaiah: "The people that walked in darkness have seen a great light." The air was full of anticipation.

When all had arrived, and a lovely quiet gathered us in, Jack or Seton read an opening Bible verse. Then we sang the first verse of the hymn, "O Come, O Come, Emmanuel." As the four Sundays progressed, going from the very dark first Sunday toward the bright fourth Sunday, when Christ's birth was imminent, we added another verse to this opening hymn. With the light of each additional Advent candle and the brightening of the room, we wanted more song and more joy.

In preparation for the homily, one of the older boys read from the Old Testament. Then, using the flame from the center candle, he lit one of the candles on the wreath. On the first Sunday, to explain the Advent wreath, one of the boys read the words:

The wreath is round, and symbolizes eternity. It is green to show the ever-presentness of God. The four candles are for each Sunday of waiting, while the middle candle, from which the others are lit, shows humanity's eternal hope in the coming of the Messiah.

Now, with two candles lit, we could see more clearly the faces of those gathered nearest to the Advent wreath. As we lighted more candles each Sunday, we eventually saw the faces of all those in the room. As we shared those winter evenings, we also came to know each other better just as the candlelight revealed us more to each other.

A New Testament reading followed the lighting of the candle. The homily followed. This was not a deep, theological document. Nor was it exegetical and full of biblical references to be carefully noted. Rather it was a personal expression of the meaning of the theme. That first year our reflections on the nativity touched on the journeys of the shepherds, the holy family, and the kings as they progressed toward the manger in the barn. Later, the thoughts turned to the coming of Christ, and its implications in our own lives and times.

I was moved by the time and thought that people put into these homilies. I realized that the church had a wealth of talent among the laity that was rarely tapped. I never heard heresy or "unbaked thought." Rather there was great humility and reverence in the handling of these themes.

The homily was followed by a "reflection," a time when any of us could add our own thoughts on the theme. Perhaps because of the dark even the children felt free to say a few words. One night one of the Ware boys—age six or so—said very simply into the darkened room, as if to state the obvious, "Well of course. God loves us." Frank McDermott, gentle scholar that he was, said in Latin, "*Ex ore infantium*" (out of the mouth of babes).

After the reflection we sang the beatiuful song, "Maranatha." Then we sang the Lord's Prayer. A small group of us, who had taken time to practice together, then sang a less familiar Christmas song, perhaps "Maria Walks amid the Thorns," "Long is Our Winter," or the lovely "Dona Nobis Pacem." After this song we passed a basket with a small token or "tangible" to concretize the theme for the evening. The token served as a souvenir that reminded us during the week of the Advent celebration and its theme.

One of the first "tangibles" that we made was a tiny crèche of straw with a small cross stitched into it to symbolize the whole story from Christmas to Easter. These tangibles were small enough to hang on a Christmas tree. On the third Sunday of Advent, known as Joy or *Gaudete* (Rejoice!) Sunday, when the "waiting" is almost over, Kathleen McDermott made a cake with cranberry frosting which the children named the "joy cake." The frosting color was similar to the church's rose-colored vestments and altar hangings on this Sunday of rejoicing. The children favored this "tangible," but they also knew that by Joy Sunday our journey toward Christmas was soon to be over.

After a closing verse, we sang the joyous "People Look East." Then we passed the Peace. Seton held the hands of one of the children, saying, "The peace of Christ be with you." The child answered, "And with you." Then, taking his neighbor's hands, the child repeated, "The Peace of Christ be with you." And this new child answered, "And with you." Once all of the children had passed the Peace, it was passed to an adult, until everyone in the room had been blessed. When the Advent celebration was over, each family left quietly, going out in to the chill December night. I remember that once there was a full moon, and the rolling fields, covered in sparkling snow, seemed to adorn our festivities.

On the last Sunday of Advent, when all the candles had been lighted, and every verse of every song had been sung—with at least two singings of "People Look East"—one of us turned on the tiny white lights of our Christmas tree that we had just set up the day before. Then we turned on the lights in the rest of the house, lit a fire in the fireplace, and had a party. After all, it was *nearly* Christmas. The dining room table was set with every kind of Christmas cake and cooky, the St. Nicholas Advent wreath over the table was lit for the last time, and we feasted. Later Kathleen McDermott sat at the piano in the living room and played all our favorite carols.

Over the years more friends came until we shared Advent with thirty people. Somehow it never lost its magic and intimacy, perhaps because of the darkness and beauty of the Farm. Even in its repetitions, it never lost its sense of belonging to another time, another place. But the season was not over yet. There were still the twelve days of Christmas.

Because we celebrated Advent, Christmas was changed, and our old nemesis was transformed into a friend. Most of it came from simply taking the emphasis off the presents, and finding a way to share the Christmas story. Now the twenty-fourth and twenty-fifth on the Farm became two days we really enjoyed. In Geneva, my family celebrated Christmas on Christmas Eve when we lit our tree with real candles, and, though they only burned a short time, I still remember the tree appearing to be alive in the light of the flickering flame. At the Farm we found a way to observe two different family traditions. On the night of the twenty-fourth we entertained my family, then spent the twenty-fifth with Jack's family.

We always enjoyed the days from December twenty-sixth to January sixth. We lit our Christmas tree every night, making the spirit or Christmas carry over into the new year. We went for walks in the big field behind the house where the grass was frozen and turned down under our feet. The branches in the trees rattled in the wind, as though the veins where the sap would run were hollow and their emptiness cried out. The sparrows congregated in the syringa bush, finding in its dense branches a perfect shelter against the cold. The dirt road to the Farm turned rock hard, and the salt from the town plows turned it white. During an ice storm the trees became ice palaces. All the grass, rocks, stone walls and steps were under glass. Then, as the temperature warmed, we heard the ice fall round the base of each tree, looking like a collection of the broken stems from wineglasses at Nature's party.

When the twelfth day of Christmas came, the lovely long season that began with Advent and the St. Eliot/St. Nicholas tea came to an end with a party. In the countries with a Spanish heritage January sixth, called the Feast of the Three Kings, is a great day of rejoicing. In other countries it is called Epiphany, "the appearance of God," when the Magi saw the Christ child. In my childhood, the bakery windows in Geneva displayed cakes with three tiny stone "kings" hidden inside. I remember the excitement of searching with my teeth, bite after bite, for the hoped-for resistance that showed that I had one of the "good luck" kings in my mouth. Those prized trophies stayed in my jewelry box for years.

Two illuminations in *Les Tres Riches Heures du Duc de Berry*—where my rigid, self-chosen faith had met my Farm world—illustrate different views of the three kings. The first shows a crossroads where the three kings meet. They are shown triumphant, "man as captain of his destiny," with magnificent crowns and prancing steeds. Banners fly, leopards come as pets, and even a dog journeyed from afar to pay homage to the child born in a stable. But in the next view of the magi they are on bended knee or prostrate before the King of Kings, their crowns in the hands of their attendants, as though their own position in human eyes was nothing by comparison to their real worth in the eyes of the Christ child.

On January sixth the Advent group gathered in the late afternoon, and, this time,

our celebration was in the entrance hall of our house. People either stood or sat for the very short service. We began by singing the hymn, "We Three Kings," men and women taking turns, and then all of us together singing the last verse. Seton read the Gospel story from Matthew 2:1-12, telling of the magi coming to Bethlehem. Then Michael Ware recited from memory T. S. Eliot's *The Journey of the Magi*, another expression of the struggle of faith as life moves from the ordinary to the extraordinary. The poem begins:

A cold coming we had of it,
Just the worst time of the year
For a journey, and such a long journey:
The ways deep and the weather sharp,
The very dead of winter.
And the camels galled, sore-footed,
    refractory,
Lying down in the melting snow.
There were times we regretted
The summer palaces on slopes, the terraces,
And the silken girls bringing sherbet....

A while later Jack stood at the front door, with its dark woodwork, and wrote in white chalk across the lintel: 19 C + M + B 80. As he wrote each letter he spoke the traditional names of the kings: Casper (sometimes referred to as Gaspard), Melchior, and Balthasar. Jack then repeated the initials with the new meaning the church had given them: *Christus Mansionem Benedicat*: Christ Bless this House. He then read the blessing:

Bless this house and each of our homes. Bless all who live in them, and bless all who pass through their doors. Bless this year for health, for peace, and for love. Bless each of our pilgrimages, and may each of us be a blessing to another along the way. Amen.

We sang again "We Three Kings," followed by the Lord's Prayer, and passed the Peace for the last time during this season.

In the old days the feast of the Epiphany was yet another cause for revelry, and we saw no reason to change the traditional theme: "When fools are kings and kings are fools." It was a time of jesters and riddles and prizes to be won. So after a buffet dinner we gathered for the serving of the King's Cake that Kathleen McDermott had baked. She cut this cake, every year running, in a magical way, so that only the children found a "king" in their portions. Then Michael Ware, the consummate actor and clown, donned a special red, white, and green jester's hat — with many points, each decorated with a tiny bell — and picked up a scepter with even more bells, to rule his court.

Before we could win a small prize, Michael put each of us to the test. Some sang, others recited or read a poem, some had to do a balancing act or to push a bean across the floor with their noses, and others had to stand still and say nothing for two minutes while the jester made hilarious faces and took wonderful poses.

The light-hearted joy of the evening bid farewell to the Christmas season. Everyone went home with a copy of the written blessing and a piece of chalk tied in a red ribbon so that they too could bless their front doors and their houses. As in *Les Tres Riches Heures,* the farm year and the church year were being played out in our lives. However, with the end of the Christmas season we were now braced for a somber time.

Grace Lee Billings lived at the Farm from 1973 to 1998. Her account of Advent and Christmas comes from an unpublished memoir, "The Season of the Green Meadows." She now lives in Boston.

Christian Creativity in a Post-Christian Ethos
QUENTIN FAULKNER

THE IDEAS I WANT TO EXPLORE IN THIS ESSAY begin with the experience of some works of art that have recently been created for St. Mark's-on-the-Campus Episcopal Church in Lincoln, Nebraska, the church of which I'm a member. All of the art you will experience has been created by active and faithful members of this church. Let me hasten to say that although I've been involved in various ways in fostering this art, I'm in no way responsible for it. That responsibility lies primarily with an insightful priest, Father Donald Hanway, who has vigorously championed the cause of the arts in the church; with my wife, Dr. Mary Murrell Faulkner, who is the church's director of music; and with various church members who have shared their talents and their support.

Please refer to the DVD that accompanies this issue: first to the visual art, in the form of altar fittings, eucharistic vestments, stained-glass, and sculpture; and then to the poetry and music, in the form of psalm settings and sung prayers. These are:

1. The altar as it was prior to the creation of new fittings

2. Advent *(Constance Backus-Yoder, fabric artist; stained-glass cross by Julee Lowe, stained-glass artist)*

3. Epiphany *(also common time; Constance Backus-Yoder, fabric artist)*

4. Lent *(Constance Backus-Yoder, fabric artist)*

5. Pentecost *(Constance Backus-Yoder, fabric artist)*

6. Altar cross *(Julee Lowe, stained-glass artist)*

7. Paschal candle *(Julee Lowe, stained-glass artist)*

8. Baptismal font *(Julee Lowe, stained-glass artist)*

9. Processional cross *(Julee Lowe, stained-glass artist)*

10. Christmas *(suspended stars designed by Julee Lowe and made by Penny Siefker)*

11. The Winged Lion of St. Mark *(sculpted by Gregg Wortham, M.F.A., University of Nebraska-Lincoln, 2002)*

12. Psalm 103: Bless the Lord, O My Soul *(music by Constance Backus-Yoder)*

13. Psalm 126: The Lord has done great things for us *(music by Constance Backus-Yoder)*

14. Come Holy Spirit *(text by Betty Sperry; musical setting by Mary Murrell Faulkner)*:

REFRAIN
Come Holy Spirit,
Come Holy Spirit,
Come Holy Spirit,
Come now.

1. Rushing winds, in anticipation of God's gift to the nations.

REFRAIN

2. Doves descending in clouds of white, a glorious sight — love unending.

REFRAIN

3. Tongues of flame, portending speaking in tongues, Spirit descending.

REFRAIN

 Holy Spirit, ever in our lives, in calm and strife. Come now.

REFRAIN

I want to use the art documented on the accompanying DVD as the basis for reflecting on several questions that have their common focus on creativity in today's church. The first question is this: Should any of the art recorded on the disk be called "great art"? To intensify that question, to up the ante, let me ask if you think the organa of Leonin and Perotin are great art? Is John Dunstable's isorhythmic motet *Veni Sancte Spiritus* great art? Is the triumphal cross at Brandenburg Cathedral in eastern Germany (see #15 on the disk) great art? All of these—Leonin, Perotin, Dunstable, the triumphal cross—are ancient artifacts from a vital culture of the past, and that automatically invests them with a certain value; but are they "great"? I think it's reasonable to label all of this art—old and new—as intense, gripping, arresting, vibrant, authentic. But great?

To get at that question, let me ask yet another: Who was the first "great composer" (great as conceived in the most usual, popular way, as in a concert program, or in an "encyclopedia of the great composers")? Handel? Perhaps, but once he moved permanently to England, Handel wasn't as widely celebrated on the continent as in his adopted country. He became great only with hindsight. The same holds true, of course, for J. S. Bach. I'd vote for Haydn. In his later years, Haydn was regularly referred to as great. Here, for example, is a poem about Haydn written by Charles Burney on the occasion of Haydn's first visit to London in 1791:

> Music! The Calm of life, the cordial bowl,
> Which anxious care can banish from the
>   soul,
> Affliction soothe, and elevate the mind,
> And all its sordid manacles unbind,
> Can snatch us from life's incidental pains,
> And "wrap us in Elysium with its strains!"
> To cultivated ears, this fav'rite art
> No *new* delight was able to impart;
> No Eagle flights its votaries durst essay,
> But hopp'd, like little birds, from spray to

> spray.
> At length great HAYDN'S new and varied
>   strains
> Of habit and indiff'rence broke the chains;
> Rous'd to attention the long torpid sense,
> With all that pleasing wonder could
>   dispense.
> Whene'er Parnassus' height he meant to
>   climb,
> Whether the grand, pathetic, or sublime,
> The simply graceful, or the comic vein,
> The theme suggested, or enrich'd the strain,
> From melting sorrow to gay jubilation,
> Whate'er his pen produc'd was Inspiration![1]

After Haydn a surge of "great" composers began to appear, first as a trickle (Mozart, Beethoven), then as a flood (Schubert, Mendelssohn, Schumann, Weber, Rossini, Chopin, Berlioz, Verdi, Liszt, Wagner, Brahms, Franck, Mahler, etc.). Now, who was the last great composer? Perhaps Igor Stravinsky? Or Benjamin Britten? Are any great composers alive and composing today? Why are certain composers great, and others before and after them not? And to further muddy the waters: are not other "composers" in our culture routinely labelled great? What about Frank Sinatra? Is Elvis Presley great? Are the Beetles great? They, and other modern popular artists as well, are regularly identified as "great" in the modern media. In fact, Elvis Presley has even had a postage stamp issued in his honor.

How do artists come to be labelled great? How do they earn that sobriquet? The answer to that question, it seems to me, ultimately boils down to this: a broad, widely accepted cultural consensus has anointed them as great. Specifically, within a given cultural context (western Europe from, say, 1790 to 1945) certain characteristics as to what in a given art form is great gained widespread acceptance among a large majority of the population—at least among those people who counted socially, especially the ascendant bourgeoisie. Once that consensus was established, then critics could identify artists whose works exhibited those characteristics of "greatness" in exemplary fashion. In the case of the great European composers, that consensus had been building for a very long time — at least since about 1100, maybe even earlier. The maturation of the Christian faith in Europe arguably had a great deal to do with that process. One of the most obvious signs that we are now living in a post-Christian era is this: that particular consensus is now unravelling in Europe. Since it was never as firmly rooted in the United States, it has already unravelled here. The great composers, then, can only rightfully be identified as great within their own cultural context. Some learned people in a subsequent cultural context (that is, you and I) may, with hindsight, also identify certain composers as great, but that greatness cannot expect to enjoy widespread cultural acceptance in a new cultural context.

Does all of this mean, then, that works of art created before that consensus — Leonin and Perotin's organa, Dunstable's *Veni Sancte Spiritus*, and that triumphal cross in Brandenburg Cathedral — are not great? It seems to me that the question is irrelevant, since no cultural context as to what was great existed when they were created; it was an idea whose time had not yet come. What about modern "classical" artists — Jackson Pollack, Andy Warhol, Philipp Glass, art created by elephants — are they great? Again, an irrelevant question, because the cultural context that once determined greatness has broken down, and no new consensus has as yet arisen to take its place. The only shred of consensus today lies in monetary value. The director of the Sheldon Art Gallery at the University of Nebraska recently admitted — rather shame-facedly — that he had silenced a women who was ridiculing a modern painting simply by telling her what it would fetch on the market.[2]

Returning to the art recorded on the disk: Is any of it great? Again, the question is irrelevant. No standard, no broad consensus exists that would establish it as great, or mediocre, or downright tawdry. It seems fair to me to call most of it competent, and perhaps some of it intense, or arresting, or vibrant, or authentic. But great? — it's beside the point.

Why is this question of "greatness" important to us as artists in the church today? Speaking as a church musician, I'd say it is because a lot of church musicians still care about great art! We study it, analyze it, perform it; we live intimately with the most intense art of all ages and cultures. It forms and informs the criteria by which we assign value, worth. How long have we been able to do this? Not very long at all — only since the widespread, cheap availability of the printed word (beginning about 1700 or so); and of color reproductions of art, music recordings, videos, the mass media, and wide-spread foreign travel, these only since the later twentieth century. I'm hardly the first to observe that our modern culture is the first culture to preserve, cultivate, and appreciate all the art forms of the past, of all cultures. This has been a splendid gift to us — but it has also led to a certain failure of nerve, one might almost say an artistic paralysis, especially in the realm of classical music. We have come to note that there is indeed nothing new under the sun, and have begun to feel that the art of the past is as good as, and perhaps better than, the art created by contemporary artists. This has to be part of the reason why we as musicians, and specifically as organists, spend so much time re-creating instead of creating, playing organ literature instead of improvising. For organists, it certainly wasn't always that way. The documentary evidence below — evidence that records the tasks required of those applying to become organists in several major European churches, from the 1500s through the 1700s — reveals vividly the improvisational hoops our earlier colleagues had to jump through!

Required for the position of second organist, Basilica of San Marco, Venice, in 1541:

1. Opening a choirbook and finding at random the beginning of a Kyrie or a motet, one copies this and gives it to the competing organist. The latter must, at the organ, improvise a piece in a regular fashion, without mixing up the parts, just as if four singers were performing.
2. Opening a book of plainchant equally at random, one copies a cantus firmus from an introit or another chant, and sends it to the said organist. He must improvise on it, deriving the three other parts [from it]; he must put the cantus firmus now in the bass, now in the tenor, now in the alto and soprano, deriving imitative counterpoint from it, not simple accompaniments.[3]

Required for the position of organist at Hamburg Cathedral in 1725, recorded by Johann Mattheson:

1. Improvise a short free prelude, approximately two minutes long, based on material "not studied beforehand." The prelude should begin in A major and end in G minor.
2. Improvise a trio "on two manuals with the pedal," approximately six minutes long, on the chorale *Herr Jesu Christ, du höchstes Gut.* The left hand should not double the pedal, and the middle voice should be artfully constructed.
3. Improvise a fugue on a given theme, with a given countersubject. The length of the fugue was left up to the candidate, whose concern should be "not how long, but how good."
4. Compose, within two days of the test, a well-worked out piece and submit it, in written form, for close scrutiny by the jury. (Note that the candidate was asked to compose the piece, not play it.)
5. Produce, at sight, an artful accompaniment (i.e., continuo realization) for an aria, approximately four minutes long.
6. Improvise, on the full organ, a ciacona on a given bass theme. The work should be approximately six minutes long, and performed in a carefully considered style. Here the applicant was given a half-hour to gather his thoughts.[4]

Required for the position of organist at St. Nicholas Church in Berlin, 1773, recorded by Bach's pupil Johann Friedrich Agricola:

Requirements to be placed before the candidate... a quarter of an hour before the audition.
1. Improvise a praeludium on the plenum, beginning in B major and ending in D major.
2. Improvise a prelude on the chorale *Christ unser Herr zum Jordan kam.* The cantus firmus, or chorale tune, must be played on a manual with a louder registration. The performer is to improvise the added contrapuntal voices on a manual with a softer registration, while paying attention to the pedal as well.
3. Play the same chorale, *Christ unser Herr,* plainly but with full chords, as it must be played for congregational singing; one verse of this will suffice.
4. To accompany from the figured bass a sung aria, or an entire cantata, which the cantor … will provide.
5. In conclusion, either play an organ piece written by a good composer (which the candidate may choose himself) using the score, or, if he wishes, improvise a free fantasy; in the latter case he should change skillfully between three manuals with different registrations.[5]

Only in the final example, in Agricola's instructions from 1773, was the candidate allowed to perform a work already composed, and even in that case the candidate was given the alternative of improvising a free fantasy. Until the twentieth century all composers of organ music were at first improvisers (including Mendelssohn and Liszt), and a major part of the literature for the instrument began its life as improvisations. Only when we compare our situation with theirs do we begin to understand what's at stake here. Great music—the organ works of the great composers—is indeed both a blessing and a curse! To the degree that it overshadows (or even stifles) improvisation—the creation of the new; indeed, the valuing of the new—it contributes to the impoverishment of the art of music as a whole, and specifically of the art of church music.

Some of the art on the disk was produced by amateur or semi-professional artists. Amateur art in the church is in part the result of the rise of the egalitarian democratic ideal and the move toward empowering every individual, toward allowing all individuals to reach their creative potential. But amateur art in the church is also in part the result of a radically new cultural phenomenon, the separation of cult and government, of church and state. Has there ever been a traditional culture in which cult and government—church and state—have been or are separated? I can't think of one. The model on which all cultures previous to our modern culture have operated is as follows: the cult (the worship of God or the gods) is indispensable to the welfare, indeed to the very survival, of the people; the role of the ruling class, the government, is to collect wealth by various methods of taxation, and to dedicate part of that wealth to the adornment of the cult; it is the duty of the ruling and priestly classes to seek out and train talented artists to create works of art in the service of the cult, and to support the artists in that endeavor. Now and then one does encounter examples of religious art created by amateurs (e.g., some medieval English devotional poetry), but in developed traditional cultures, amateur art in public cultic observances is the exception rather than the rule.

The model on which modern culture operates hardly needs to be described in detail. It's quite familiar to everyone living in the United States today: rigorously enforced separation of cult and government; cult (now actually many cults) supported by free-will offerings of adherents, etc. Neither of these models—the traditional or the modern—is inherently more friendly to art than the other, but the first has shown itself to be, on the whole, better funded and more congenial to professional artists; that is, friendlier to fine art.

It seems to me that it has now become vastly more important for Christians in the modern world to encourage amateur or semi-professional artists, for two reasons: (1) we need what they create, and (2) we need a broad base of discerning, committed amateurs as a fertile matrix for the development and support of professionals.

BUT! what do we do about the disasters, the failures, the trite, the second- and third-rate art that are an inevitable by-product of encouraging amateur art? Well, first we have to acknowledge that professional artists don't always create masterpieces either. And with that in mind, I can only recommend to you what we've been doing at St. Mark's: identify artists with talent, offer them guidance and support, and retire the ill-begotten as soon as is prudently and diplomatically possible—and above all, keep on encouraging more and better art to take its place. Granted, it's a messy business, but I think it's a risk we simply have to take. For me, a maxim (sometimes attributed to St. Augustine) comes to the rescue, reminding me that "we should not allow ourselves to be distracted by the imperfect as we strive for the perfect."

Should everybody in the Church be an artist? Clearly not. Should every individual church be in the business of identifying, encouraging, and supporting the artists in its midst? I think so.

It occurs to me at this point that I'm operating on a number of assumptions. Let me, in the interest of honesty and candor, make them clear to you now:

1. Christians, like all human beings, are subject to the creation mandate: since they're made in the image of God, they are, like God, creators. And, being made in God's image, they should exercise their creativity fully and continually.

2. The locus of human artistic creativity in the context of religion, viewed both historically and rationally, is principally in the service of the cult, i.e., of public worship—when imagination, impelled by intensity of love and devotion, takes wing.

3. Creative intensity is as good an indicator of intense religious conviction as any I know: we adorn what we love. We adorn by expending on what we love time, creative energy, effort, and resources. The truth of this statement is best understood when, viewed historically, we recognize and gauge the intensity of religious faith in past cultures largely by the creative uniqueness and intensity of their religious art: Mayan temples, Tibetan monasteries, Gothic cathedrals. Now, if we hold up the music of Christianity in the modern world to that standard we have a problem, because (in the words of Calvin Johansson) "if a knowledgeable observer were asked to name the institution in our society that clearly utilizes the highest musical creativity, we can be sure it would not be the contemporary church."[6]

4. The fourth and final assumption is this: religious creativity, at its most intense and vital, forges its own unique artistic stylistic norms, conditioned by its passionately held religious convictions. Those stylistic norms are always based in some way on the art of the past, but they always embody something new and original as well, in order to mirror a given religion's unique identity. Conjure up in your mind, for example, an image of the nave of a medieval Gothic cathedral. What's holding up its stone-vaulted ceiling? Columns. Are columns indigenously Christian? Of course not—the Gothic style inherited them from the earlier Romanesque, which in turn borrowed them from Greek and Roman architecture, which in turn … So Gothic architecture uses elements that are derived from the art of past cultures (we can trace that same process with the stone vaulting, and with the arches). The borrowing is not important, though. What the Gothic style does with what it borrows is important. We should ask: Does Gothic architecture incorporate those borrowed elements into something new and unique to its own culture (that is, to medieval Christianity)? Would you ever mistake a Gothic cathedral for a Greek or Roman temple? Would you ever mistake it for anything but a medieval Christian place of worship? Hardly! Most people the world over would immediately identify it as such. What makes a religious art form a truly indigenous expression of a particular religious faith, then, is not its individual elements, but the way those elements are put together, and the degree to which the resulting synthesis is truly a hallmark of a given religious identity.

If this final assumption of mine is true, then the music of modern Christianity has more than a problem; it has a major dilemma! The music available to us as modern Christians is either cloned from the art of a former Christian culture, or it's borrowed lock, stock, and barrel from the surrounding secular culture, which is driven by ideals and assumptions that can hardly be considered Christian. Judging from the present state of its music (and other arts as well), Christianity in the modern world is to a large degree impotent, sterile; it has lost its zeal and vitality, its inner conviction, its confidence, its consistency.

Such a claim may be exaggerated, I'll grant—but a candid assessment of our present situation will confirm, I believe, that it is not entirely baseless. It is not the threat of a "take-over" by popular music that we as church musicians should fear—that is, in my opinion, a red herring. The importation of popular music into the church is not a cause but a symptom. The secular culture of the modern world is not fundamentally the problem. If by waving a wand we could suddenly banish it from our modern churches, what creative intensity could today's churches muster to produce something viable in its stead? No past art form alone can adequately serve the modern church. Just like the church in every age, today's church requires art that is indigenous—native to Christianity—and modern—of our time—and we don't have it: that's the dilemma!

How do we surmount this impasse? We can't go back—that leads ultimately to creativity stifled, to stagnation, to epigonism. Neither can we uncritically adopt the alien secular musical styles that surround us—that would brand us as sterile, exhausted, without prophetic power. How do we surmount this impasse?

If I knew the answer to that, I'd be a prophet—and I'm not a prophet. I don't know. But I suspect that some part of the eventual answer is to begin again at a grass roots level to identify and empower the artists in our midst; to encourage a vital artistic expression within the churches we serve, an expression that is driven by a community's faith, and that intensifies that faith; to build a broad-based, creatively aware constituency, people who intuit what's at stake here. And that brings us full circle to the ideas I put forth earlier in this address; those are:

• put greatness into proper perspective. In fact, retire it from our modern religious artistic vocabulary. Talk instead about *vital* or *intense* or *convincing* art, so that we can take a load off our backs and move ahead;

• support and encourage artistic activity at all levels—amateur, semi-professional, professional—wherever we find it in the church—in our church! Showcase it, celebrate it, treasure it;

• and finally, have the courage to take risks, and to allow ourselves not to be distracted by what is less good as we strive for what is better.

ENDNOTES

1. From Piero Weiss and Richard Taruskin, *Music in the Western World* (New York: Schirmer Books, 1984), 313-14.

2. L. Kent Wolgamott, " What is Art," *Lincoln Journal Star* (August 3, 2002): K 2. Art painted by elephants is now bringing up to $500 a painting—check it out on the web: www.elephantart.com/catalog/

3. Quoted after Haar, "The *Fantasie et recerchari* of Giuliano Tiburtino," *Musical Quarterly* 59 (1973): 223-38

4. Johann Mattheson, *Grosse General-Bass-Schule* (Hamburg, 1731), 34-35, as translated and condensed by George B. Stauffer, "J.S. Bach as Organ Pedagogue," in *The Organist as Scholar*, ed. Kerala J. Snyder (Stuyvesant, N.Y.: Pendragon Press, 1994), 37-38.

5. See Quentin Faulkner, "Die Registrierungen der Orgelwerke J.S. Bachs," *Bach-Jahrbuch* (1995): 29-30.

6. *Music & Ministry: A Biblical Counterpoint*, 2nd ed. (Peabody, Mass.: Henderson, 1998), 26.

Quentin Faulkner is Larson Professor of Organ and Music Theory/History at the University of Nebraska-Lincoln, where in addition to teaching organ he has developed a series of courses in church music. He is the author of Wiser than Despair, *a book on the history of ideas in church music (1996). During the winter semester 1998-9 he was Fulbright Guest Professor at the Evangelische Hochschule für Kirchenmusik, Halle/Saale, Germany. He and his wife, Mary Murrell Faulkner, serve together as musicians for St. Mark's-on-the-Campus Episcopal Church in Lincoln.*

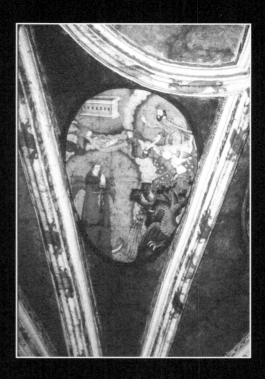

Johann Sebastian Bach's Mass in B Minor: The Greatest Artwork of All Times and All People

MARKUS RATHEY

The Tangeman Lecture delivered April 18, 2003

I.

WHEN WE GO TO THE MOVIES OR WATCH television, the first things we encounter are — commercials. No place in our life is uncontaminated by sentences like "Buy me — I'm the best you can get," or "You will be most satisfied with this item." Commercials surround us — except in the sphere of high art, of classical music, the place of purity. But we all know that this is not entirely true. The title of this article proves the contrary: "Johann Sebastian Bach's Mass in B Minor: The Greatest Artwork of All Times and All People." That sounds just like the slogan from a commercial. Replace "artwork" by "shampoo" and you could use the sentence on television.

The title, however, was not my idea. The Swiss composer and publisher Hans Georg Nägeli (1773–1836)[1] used it first, in 1818, in an advertisement. Nägeli had bought the original manuscript of the B Minor Mass from the heir of Carl Philipp Emanuel Bach, and intended to edit the first edition of the work.[2] He was unsuccessful. In 1832 the German publisher Simrock printed a piano reduction of the work, and in 1833 the first half of the score was published by Nägeli. He advertised the second half for 1834, but when he died two years later it had not yet been printed. Finally in 1845 the whole score was published.[3]

Two other nineteenth century editors also failed when planning to publish the Mass, or at least parts of it. In 1816 the English composer Samuel Wesley (1766–1837), a forerunner in the rediscovery of Bach on the British islands,[4] made an attempt to publish the Credo of the Mass, but was unsuccessful.[5] And in 1818, only a month later than Nägeli, Georg Johann Daniel Poelchau (1773–1836), a member of the Berlin Singakademie and an important collector of Bach's manuscripts,[6] considered printing the score of the work — a plan that was never put into effect.[7]

The reason for the lack of success was that in 1818 only composers and music historians were interested in Bach's music, and the entire Mass had never been performed. Although his music was never completely forgotten, Bach was a composer for specialists, a model for composers; his works were rarely performed in public.[8] The few pieces by Bach published during the first third of the nineteenth century served primarily as examples for polyphonic composition, or were understood as cornerstones of music history,[9] but were not to be played in public.[10]

This situation changed when Felix Mendelssohn Bartholdy (1809–1847) performed Bach's St. Matthew Passion in Berlin in 1829, introducing Bach to the concert hall.[11] Even then, however, it was long before Bach's large-scale works were an integral part of the concert repertoire, and even longer until as complicated a piece as the B Minor Mass was performed in a public concert. Although several movements had been performed in the first half of the century, the first performance of the entire B Minor Mass was no earlier than 1859.[12]

Nägeli's unsuccessful campaign was not the first time that the B Minor Mass was the subject of advertising. Bach himself created the first parts of the Mass, the Kyrie and Gloria, in order to apply for the position as court composer in Dresden in 1733. He was dissatisfied with his position as cantor at St. Thomas in Leipzig,[13] and since the old Elector of Saxony, Friedrich August I (the Strong, 1670–1733), had died that year, and his son, Friedrich August

II (1696–1763), had just been enthroned, Bach offered his services to the new ruler and sent him the following letter:

> To Your Royal Highness I submit in deepest devotion the present small work of the science which I have achieved in musique, with the most wholly submissive prayer that Your Highness will look upon it with Most Gracious Eyes, according to Your Highness's World-Famous Clemency and not according to the poor composition; and thus deign to take me under Your Most Mighty Protection.[14]

The music Bach mentions in the letter, and that he sent to the Duke of Saxony, was the first half of the B Minor Mass, the Kyrie and the Gloria. Although the pieces were not entirely new (some movements were taken from earlier cantatas; see the table at the end of this essay), the Mass was a showpiece for Bach's compositional skills.

But Bach did more than just present some of his most demanding pieces. It is obvious that he knew the style of Mass composition that was popular in Dresden at his time, and that he tried to compose in a similar idiom. He used, for example, a five part choir, which is unusual in his own compositions but rather frequent in Dresden masses; he composed several movements in the old *stile antico*, a polyphonic style that was rooted in the music of the sixteenth century and was also popular in some of the masses at the court in Dresden; finally, the division of the Mass into several independent movements alluded to Dresden models as well.

The letter and the Kyrie-Gloria Mass formed an advertisement, saying, "Take me as your new court composer." But, like Nägeli's eighty-five years later, Bach's advertising campaign was not successful, and only in 1736 did Bach received the title "court composer."[15]

The B Minor Mass was in its first centuries an unsuccessful piece. But something in the music made Hans Georg Nägeli believe that it was worthy to be published, and that something has inspired generations of choirs since the second half of the nineteenth century to perform it again and again. The slogan "The Greatest Artwork of All Times and All People" might have been written to sell something, but it must contain a grain of truth. The following view of the Mass, of its genesis and peculiarities, will show how Bach built this artwork, and will try to reveal the unique character of the composition.

II.

The music and architecture of the baroque period shared the same ideas. One of the basic principles of baroque architecture is the symmetric ground plan. The palace of Versailles in France served as a model for many other buildings. Its centerpiece is the main building, which is itself axial-symmetric; this is framed by two huge wings. Norbert Elias has noted in his study *The Court Society* to what extent the architecture of Versailles reflected (and shaped) society, and how the European nobility, by imitating the architecture of the palace, took over the sociological paradigms of the French court.[16] Thus the palace served not only as an architectural paradigm but was an emanation of the sociological structure of the late seventeenth and early eighteenth centuries. In Germany several residences were built, or re-built, according to this model, although in a much smaller size, but with the symmetric outline preserved. We know that Bach was familiar with this type of architecture since the palace of Friedrichsthal in Gotha, close to Weimar, was constructed about 1710 according to the model.[17]

Even apart from architecture, symmetry was seen in the baroque world as a sign of perfection, mirroring the beauty and perfection of the divine creation. An example is the title page of Michael Praetorius's *Musae Sioniae*, one of the most successful music collections of the seventeenth century, of which the first part was published in 1605.

In the upper register we see God Father represented by the divine name in Hebrew letters, and underneath is the lamb, Jesus Christ. God is framed by the evangelists, two on either side, and he and Christ are surrounded by the heavenly choirs. The music-making on earth is a reflection of this heavenly scenario, with a choir on a balcony on either side, and in the middle the great organ. The symmetry on earth mirrors the symmetric perfection of heaven.[18] The purpose of art at this time—in architecture, the visual arts, and music—was not to create something entirely new, but to reflect this divine perfection, and in this way to praise God. We find such a symmetric outline in many pieces by Johann Sebastian Bach,[19] but only in a few cases is this outline as consequent as in the B Minor Mass.

Kyrie
Christe
Kyrie

The first example is the Kyrie. Its middle section, the *Christe eleison* (Christ, have mercy), is framed by two huge movements for choir and orchestra, each presenting the phrase *Kyrie eleison* (God, have mercy) in a polyphonic fabric. But there is a significant difference between these two movements. The first *Kyrie* is composed as a modern fugue with an instrumental theme and—at least at the beginning—independent instrumental voices. When the *Kyrie eleison* is repeated after the *Christe eleison*, the texture is again polyphonic, but in quite a different way. While the first *Kyrie* had an instrumental character, the second is influenced by the polyphonic vocal style of the early modern period; this is known as "Palestrina style" after the famous Roman sixteenth century composer Giovanni Pierluigi da Palestrina (1525–1594), or *stile antico*.[20] The instruments in the second *Kyrie* basically follow the vocal parts, and the whole piece could easily be performed without the instruments.

Bach had several reasons for using this compositional technique. One is his interest in different musical styles, and his desire to improve his own style during his lifetime. He was always looking for compositional challenges, and to compose a movement in this elaborate vocal style was a challenge. His other motivation follows from the purpose of the Mass as a "job-application" for the court in Dresden: Bach knew the musical style the court in Dresden preferred. Because the *stile antico*, or Palestrina style, was very frequently used by composers in Dresden at this time,[21] Bach likely used it to improve his chances of getting the position he wanted. In other words, writing some movements of the Mass in Palestrina style was a part of his advertising strategy.

The first music example shows the beginning of the second *Kyrie*. The bass begins with a long *soggetto*, sharpened by chromaticisms and supported by the bassoon. The tenor enters with the same *soggetto* and is accompanied by the viola. The different timbres of the reed instrument and the string instrument make the polyphonic fabric even more transparent. The same is true when eventually the alto (with the oboe) and the soprano (with oboe and flute) enter. The instrumentation, characteristic of the German seventeenth century ideal of *Spaltklang*, underscores the polyphonic texture of the setting (see Example 1).

Several other aspects of the Kyrie refer to models in the Saxon capitol. One is the slow introduction opening the whole piece. We find similar introductions in other masses in Dresden; one, composed by Johann Hugo von Wilderer (1670/71–1724), is so much the same that it likely served as a model for Bach. Even the theme of the first fugue in Bach's mass is similar to Wilderer's *Kyrie*-fugue (see Example 2). [22]

Bach copied the mass by Wilderer around 1730 so that we are sure that he knew it.[23] On the other hand, Bach did not just imitate the model, but composed a much more complex setting. While Wilderer's introduction is a straightforward accordic piece,

EXAMPLE 1

EXAMPLE 2

EXAMPLE 3

EXAMPLE 4

Bach's introduction also starts with a dense accordic texture, but enriches the setting with syncopations and sharp chromaticisms.

Kyrie I and *Kyrie II* represent the two side wings of our "palace." The central section of the building, the *Christe eleison*, is composed as a contrast. It is set for two soprano voices and violins. The character is quite intimate. Again, models from Dresden have shaped the movement, but in this case not only sacred compositions but secular pieces as well. Dresden was at this time a center for the Italian opera in Germany. Although Bach never composed an

opera himself, he possessed a deep knowledge of this genre.[24] In the case of the *Christe*, the love-duet of Neapolitan opera might have served as a model. We find several characteristics of this duet style in the *Christe*: "parallel thirds and sixths (emphasized here through sustained notes), diatonic melodic lines, a *galant* mixture of duple and triple figures, straightforward harmonies, expressive appoggiaturas, and weak-beat phrase endings that resolve downward as 'sighs.'"[25] Bach used this style in several duets in his cantatas to depict the love between two persons, or between God and humanity, so that we can be sure that he was aware of possible connotations, and used these stylistic devices on purpose.[26]

The relationship between this type of duet and love becomes clear when we compare a section from the secular cantata *Lasst uns sorgen, lasst uns weichen* (BWV 213), composed in September 1733, with the duet in the Mass. The cantata was written for the birthday of Prince Friedrich Christian of Saxony (1722–1763). The text of the duet is "I am yours and you are mine; I kiss you, kiss me" (see Example 3).

This may again be a reference to a popular style in Dresden; both these compositions were composed for the court of Saxony, and thus reflect its preferences. But besides this another, a theological, layer of understanding is important for the interpretation of the *Christe* duet. Protestant theology of Bach's time was shaped by the idea of an intimate relationship between Jesus and the believer. Jesus was seen as bridegroom, and the believer as bride. A central biblical text for this theology was the Song of Songs, with its dialogs between a lover and his beloved. Bach employed texts from this book in several of his compositions, but most obviously in the cantata *Wachet auf, ruft uns die Stimme* (BWV 140). Using motives from the Song of Songs, the unknown librettist wrote the following duet:

Soprano	Bass
My beloved is mine!	And I am yours!
Love shall by naught be sundered!	
I will join thee	thou shalt join me
To wander through heaven's roses,	
Where pleasure in fullness, where joy will abound.	

The two "lovers" in this duet sing the way we have seen in the musical examples above.[27] This kind of deep love is expressed in our love-duet, the love between Christ and humanity (see Example 4). We do not have to understand the two voices in the *Christe eleison* as two lovers

personified, the first soprano as Jesus, the second as the believer; the idea of love in general is depicted in this movement.

Returning to our comparison of Bach's music with a baroque building, we see another similarity: the central position of this duet, expressing the concept of humanity's relationship to God, corresponds with a central theological idea of this time.

> *Gloria in excelsis*
> *Et in terra pax*
> *Laudamus te*
> *Gratias agimus*
> *Domine Deus*
> *Qui tollis*
> *Qui sedes*
> *Quoniam tu solus*
> *Cum Sancto Spiritu*

The Gloria consists of nine movements. Again, this section of the Mass is framed by two huge movements for choir and orchestra which in this case are stylistically equivalent. Both are inspired by instrumental concertos of the eighteenth century.[28] The first movement, *Gloria in excelsis Deo*, even starts as an instrumental concerto, with the orchestra presenting the musical material before the voices develop this motivic material in a dense dialogue with the instruments. The jubilation of the angels is expressed by the use of trumpets and drums.

The last movement of the Gloria, the *Cum Sancto Spiritu*, has the same character, again a concerto, and again the sound is shaped by the use of trumpets and drums. These two side wings frame the rest of the Gloria, which, as we will see, again revolves around a central piece.

The second movement is the *Et in terra pax* (And peace on earth). Since the text talks about people on earth, the human element, the voice, is emphasized by Bach. While in the *Gloria in excelsis* the music was shaped by musical material presented and developed by instruments in the long instrumental introduction, now the voices start in a quiet four part setting without the instruments. Those only enter one measure later, using the motivic material of the vocal choir (see Example 5).

After this juxtaposition of heavenly orchestra and earthly voices, the solo soprano and a solo violin enter in the *Laudamus te* with a virtuoso aria. Some Bach scholars have argued that this movement was also composed to fit the taste of the court in Dresden, and that the composer might have had in mind one particular soprano, Faustina Bordoni (1697–1781), when he wrote the piece.[29] Indeed, what we know of her singing from Bach's contemporary Johann Joachim Quantz (1697–1773), fits perfectly the demands of this aria:

Her execution was articulate and brilliant. She had a fluent tongue for pronouncing words rapidly and distinctly, and a flexible throat for divisions, with so beautiful and quick a shake, that she could put it in motion upon short notice, just when she would. The passages might be smooth, or by leaps, or consist of iterations of the same tone—their execution was equally easy to her.[30]

Just as the transition from Kyrie to Gloria is full of contrast, so is the *Gratias agimus* stylistically different from the preceding aria. Bach turns back again to the *a cappella* style of the Renaissance, which had already shaped the second *Kyrie*. The vocalists are accompanied

EXAMPLE 5

by instruments, and Bach's aim is to reach the highest degree of transparency in polyphonic texture by supporting every human voice with a different instrumental timbre. He is reusing here a polyphonic movement from the cantata *Wir danken dir Gott* (BWV 29),[31] composed in 1731, overlaying it with the Latin text. Interestingly, Bach not only parodies an older movement — something he does in many other pieces[32] — but the older cantata movement has nearly the same text as the movement in the Mass. *Gratias agimus tibi* and "Wir danken dir Gott" both mean "We thank you."

Although we have no sources, very likely the music of the *Domine Deus* was taken from an earlier composition as well, perhaps from the now lost cantata *Ihr Häuser des Himmels* (BWV 193a) from 1727 (see Example 6).[33] It is a movement for a solo instrument, this time the flute, which begins a concerto-like dialogue with

the orchestra, until soprano and tenor enter to engage with the instrumental soloist and the orchestra. With its many parallel thirds and sixths, the movement has again the character of a "love-duet," like the *Christe eleison*; in both movements the text speaks directly to Jesus Christ. *Domine Deus* is similar to the *Christe* in another way: in both cases the love-duet is the central movement of a larger work.

The instrumentation of this movement is theologically very subtle. One might expect that the text *Domine Deus, Rex coelestis, Deus Pater omnipotens* would be set with a scoring that involves the trumpets, drums, and the whole choir, to express the power of God, Father and Son. The movement begins with a single flute, however, accompanied only by the basso continuo, and when the string instruments enter one measure later, they have to play *con sordino* (with the mute).

EXAMPLE 6

The soft sound does not fit the first part of the movement, *Domine Deus, Rex coelestis, Deus Pater omnipotens*, as much as its end, *Domine Deus, Agnus Dei, Filius Patris*. The musical expression of this movement is thus developed with respect to the *theologia crucis* at the end of the text. In other words, the omnipotent God is understood as the very God who reveals himself on the cross. The Lutheran *theologia crucis* is expressed by means of the music. Martin Luther wrote in his "Heidelberg Disputation" of 1518:

> He deserves to be called a theologian, however, who comprehends the visible and manifest things of God seen through suffering and the cross. . . . Now it is not sufficient for anyone, and it does him no good to recognize God in his glory and majesty, unless he recognizes him in the humility and shame of the cross. . . . A theologian of glory calls evil good and good evil. A theologian of the cross calls the thing what it actually is.[34]

According to Luther, we only understand God when we see him revealed in the crucified Jesus Christ. In the seventeenth century the theological interpretation of the passion of Jesus Christ underwent a re-interpretation. The *theologia crucis* was still an integral part, but the love of God expressed in the passion was emphasized even more.[35] Thus the German theologian Heinrich Müller (1631–1675), one of the most influential preachers at that time, wrote in a sermon published in 1679:

> The Apostle Paul admonishes his Timothy that he should always keep in mind Jesus, the crucified one. . . . By this we recognize his love, that he gave his life for us when we were still his enemies. Thus it is proper that we repay his love with love. It is the character of love to keep always in mind what is loved. Whether walking or standing, love sees the beloved in thought.

> We who love the Lord Jesus should keep him in remembrance. The crucified Jesus is the only comfort for our souls. [36]

The cross is the sign for God's love for humanity, and our appropriate reaction is to answer this love with love.

The *Qui tollis*, a gloomy, harmonically rich movement that expresses the crucifixion and death of Jesus Christ, is taken from the 1723 cantata *Schauet doch und sehet* (BWV 46). The cantata text stems from the Lamentations of Jeremiah 1:12: "Behold and see if there be any sorrow like unto my sorrow, which is done unto me; herewith the Lord hath afflicted me in the day of his fierce anger." The text has thus a similar character of grief, and it was easy for Bach to adjust the music to the new text.[37]

This movement is followed by an intimate aria on the text *Qui sedes ad dexteram Patris* for alto, accompanied by solo oboe d'amore and strings. Most of the masses from the repertoire of the Dresden court, and Bach's own Kyrie-Gloria Masses (BWV 233–236), composed a short time before the B Minor Mass, treat the *Qui tollis* and the *Qui sedes* as one movement.[38] Here Bach splits up the text in order to give each its appropriate treatment. While the *Qui tollis* was mournful in tone, the *Qui sedes* has a dance-like character, celebrating the elevated Christ. It was Bach's biographer Philipp Spitta (1841–1894) who in 1870 interpreted this as resulting from theological reflection:

> Here his theological learning . . . stood him in good stead. Doctrinal theology assigns to Christ a three-fold office—as Prophet, High Priest, and King. The text offered no opening for treating the prophetic aspect—only the priestly and kingly. As, in considering Christ as a priest, there is again a distinction between Atonement and Mediation (*munus satisfactionis* and *intercessionis*), Bach has figured the former by the chorus *Qui*

tollis, and the latter by the alto aria *Qui sedes*, but in close connection, for the key is the same in both.[39]

We may doubt that the dogma of the three-fold office formed the background of these two movements, since one of the offices is missing, and we have no evidence that Bach wanted to allude to this theological concept. But obviously Bach has built up a contrast between the suffering of Christ in the *Qui tollis*, and the elevated Christ, sitting next to his Father, in the following movement. Instead of the offices, the binary opposition of the two movements supports another thesis: here Bach is emphasizing the difference between the human nature of Christ, visible in his suffering, and the divine nature, expressed by his ascension and his sitting at the right hand of God the Father. This is of crucial importance in Martin Luther's theology. In his explanation of the second article of the Creed in his "Small Catechism," the reformer stated:

I believe that Jesus Christus, true God, begotten of the Father from eternity, and also true man, born of the virgin Mary, is my Lord, who has redeemed me, a lost and condemned creature, delivered me and freed me from all sins, from death, and from the power of the devil, not with silver and gold but with his holy and precious blood and with his innocent sufferings and death, in order that I may be his, live under him in his kingdom, and serve him in everlasting righteousness, innocence, and blessedness, even as he is risen from the dead and lives and reigns to all eternity.[40]

I have already pointed out the importance of the *theologia crucis* for Luther's theological thinking, and how it might have shaped Bach's Mass. The dual nature of Christ is the precondition for humanity's salvation, and it is possible that Bach wanted to reflect this duality in his music, and in the structure of his Mass as well.

The Gloria's second last movement is the *Quoniam tu solus sanctus*, sung by the bass, and accompanied by the corno da caccia and two bassoons. This combination gives it a solemn character, corresponding with the text set in this section of the Mass, before the whole Gloria ends with a concerto grosso-like movement, *Cum Sancto Spiritu*, performed by the choir and full orchestra with trumpets, timpani, flutes, oboes, strings, bassoon, and basso continuo.

The architecture of this "building" is obvious: framed by the concerto-like side wings, and the other outer movements praising God, the central section speaks of the believer's relationship with God, which is — in the contemporary theology — a relationship of deepest love, rooted in Christ's suffering. And this love is expressed by a love duet.

With the *Cum Sancto Spiritu* the Mass Bach composed for the court in Dresden in 1733 ends. We do not know whether or not these pieces were ever performed in Dresden or in Leipzig.[41] It was nearly fifteen years before Bach began to complete his Mass cycle. When he returned to work on the Mass in the late 1740s, he again recycled several older cantata movements, and provided them with the Latin texts of the Mass.

Credo in unum Deum
Patrem omnipotentem
Et in unum Dominum
Et incarnatus est
Crucifixus
Et resurrexit
Et in Spiritum Sanctum
Confiteor
Et expecto resurrectionem

The introductory movement of the Credo, *Credo in unum Deum*, a polyphonic piece with a walking bass, was — according to recent research — composed about 1747/48, and might have served as a slow introduction to a Credo by another composer.[42] Only a short time later, however, Bach began to complete his Mass, and he used this movement in his own Credo (see Example 7). The following *Patrem omnipotentem* is a parody of a movement composed in 1729, *Gott, wie dein Name, so ist auch dein Ruhm* (BWV 171).[43] To remodel this older piece was not difficult because the mood and the contents are similar: in both cases the power and might of God are praised.

Again, as in the Kyrie, Bach juxtaposes two musical styles, the *stile antico* in the introduction, and a modern, concerto-like texture in the *Patrem omnipotentem*. This is a juxtaposition of old and new musical material as well: the *stile antico* movement is not only composed in an older musical technique, but Bach adopts an old Gregorian chant, a melody used in the Leipzig worship at Bach's time.

The beginning of this part of the Mass is mirrored at the end. The final movements are a piece in an old, motet style, with the text *Confiteor unum baptisma*, and a modern, concerto-like movement, *Et expecto resurrectionem peccatorum*. Thus the Credo starts with a couple of movements for choir in different styles, and it ends with the same combination of styles. But the connection between beginning and end is deeper. Both *stile antico* movements employ the same chant melody. This is obvious in the *Credo*, since Bach uses it as the main musical idea in all the voices. In the *Confiteor*, however, the melody of the Gregorian chant that was used in Leipzig for the words of the *Confiteor* is hidden in the lower voices and treated as a canon.[44]

These observations are still on a technical level. A third, theological connection exists between the beginning and the end of the Credo. The two movements Bach composed in *stile antico* have a similar aspect: *Credo*–I believe… *Confiteor*–I confess. Both express the human reaction to the divine mystery: I believe and I confess.

EXAMPLE 7

These two side wings of the Credo-"palace" embrace seven single movements. Like the Kyrie and the Gloria, the Credo has a centerpiece as well, focused on a central theological idea. Here it is not a love-duet, but the text expresses the love between God and humanity in the most intense way: *Crucifixus etiam pro nobis* (Crucified for us). If we take into account that the *theologia crucis* was a cornerstone in Lutheran theology in the time of Bach, this choice is not surprising. The genesis of the Credo makes clear how important this aspect was for Bach. In an earlier version he composed just eight movements, but when he reworked the piece he inserted a separate *Et incarnatus est* to make sure that the *Crucifixus* was indeed the middle of the whole Credo.[45]

The *Crucifixus* is the oldest movement in the entire Mass. Bach composed it in 1714 in Weimar for the Cantata *Weinen, Klagen, Sorgen, Zagen* (BWV 12), and reworked it for his Mass. Some scholars have identified the repeated quarter notes in the bass of the *Crucifixus* as the hammering of the nails, and the flutes as drops of Christ's blood. But even without these metaphorical explanations, the movement, with a chromatic voice leading, dissonant harmonies, and a sigh-motive at the end of the word *crucifixus*, reflects the text, telling the death and suffering of Jesus Christ, in an exemplary manner.

Although the center piece of the Credo is not a love-duet, something similar is here as well. It is the third movement, *Et in unum Dominum* (And I believe in the one Lord, Jesus Christ). Again, devotion to Christ—and in contemporary theology that meant love—is expressed in a style close to a love-duet.

The center-piece, *Crucifixus,* is followed by the *Resurrexit,* composed in the style of a concerto grosso. It musically "paints" the resurrection of Christ with ascending motifs. The adoration of the Holy Spirit (*Et in Spiritum Sanctus*) serves as a point of repose. It is a calm aria, sung by the bass and accompanied by two oboes d'amore, serving as a counterpart to the duet *Et in unum Dominum,* and balancing the symmetric outline of the whole Creed: Choir—Choir—Duet—Choir—Choir—Choir—Solo—Choir—Choir

> Sanctus
> Osanna
> Benedictus
> Osanna

While the *Sanctus* was already composed in 1724, the *Osanna, Benedictus,* and *Agnus Dei* were written at the same time as the Credo in the late 1740s. The *Sanctus* employs a six-part choir, accompanied by trumpets, timpani, oboes, strings, and basso continuo. Thus the movement demands a slightly larger ensemble than the previous pieces, which used only up to five voices. One reason for this discrepancy is of course that Bach used a setting that already existed, but there might be a symbolic reason as well. The beginning of the liturgical *Sanctus* is taken from the prophecy of Isaiah, chapter 6. It is the song of the celestial Seraphim which, according to this text, have six wings. The number of voices reflects this biblical number.

The following *Osanna* further expands the vocal forces. It is a polychoral concerto for two four-part choirs and instruments. It is quite certain that this movement is also based on an older model.

The *Benedictus* is an aria for a solo instrument, probably the flute, and tenor. Stylistically it is one of the most progressive parts in the Mass. The flexible rhythm of both voice and instrument, significantly different from the rather motoric and stereotypical rhythms of the other movements of the Mass, is influenced by the modern *Empfindsamer Stil* (sensitive style). It is as though Bach had wanted to prove his command of this style in the last aria of the Mass.

Bach completed this part of the Mass without having in mind the architectural plan that shaped the first parts of the composition.

The symmetrical plan of the Kyrie, Gloria, and Credo, is absent here, and we have no love-duet. But Bach still tries to express the meaning and mood of the text in the music. The *Sanctus* and the *Osanna* are extroverted concerto movements, while the *Benedictus*—like similar movements in masses by Dresden composers—has a more intimate character.

> *Agnus Dei*
> *Dona nobis pacem*

After a repetition of the *Osanna*, the *Agnus Dei* is performed by the alto, accompanied by violins. This movement, about the Lamb of God who died for the sins of the world, is a dialogue between voice and instruments that lacks the virtuoso character of earlier arias in this Mass. The death of Christ is a place for meditation, not for extroverted virtuosity. It is a parody of a now lost aria. Bach has taken the same aria as a model for his *Ascension Oratorio* (BWV 11), from 1735, where the text is "Ach bleibe doch, mein liebstes Leben" (Oh stay with me, my dearest life).[46] Both pieces have a lamenting tone and a

MODELS AND PARODIES IN BACH'S B-MINOR MASS

		1.1. Kyrie eleison
		1.2. Christe eleison
		1.3. Kyrie eleison
		1.4. Gloria
		1.5. Et in terra pax
		1.6. Laudamus te
29/2: Wir danken dir Gott, wir danken dir (1731)	1733	1.7. Gratias agimus tibi
[193a/5: Ihr Häuser des Himmels, ihr scheinenden Lichter (1727)]		1.8. Domine Deus
46/1: Schauet doch und sehet, ob irgend ein Schmerz sei (1723)		1.9. Qui tollis
		1.10. Qui sedes
		1.11. Quoniam tu solus sanctus
		1.12. Cum Sancto Spiritu
[earlier version about 1747/48]		2.1. Credo
171/1: Gott, wie dein Name, so ist auch dein Ruhm (1729)		2.2. Patrem omnipotentem
		2.3. Et in unum Dominum
		2.4. Et incarnatus
12/2: Weinen, Klagen, Sorgen, Zagen (1714)	1748/1749	2.5. Crucifixus
Anh. I 9/1:Entfernet euch ihr heitern Sterne (1727)		2.6. Et resurrexit
		2.7. Et in Spiritum sanctum
		2.8. Confiteor
120/2: Gott, man lobt dich in der Stille (1729)		2.9. Et expecto
	1725	3. Sanctus
Anh. I 11/1: Es lebe der König, der Vater im Lande (1732)		4.1. Osanna in excelsis
		4.2. Benedictus
	1748/1749	4.3. Osanna [=IV.1.]
Anh. I 196/3: Auf, süß entzückende Gewalt (1725)		4.4. Agnus Dei
		4.5. Dona nobis pacem [=1.7.]

pleading character, expressed by chromaticisms in the bass-line and leaps that expose dissonant intervals.

At the end of the whole Mass Bach repeats the *Gratias* from the Gloria, now with the text *Dona nobis pacem*. He thus makes a connection between the older parts of the Mass and the newly composed ending.

III.

The B Minor Mass is a showpiece in several respects. At least a third of the twenty-seven movements are taken from earlier compositions (see the table below), but Bach is very careful in the way he reuses the older pieces. He never takes two movements from one model, as he does in several cantatas, his Christmas Oratorio, and his smaller Kyrie-Gloria Masses. Furthermore, in several cases Bach parodies movements in the B Minor Mass that had nearly the same text in the original version as in Latin. He tries to keep the relationship between music and words as close as possible.

Another important point to note is how Bach combines the newer and older parts of the Mass. In the Kyrie, Gloria, and Credo he creates a symmetric architectural form that is framed by vocal-instrumental movements and has a Christological section as centerpiece. The movements of the Mass might have their own history, but the way Bach combines them is unique and new.

To know the history of the piece, the different steps of its genesis, is useful, but that does not describe the artwork as it is now. The whole is more than the sum of its parts. I started this essay with some remarks on commercials. Bach composed the first half of the Mass when applying for the title of court composer in Dresden. In order to support his application he employed several stylistic devices he knew from masses in Dresden. But he did not simply imitate them. He combined these devices with his own musical language, his Lutheran theology, and his own sense of musical architecture. He was

not successful. Naegeli, despite his advertising campaign, was not successful when he tried to publish the piece at the beginning of the nineteenth century. Is Bach's Mass in B Minor the greatest artwork of all times and all people? A commercial would have to say, "Yes, it is." I'm not going to answer that question. Music is not about better, faster, louder. Listen to the piece yourself; try to hear how Bach builds his baroque palace, his musical Versailles.

ENDNOTES

The lecture was originally followed by a performance of Bach's B Minor Mass, given by the Yale Camerata and conducted by Marguerite Brooks. This published version of the talk maintains the lecture's introductory character.

1. A short survey on Nägeli and his commitment to Bach's music is given by Karen Lehmann: "Nägeli, Hans Georg," in *Das Bach-Lexikon: Bach-Handbuch* 6, ed. Michael Heinemann (Laaber: Laaber-Verlag, 2000), 382–83.

2. George B. Stauffer, *Bach: The Mass in B Minor: The Great Catholic Mass* (New Haven: Yale University Press: 2003), IX.

3. See Walter Blankenburg, *Einführung in Bachs h-moll-Messe*, 5th ed. (Kassel: Bärenreiter, 1996), 16–18.

4. Samuel J. Rogal, "For the Love of Bach: The Charles Burney–Samuel Wesley Correspondence." *Bach* 23 (1992): 31-37; and Michael Kassler, Philip Olleson, *Samuel Wesley (1766-1837): A Source Book* (Aldershot: Ashgate, 2001).

5. See Stauffer, *Bach*, 190.

6. See Klaus Engler, *Georg Poelchau und seine Musikaliensammlung: Ein Beitrag zur Überlieferung Bachschen Musik in der ersten Hälfte des 19. Jahrhunderts*. Ph.D. diss., University of Tübingen, 1974.

7. See Stauffer, *Bach*, 190.

8. Christoph Wolff, *Johann Sebastian Bach: The Learned Musician* (New York: Norton, 2000), 471.

9. This is true, for example, of an edition of Bach's smaller Masses in A major (BWV 234) from 1818 and G Major (BWV 236) from 1828, both edited by

Poelchau; they were not intended as enrichments of the repertoire of liturgical music but as compositional models.

10. See Karen Lehmann, *Die Anfänge einer Bach-Gesamtausgabe: Editionen der Klavierwerke durch Hoffmeister und Kühnel (Bureau de Musique) und C.F. Peters in Leipzig 1801-1865: Ein Beitrag zur Wirkungsgeschichte J.S. Bachs.* Leipziger Beiträge zur Bach-Forschung 6 (Hildesheim: Olms, 2004), passim, and Markus Rathey, "Bach-Renaissance, Protestantismus und nationale Identität im deutschen Bürgertum des 19. Jahrhunderts," in *Protestantische Identität und Erinnerung: Von der Reformation bis zur Bürgerrechtsbewegung in der DDR.* Formen der Erinnerung 16, ed. Joachim Eibach and Marcus Sandl (Göttingen: Vandenhoeck & Ruprecht, 2003), 177–90.

11. See Martin Geck, *Die Wiederentdeckung der Matthäuspassion im 19. Jahrhundert: Die zeitgenössischen Dokumente und ihre ideengeschichtliche Deutung.* Studien zur Musikgeschichte des 19. Jahrhunderts 9 (Regensburg: Bosse, 1967).

12. The piece was performed by Karl Riedel and the *Riedel-Verein*, Leipzig; see Gerhard Herz, "The Performance History of Bach's B minor Mass." *Studies in Musicology* 73 (1985): 202.

13. In a letter of 1730 to his friend Georg Erdmann, who was at this time Imperial Russian Residence agent in Danzig, Bach complained about his situation in Leipzig, and asked if he could find him a decent position. The whole text is published in *The New Bach Reader: A Life of Johann Sebastian Bach in Letters and Documents*, ed. Hans T. David and Arthur Mendel, revised and enlarged by Christoph Wolff (New York: Norton, 1998), 151–52.

14. *The New Bach Reader*, 158.

15. Wolff, *Johann Sebastian Bach: The Learned Musician*, 371.

16. *The Court Society*, trans. Edmund Jephcott (New York: Pantheon Books, 1983), 41–45.

17. See Blankenburg, *Einführung* (note 3), 59.

18. Rolf Dammann, *Der Musikbegriff im deutschen Barock*, 2d ed. (Laaber: Laaber-Verlag, 1984), 80-86.

19. See Nors S. Josephson. "Formale Symmetrie und freizyklische Gesamtstruktur in einigen Vokalkompositionen Johann Sebastian Bachs." *Jahrbuch des Staatlichen Instituts für Musikforschung*

2000: 150–74; and Werner Breig. "Bemerkungen zur zyklischen Symmetrie in Bachs Leipziger Kirchenmusik." *Musik und Kirche* 53 (1983): 173–79.

20. See Christoph Wolff, *Der stile antico in der Musik Johann Sebastian Bachs: Studien zu Bachs Spätwerk.* Archiv für Musikwissenschaft, Beihefte 6. (Wiesbaden: Steiner, 1968).

21. Wolfgang Horn. *Die Dresdner Hofkirchenmusik 1720–1745: Studien zu ihren Voraussetzungen und ihrem Repertoire* (Kassel/Basel: Bärenreiter; Stuttgart: Carus, 1987), 97–99, 150–53.

22. Christoph Wolff has pointed out this similarity in his article "Origins of the Kyrie in the B Minor Mass," in *Bach: Essays on his Life and Music* (Cambridge: Harvard University Press, 1991), 141–51.

23. Kirsten Beißwenger, *Johann Sebastian Bachs Notenbibliothek.* Catalogus Musicus 13 (Kassel: Bärenreiter, 1992), 322–23, and "Bachs Eingriffe in Werke fremder Komponisten. Beobachtungen an den Notenhandschriften aus seiner Bibliothek unter besonderer Berücksichtigung der lateinischen Kirchenmusik." *Bach Jahrbuch* 77 (1991): 127–58.

24. On Bach's knowledge of the opera see Wolfgang Osthoff. "Bach und die Oper," in *Festschrift Heinz Becker zum 60. Geburtstag*, ed. Jürgen Schläder and Reinhold Quandt (Laaber: Laaber-Verlag, 1982), 38-55; and Georg von Dadelsen. "Wenn Bach Opern geschrieben hätte," in *Johann Sebastian Bachs Spätwerk und dessen Umfeld* (Kassel: Bärenreiter, 1988), 177–83.

25. Stauffer, *Bach* (note 2), 57.

26. Regarding Bach's use of duets in his sacred music see the overview by Mary J. Greer, *The Sacred Duets and Terzets of Johann Sebastian Bach: A Study of Genre and Musical Text Interpretation.* Ph.D. diss., Harvard University, 1996.

27. See the description of the piece in Greer, 298–302.

28. John Butt, *Bach: Mass in B Minor* (Cambridge: Cambridge University Press, 1991), 60-69. A more critical position on Bach's use of concerto-form in his vocal music was recently taken by Miriam K. Whaples in "Bach's Recapitulation Forms." *Journal of Musicology* 14 (1996): 475–513.

29. See Robert L. Marshall, "Bach the Progressive: Observations on His Later Works." *Musical Quarterly* 62 (1976): 341; and Stauffer, *Bach*, 72.

30. Quoted by Charles Burney in *A General History of Music from the Earliest Ages to the Present* (London 1776–1789; reprint, ed. Frank Mercer, New York: Harcourt, Brace, 1935). 2:736-37.

31. See Alfred Dürr. *Die Kantaten von Johann Sebastian Bach*, 6th ed. (Kassel: Bärenreiter, 1995), 808–11.

32. Regarding Bach's parody-technique see Hans-Joachim Schulze. "The Parody Process in Bach's Music: An Old Problem Reconsidered." *Bach* 20 (1989): 7-21.

33. Only the text of this cantata has come down to us, but Klaus Häfner has convincingly argued that the common structure of the texts of the *Domine Deus* and the duet *Ich will/Du sollst rühmen* points to a relationship between these two pieces. See Häfner, "Über die Herkunft von zwei Sätzen der h-moll-Messe." *Bach-Jahrbuch* 63 (1977): 56–64.

34. Martin Luther. "Heidelberg Disputation (1518)," in *Martin Luther: Basic Theological Writings*, ed. Timothy F. Lull (Minneapolis: Fortress Press, 1989), 43–44; see Jos E. Vercreysse, "Luther's Theology of the Cross at the time of the Heidelberg Disputation." *Gregorianum* 57 (1976): 523–48.

35. See Elke Axmacher, *Johann Arndt und Paul Gerhardt: Studien zur Theologie, Frömmigkeit und geistlichen Dichtung des 17. Jahrhunderts*. Mainzer hymnologische Studien 3 (Tübingen/Basel: Francke, 2001), 217–20.

36. "Der Apostel Paulus vermahnet seinen Thimotheum / daß er stets solle im Gedächtniß tragen Jesum / den Gecreutzigten. [...] Daran erkennen wir seine Liebe / der sein Leben hat für uns gelassen / uns zwar / da wir seine Feinde waren. So ists je billich / daß wir Liebe mit Liebe vergelten. Das ist aber der Liebe Art / daß sie das Geliebte stets trage im Gedächtniß. Wie sie gehet und stehet / da erbildet sich das Geliebte in ihren Gedancken. Die wir den HErrn Jesum lieben / sollen ihn auch stets im Gedächtniß tragen. Der gecreutzigte Jesus ist der einzige wahre Trost unserer Seelen" [translated by MR]. Heinrich M ller, "Der Leidende Jesus / Oder Das Leiden unsers Herrn und Heylandes Jesu Christi," in *Evangelischer Hertzens=Spiegel / Jn Offentlicher Kirchen=Versammlung / bey Erklärung der Sonntäglichen und Fest=Evangelien / Nebst beygefügten Passions=Predigten* (Frankfurt: Wust, 1679), 981, quoted by Renate Steiger, "Vom Sieg Singen – den Frieden austeilen. Die Kantate 'Halt im Gedächtnis Jesum Christ' BWV 67 auf den Sonntag nach Ostern." in

Gnadengegenwart. Johann Sebastian Bach im Kontext lutherischer Orthodoxie und Frömmigkeit. Doctrina et Pietas II/2 (Stuttgart-Bad Cannstatt: Frommann-Holzboog, 2001), 6.

37. See Stauffer, *Bach* (note 3), 82–83 regarding the changes Bach made.

38. See Stauffer, *Bach*, 85.

39. Philipp Spitta. *Johann Sebastian Bach: His Music and Influence on the Music of Germany, 1685–1750*, trans. Clara Bell and J. A. Fuller-Maitland (London: Novello, 1889; reprint, New York: Dover, 1979), 3:50.

40. Martin Luther, "The Small Catechism," in *Basic Theological Writings*, 480.

41. Regarding putative performances in Leipzig or Dresden see Stauffer, *Bach*, 34–37.

42. Peter Wollny, "Ein Quellenfund zur Entstehung der h-Moll-Messe." *Bach-Jahrbuch* 80 (1994): 163-69.

43. It is possible that the cantata was composed in the following years; see Dürr, *Die Kantaten* (note 31), 188.

44. See Blankenburg, *Einführung*, 85–87; and Stauffer, *Bach*, 131–35.

45. Eduard van Hengel and Kees van Houten have recently contradicted this assumption and proposed that the *Et incarnatus* was not added but was already a part of Bach's original version: "'Et incarnatus': An Afterthought? Against the 'Revisionist' View of Bach's B-Minor-Mass." *Journal of Musicological Research* 23 (2004): 81–112.

46. Christoph Wolff, "The Agnus Dei of the B Minor Mass: Parody and New Composition Reconciled," in *Bach. Essays on his Life and Music* (Cambridge: Harvard University Press, 1991), 332–39.

Markus Rathey is Assistant Professor of Music History at the Institute of Sacred Music, the Yale School of Music, and the Divinity School. Before he joined the Yale Faculty in 2003 he was a research fellow at the Bach Archive in Leipzig. Professor Rathey has published extensively on Johann Sebastian Bach and European music of the 17th and 18th centuries. His research focuses especially on the relationship between music, theology, and intellectual history in the 18th century.

From Resistance to Jubilee: Prophetic Preaching and the Testimony of Love

JOHN S. MCCLURE

IN RECENT YEARS HOMILETICIANS HAVE FOCUSED a good deal of attention on ethical models for preaching that accentuate the task of prophetic resistance. In most cases these models involve esthetic or rhetorical strategies through which preaching becomes, and attempts to promote, a re-scripting of reality in order to resist the dominant materialistic and oppressive discourses of modernity in the West. While all of these ways of preaching can help preachers create sermons that do battle with significant evils in society, it will become evident in what follows that homiletical strategies of resistance leave largely untouched a deeper substratum of forces that conspire to corrupt the benign, defensive way that we use language, or what the developmental psychologist Jean Piaget calls the human "semiotic function,"[1] for idolatrous purposes. Paradoxically, these forces are supported and maintained precisely by the (appropriately) defensive language of prophetic resistance. What is required, therefore, in order to overcome these forces, is sustained attention to transforming the way that we use language, including the language of resistance. This can be accomplished by re-framing the interhuman context for resistance in worship and preaching, moving from one dominated by the defensive self-securing of identity to the celebration of the self's and community's ability, in response to the Word, to move beyond the securing of identity, and to respond to others in love. Testimony helps to accomplish this because of its unique role in creating a context for the repair of speech by heightening awareness of the reality of sheer interhuman proximity (being-with, affinity) in church and society. Testimony, in the first instance, is a "language of jubilee." At the heart of this language of jubilee is a second language through which the human semiotic function is actually released from its defensive posture and

reoriented toward others through the giving and receiving of signs of peace and love. This is testimony as the "language of love."

Preaching as a Language of Resistance

Christine Smith, in her book *Preaching as Weeping, Confession, and Resistance: Radical Responses to Radical Evil*, asserts that in our day and age preachers must learn to speak the language of resistance, of prophetic assertion. This is the language of refusal and reclamation, in which the potentially violent references and rhythms within our common language are taken to task, exposed for what they are, and re-scripted. Currently a variety of homiletical models encourage preachers to engage in prophetic resistance through re-scripting or "re-languaging." In some of these models (Black, Smith) the focus is placed on scripting an inclusiveness that will resist discourses of patriarchy, ageism, ableism, heterosexism, etc.[2] In other models (Bond, McClure, Ramsay) preachers are encouraged to script new, non-oppressive theologies that will defend against theological ideas that may condone abusive power and increase the likelihood of suffering.[3] In still other approaches (Hauerwas, Willimon, Brueggemann, Campbell) biblical-rhetorical metaphors such as "resident alien," "exile," and "principalities and powers" are used to evoke alternative forms of imagination that will resist prevailing worldviews.[4]

Another, more subtle strategy is required, however, if preachers are to resist, not only the content of discourse, but also its embeddedness within unredeemed interhuman (intersubjective, interpersonal, and social) structures.[5] A large body of research that extends through the psychoanalysis of Anna Freud and Jacques Lacan, the cultural anthropology of René Girard and Eric Gans, the practical theology of James E. Loder, and the biblical theology of Regina Schwarz, indicates a profound susceptibility within the human unconscious to give over the way that we use language relationally to the business of securing the ego and its identity in the world.[6] It appears that one way humans orient themselves toward and within language and speech is in a defensive and self-securing posture. Words are used to cut boundaries between people, and to attach us to things that we believe will secure us in the world. Language becomes something to ward off perceived dangers, and to link us to persons, ideas, or groups that we think will provide us with the security that we need. Although this natural defensive orientation of the way that we "language" ourselves and the world in which we live is not in itself evil or immoral, and in spite of the fact that it serves a necessary function as one tool for self-preservation, we can easily to see how this way of using language can be derailed toward any number of would-be idolatries that promise to secure us in the world: consumer goods, military or social power, racism, etc.

According to the political philosopher Louis Althusser and the psychoanalyst Jacques Lacan, part of the trickery and deception of language within the larger social setting is the way that semiotic socialization creates a mirroring process through which the dominant ideologies within a culture "hail" or whisper to us as individuals and groups, telling us who we are or should be, and encouraging us through thousands of different attractions to identify ourselves within a certain range of self-images or identities.[7] Althusser calls this process "interpellation."[8] This is a kind of "fitting" process, similar to trying on clothes. As one comes closer and closer to fitting within the dominant ways of using language for becoming a "subject" within society, one feels more comfortable and secure.

Antonio Gramsci developed this further

with his idea of "hegemony."[9] Hegemony is simply the established set of notions that constitute common sense within a society. It includes those values, beliefs, practices, and forms of knowledge that "go without saying." This language that goes without saying constitutes a massive hidden script for all of our lives. Most important for our purposes, however, is the way that this script works in relation to the human semiotic function—what it does to the way that we think we have to "use" language. Semiotic hegemonies establish themselves, in large part, by preying upon and exploiting the natural defensive quality of the way that humans use language, promising comfort and security in exchange for allegiance or interpellation. This has the cumulative effect of establishing the defensive, identity-securing aspect of the semiotic function as primary to the way that we use language, at the expense of ways that language can be used to move beyond the securing of identity on behalf of others. At a communal or social level, this amounts to a persistent *saming* of language-use at the expense of its *othering*.

What this means is that preachers are not up against potentially dangerous everyday language scripts alone. They are also up against the myriad ways whereby a set of dominant ideologies seduces the benign defensiveness of the human semiotic function, potentially turning it into a malignant interhuman structure of self-securing idolatry. It is crucial to realize that this structure exists as the larger complex within which all of our "scripts" find themselves embedded. Regardless of the languages or scripts that we adopt and use, this deeper structure is busy undermining the way that we use language, including these scripts, toward forms of interhuman defensiveness, separation, and distance that promise to better secure us in this world. As this structure attaches itself to univocal ecclesial, racial, national, gender identities it co-opts the redemptive scripts we preach in increasingly sophisticated ways, shaping our experience toward exclusion, oppression, and violence.

Although re-scripting our language will offer some help, providing an initial line of defense against the dangerous scripts of materialism, patriarchy, racism, etc., which confront us, it does not go to the core of the issue. This is because even if we are able to re-imagine, re-script, and re-language the world in which our congregations live we cannot assume that this will adequately address the deeper unconscious binding of the semiotic function itself by this malignant defensive structure of semiotic interpellation.

This problem becomes even more complex when we consider that the appropriate justice-seeking defensiveness[10] inherent in homiletical practices of prophetic resistance mirrors and supports precisely the defensive orientation of the semiotic function required by hegemonic semiotic interpellation. Paradoxically, practices of prophetic resistance support precisely the defensive identity-preservation-through-boundary-cutting way of using language that semiotic interpellation relies upon in order to function properly as an interhuman structure.

Here we confront, on a contiguous track, an insidious double-bind in the way that cultural hegemony, the language "center" in society (our common sense language), actually requires the language of resistance to further its own purposes. The heart of the problem is this: the center (semiotic hegemony, set of dominant ideologies) in a society requires the margins in order to be the center. This creates a double-bind, because any struggle against the center (re-scriptings, re-languaging, inclusive language, etc.), indeed all of our strategies of resistance, paradoxically prop up the center as the center. All of these efforts ultimately only set off the center in more bold and striking relief.

To use only one small example, this is what has happened to the inclusive language movement in worship and hymnology on many seminary and college campuses. It appears that these good efforts at resistance and the reclamation of language have had the reverse effect in many situations, reinforcing a dominant idea of the language-center or tradition. In some instances efforts at re-scripting have spawned a powerful backlash from people representing the language center against so-called "politically correct" language, and against those representing the language margins who insist upon such language.

What preachers and liturgists are up against is this: the lived experiences and language of everyone are only made sense of from the cumulative linguistic vantage point of an all-defining center. The realization of this, of course, elicits a deeper and more volatile struggle from many who are a part of the speech and language resistance. This resistance is sometimes met by an increasingly strident response from those who choose to represent the center as language police. And so preachers and liturgists find themselves deeply within a spiraling double-bind, a situation in which they are damned if they do and damned if they don't. We know now that no matter how re-scripting is done, it doesn't go far enough. It leaves the deeper, unconscious problem of defensive self-securing in relation to what is "other," and the parallel problem of the language center and language-margins, virtually untouched.

Preaching as the Language of Jubilee

In the face of this double-binding problem, it is possible that a new opportunity for preaching, and perhaps for liturgy and music, can emerge from listening to marginalized persons in society who have, out of many years of experience, created ways to unravel this self-perpetuating center-margin double bind and the malignant defensiveness that underpins it. In homiletics we have begun to ask with real seriousness: What do persons of color, women, and other so-called marginalized folk have to say that might help us to deal with this larger unconscious and pervasive problem that is co-opting even our best prophetic strategies of communication?

To summarize, these friends are teaching us that our languages of resistance can and should be re-framed entirely by being placed within the larger context of liturgical and homiletical languages of jubilee. Jubilee is an opening or space within social and semiotic reality in which there is an opportunity and a vision for repair. It is a language-constructed "time out" in which a reorientation within language becomes possible. In our case, what is to be repaired is the violent rhythm or double-bind that exists between the center and the margins, the same and the other, that dominates human speaking. And what is reoriented, ultimately, is the human semiotic function itself, the way that we speak and "language" our lives, from a defensive and self-securing orientation, to an orientation toward others in compassion.

Within homiletics today, there seems to be some convergence by those who are seeking to identify this language-redemptive form of proclamation around the word "testimony."[11] This is not simply personal testimony, at least not exclusively. Testimony is a powerful speaking out of the context of one's life, but it is done on behalf of an entire community who are struggling for speech, for words, and for the acknowledgement and reception of new traditions of interpretation and meaning beyond the center-margin double-bind.

There is a crucial theological difference at the heart of this kind of testimony that is not found in most preaching today, including prophetic preaching, a difference that is important for undoing the largely unconscious double-bind between the language-center and the language-margins. At the deepest possible level, testimonial preaching relies on a very different understanding of the Word of God than we find in our usual theologies of preaching. Typically the Word of God is closely associated with a particular core message of preaching, the *kerygma*: the identifications and

representations of the Word of God in and through Christ as disclosed in Scripture and the Church's proclamation (what the theologian Karl Barth called the threefold form of the Word of God). One implication of this has been the powerful impetus toward Logos as the hub of a comprehensive set of rhetorical *topoi* (Newman), a dogmatic system (Barth), a cultural-linguistic totality (Lindbeck), and supervenient models of rheotorical rationality and truth (Murphy).[12]

For those within testimonial traditions of preaching, however, Logos is understood not so much as an "ordering" element as a re-ordering, converting, and re-creating element in human speech. Its rhythms are less appropriate to myth, epic, and the beautiful, and more inclined toward the parabolic, the ironic, and the sublime.[13] Rebecca Chopp has done an admirable job of re-defining how the Word of God is understood within so-called marginal traditions of testimonial speaking. She calls the Word of God a "perfectly open sign,"[14] and places it within the economy of an infinite God's infinite ethical re-ordering of human life.

Why is it important in a world of increasing center-toward-margins violence that the Word of God be considered a "perfectly open sign" within an ethical infinity, rather than the guiding force of rationality and order within a theological system seeking comprehensiveness and totality? The primary reason is that as an open sign the Word refuses to secure referencing for God's redemptive activity in Christ to only one hitching post liturgically, existentially, theologically, socially, etc. The "perfectly open" dynamic within the Word introduces a wholly non-defensive, "othering" (*kenotic*) way of signifying God's redemptive relationship to the world.[15] Emmanuel Levinas has argued that it is God moving toward humanity under the aspect of "infinity," rather than God moving within and toward God's own being under the aspect of "totality," who determines testimonial speech inasmuch as it has the power to interrupt dangerous linguistic and structural totalities.[16]

In short, the Word of God as perfectly open sign is a word of *shalom* to others, a sign that opens itself toward an infinity of human others and their ways of speaking and hearing the redemptive activity of God in (and into) the world. This is not simply a word of "inclusion" in a pre-established system of communication. It is rather recognition that there are, and indeed always have been, others (other faces, other voices, other words) on the originary Logos-scene, on the scene of verbal-linguistic representation itself. This means nothing less than recognizing all other origins of speaking, and speaking of God, in this world, a deeper and richer intertextuality and heteroglossia[17] than is usually admitted, and thus other origins of distinctively Christian speech, beyond and beneath those usually heard.

Anna Carter Florence makes use of Rebecca Chopp's language to describe what she thinks is happening throughout the history of women's testimonial speech with respect to the homiletical appropriation of this kind of Word. Speaking of the testimonies of women, and her own life, Florence asserts that "our lives are not the testimony, and our lives do not prove the testimony; rather our lives are sealed to the testimony [and here's the crucial part of the sentence], sealed to the narrated and confessed freedom the testimony proclaims: the Word as perfectly open sign." [18] In other words, women's testimonial speech is sealed to a Word of jubilee that is absolutely free from the violent rhythm that exists between the center and the margins. When women preach, there is a tacit understanding among the women who preach and listen that the Word that they are speaking and hearing is open, "testifying" them, along with an infinity of others far and near, into God-speech. This testimonial Word opens up a new space in worship and preaching, not simply a space in which to re-script faith and reclaim symbols, but an infinite space of interhuman proximity (being with), or affinity[19] that makes the space occupied by the defense-driven warfare

between the center and the margins seem small, insignificant, even irrelevant. In this space there exists no longer any center and margin, same and other, just the faces and words of "others" and of other others: sheer, infinite, interhuman proximity such as one might experience within a huge cosmic conversation.

In a different way, African-American homileticians have highlighted a kind of absolute freedom or openness that accompanies the liberating Word, a freedom that marks the "celebration" that occurs within many traditions of black preaching. Part of what is happening in these moments of celebration is that the infinity of the Logos (indicated, but not exhausted, in things like spiritual glossalalia and ritual ecstasy) is intervening and shattering all forms of linguistic and communicative totality. Similar to Florence's idea of "sealing" preaching to the Word as a perfectly open sign, Henry Mitchell speaks of a deep "internalization" of and "saturation" by God's liberating Word.[20] Warren H. Stewart calls this a deep and sudden awareness that God is involved in one's "wholistic liberation."[21] Olin P. Moyd tells us that this experience at the heart of preaching is literally unstoppable, another way of expressing the infinite and expanding welcome at the heart of this understanding of God's Word.[22]

These forms of testimonial preaching open up something like what is described in the Bible as jubilee.[23] Testimonial preaching creates a new non-defense-driven, "othering" context for the use of language, a context in which there is a divinely sponsored freedom for repair, especially freedom to repair the double-bind that exists between the center and the margins, and in the space of that freedom, a place in which perhaps the defensive orientation of the human semiotic function itself can be redeemed.

The Language of Love

We now need to ask if yet another language can emerge within the context of repair opened up by language of jubilee. This would be a language that actually releases the human semiotic function from its defensive posture and brings it onto the ground of others and otherness. Is there a language that we would speak in preaching and worship that can transform the way that we use language from boundary-cutting, grasping, and self-securing functions in relation to others, into a "letting be," a "letting flourish" compassionate aspect with others? Can preaching harbor a separate non-defensive, or defense-transforming, language that can even transfigure the self-securing aspect residing within the language of prophetic resistance? Is there a language that may draw forth the kenotic, self-giving aspect of the prophetic word within a new freedom from the center/margin double-bind brought into existence by the perfectly open sign?

The answer to this question is this: This almost unspeakable language is the language of love, because it is love that seals preaching to the Word as perfectly open sign. We are not here talking about a verbal language, or not that only, but about a particular "signing" of love. This signing of love is desperately essential if we are to keep the human semiotic function turned toward its deepest purpose – the one that is waiting on the other side of its defensive posturing.[24] This signing, or what can now be called "the testimony of love," is a direct and in most cases simultaneous extension of the jubilee-testimony that brings the perfectly open sign into preaching.[25] The testimony of love exists as the final signifying form that is assumed by the divine infinity that invades preaching when it is sealed to the perfectly open sign as the Word of God.

The testimony of love exists as a largely passive language through which our preaching becomes a signing or saying to others of love, of our proximity to one another, our infinite and mutual exposure and vulnerability. When this signing of love begins to appear in preaching, it signals that in this moment the semiotic function, the way that I "language" myself and

the world, has turned — turned away from self-securing idolatry toward the faces of others, and toward the God who passes by every time that turning, the turning of love, occurs. The signing of love in preaching signals a disruption and undoing of the double-bind between the semiotic center and the semiotic margins. It is a signing of our freedom from the power of the double-bind and of our ability, as those whose lives are sealed to the Word as perfectly open sign, to use language solely as a means to respond to one another in love.

How can our preaching become a testimony of love? In many respects this is the fundamental question behind the tremendous turn toward the listener in recent homiletic theory. These homiletic theories are straining, sometimes in a kind of excessive, overdrawn way, toward the other (meaning toward all others) in the preaching event and beyond. Recent efforts go far beyond the measured move toward the listener in Fred Craddock's inductive method, which intended, through a kind of Burkean identification, to bring the hearer into a more participatory role in preaching. Ronald Allen and Lucy Rose have created different forms of conversational and testimonial homiletics;[26] Nora Tubbs Tisdale works to integrate congregational studies and local theology into homiletics in order to promote a kind of folk dance between preacher and listener;[27] Chuck Campbell and Stanley Saunders take preaching students into the homeless shelters and onto the streets of Atlanta where they preach to the powers;[28] Kathy Black encourages preachers to listen to the lives of those who are most marginalized in society and congregations, especially persons with disabilities;[29] Christine Smith urges preachers to stand in solidarity with the oppressed, especially victims of classism, ageism, homophobia, and sexism;[30] and I have supported methods of collaborative preaching in which lay people, and even the un-churched, are involved in sermon brainstorming.[31] All of these are attempts to bring the barest glimmer of *shalom* into the preaching process, *shalom* that has the potential, in some cases, to signify love. These are, of course, only methods. They require certain forms of character and rhetorical ethos, as well as attention to a new range of emotions or pathos in preaching. In short, we in homiletics have only begun to scratch the surface of how a signing of love might be "mid-wifed" into preaching (or worship).

In conclusion, in a world increasingly shaped by violence toward others, preaching can and should pay close attention to the business of reshaping our experience as users of language, speaking agents, at the deepest possible levels. Preaching can help us to consciously resist the scripts of greed, violence, and loveless power that dominate our interpersonal, social, and political consciousness. But most important in our generation, preachers will have to begin to address these deeper questions: How can preaching become a form of speech that unravels the violent rhythm between language-center and language-margin? And how can preaching help to shift the balance and turn the ways that we use language away from strategies of self-securing defensiveness toward ways of speaking that will foster jubilee and signings of love?

ENDNOTES

1. For more on the semiotic function see Jean Piaget, *The Language and Thought of the Child* (New York: Meridian Books, 1955), and Jean Piaget and Barbel Inhelder, *The Psychology of the Child* (New York: Basic Books, 1969), 51ff.

2. Kathy Black, *A Healing Homiletic: Preaching and Disability* (Nashville: Abingdon Press, 1996); Christine L. Smith, *Preaching as Weeping, Confession and Resistance: Radical Responses to Radical Evil* (Louisville: Westminster John Knox Press, 1992).

3. L. Susan Bond, *Trouble with Jesus: Women, Christology, and Preaching* (St. Louis: Chalice Press, 1999); John S. McClure and Nancy Ramsay, eds., *Telling the Truth: Preaching about Sexual and Domestic Violence* (Cleveland: United Church Press, 1998).

4. Stanley Hauerwas and William Willimon, *Resident Aliens, Life in the Christian Colony: A Provocative Christian Assessment of Culture and Ministry for People Who Know that Something is Wrong* (Nashville: Abingdon Press, 1995), and *Preaching to Strangers* (Louisville: Westminster John Knox Press, 1992); Walter Brueggemann, *Cadences of Home: Preaching Among Exiles* (Louisville: Westminster John Knox Press, 1997); Charles L. Campbell, *Preaching Jesus: New Directions for Homiletics in Hans Frei's Postliberal Theology* (Grand Rapids: Eerdmans, 1997), and *The Word Before the Powers* (Louisville: Westminster John Knox Press, 2002) .

5. For more on the concept of the interhuman, see Edward G. Farley, *Good and Evil: Interpreting A Human Condition* (Minneapolis: Fortress Press, 1991); and *Theology and the Interhuman: Essays in Honor of Edward Farley*, ed. Robert R. Williams (Valley Forge, Pa.: Trinity Press International, 1995).

6. See Anna Freud, *Ego and the Mechanisms of Defense* (New York: International Universities Press, 1946); Jacques Lacan, *Écrits: A Selection*, trans. Alan Sheridan (London: Tavistock/Routledge, 1977); René Girard, *Violence and the Sacred*, trans. Patrick Gregory (Baltimore: Johns Hopkins University Press, 1979); Gil Bailie, *Violence Unveiled: Humanity at the Crossroads* (New York: Crossroad/Herder and Herder, 1997); Mark I. Wallace, *Fragments of the Spirit: Nature, Violence, and the Renewal of Creation* (New York: Continuum, 1996); Eric Gans, *The End of Culture: Toward a Generative Anthropology* (Berkeley: University of California Press, 1985); Regina M. Schwarz, *The Curse of Cain: The Violent Legacy of Monotheism* (Chicago: University of Chicago Press, 1998); James E. Loder, *The Transforming Moment*, 2d ed. (Boulder, Colo.: Helmers and Howard, 1989).

7. See especially Louis Althusser, "Ideology and Ideological State Apparatuses (Notes Towards an Investigation)," in *Essays on Ideology* (London: Verso, 1984), 41. See also Lacan, *Écrits*; Antonio Gramsci, *Selections from the Prison Notebooks* trans. Quentin Hoare and Geoffrey Nowell Smith (Newark: International Press, 1971); Ernesto Laclau and Chantal Mouffe, *Hegemony and Socialist Strategy: Towards a Radical Democratic Politics* (London, Verso, 1985); and Rosemary Hennessy, "Subjects, Knowledges,… and All the Rest: Speaking for What?" in *Who Can Speak: Authority and Critical Identity*, ed. Judith Roof and Robyn Wiegman (Urbana: University of Illinois Press, 1995), 137-49.

8. *Lenin and Philosophy and Other Essays*, trans. Ben Brewster (New York: Monthly Review Press, 2001), 118.

9. See *Selections from the Prison Notebooks*; also Robert Bocock, *Hegemony* (New York: Tavistock Publications, 1986).

10. I do not support a rejection of prophetic resistance, which is appropriate in situations in which there is a struggle to establish identity where it is in the process of being de-created or in which identity has been long denied; see McClure and Ramsay, *Telling the Truth.*

11. See especially Lucy Atkinson Rose, *Sharing the Word: Preaching in the Roundtable Church* (Louisville: Westminster John Knox Press, 1997); Anna Carter Florence, *Preaching as Testimony, Toward a Women's Preaching Tradition and New Homiletic Models* (Ph.D. dissertation, Princeton Theological Seminary, 2000); and John S. McClure, *Otherwise Preaching: A Postmodern Ethic for Homiletics* (St. Louis: Chalice Press, 2001).

12. See John Henry Newman, *Grammar of Assent* (Notre Dame: University of Notre Dame Press, 1978); Karl Barth, *Church Dogmatics* 1.1, trans. G.W. Bromiley (Edinburgh: T. &T. Clark, 1975), 99-111; George Lindbeck, *The Nature of Doctrine: Religion and Theology in a Postliberal Age* (Louisville: Westminster John Knox Press, 1984); Nancy Murphy, *Reasoning and Rhetoric in Religion* (Harrisburg, Pa.: Trinity Press International, 1994).

13. See David Jasper, *Rhetoric, Power and Community* (Louisville: Westminster John Knox Press, 1993); Graham Ward, "The Revelation of the Holy Other as the Wholly Other: Between Barth's Theology of the Word and Levinas's Philosophy of Saying," *Modern Theology* 9:2 (April 1993), 159-80.

14. *The Power to Speak: Feminism, Language, God* (New York: Crossroad Press, 1991), 30-39.

15. By non-defensive, I do not want to imply or promote any form of abusive annihilation of the self motivated by fear, avoidance of self (Plaskow's "hiding"), or loss of self (the self that goes nowhere, rather than toward neighbor). The *kenotic* move toward neighbor envisioned here would be when the self comes out of hiding (in the abused self) and, out of responsibility to and for others, challenges abusive power in the neighbor (or spouse), and participates in the re-creation of what has been de-created through the giving and receiving of compassion. See Judith

Plaskow, *Sex, Sin and Grace: Women's Experience and the Theologies of Reinhold Niebuhr and Paul Tillich* (New York: University Press of America, 1980). For an excellent reassessment of the *kenosis* of Christ see Mary M. Solberg, *Compelling Knowledge: A Feminist Proposal for an Epistemology of the Cross* (Albany: SUNY Press, 1997). See also Sally B. Purvis, *The Power of the Cross: Foundations for a Christian Feminist Ethic of Community* (Nashville: Abingdon Press, 1993), and Sally H. Brown, *Preaching Ethics Reconsidered: The Social Construction of Christian Moral Reasoning and the Reimagining of Power in Preaching According to the Cross* (Ph. D. diss., Princeton Theological Seminary, 2001), 200-24.

16. Levinas locates the priority for the human other in the Old Testament commandment "Thou shalt not kill" as the ultimate command against making "same" that which is "other," or making a totality out of that which is infinite. Thus the priority of the human other achieves proto-theological status. See *Totality and Infinity: An Essay on Exteriority*, trans. Alphonso Lingis (Pittsburgh: Duquesne University Press, 1969), 198, 232-37. See also Emmanuel Levinas, *Otherwise Than Being*, trans. Alphonso Lingis (The Hague: Martinus Nijhoff, 1987); and O. E. Ajzenstat's excellent essay "Beyond Totality: The Shoah and the Biblical Ethics of Emmanuel Levinas" in *Strange Fire: Reading the Bible after the Holocaust*, ed. Tod Linafelt (Sheffield, England: Sheffield Academic Press, 2000), 206-13. Rebeccas Chopp's work is rooted to some extent in Paul Ricoeur's reflections on the work of Emmanuel Levinas, whom Ricoeur calls the "thinker of testimony" par excellence; see Ricoeur, "Emmanuel Levinas: Thinker of Testimony," in *Figuring the Sacred: Religion, Narrative, and Imagination*, ed. Mark I. Wallace (Minneapolis: Fortress Press, 1995).

17. For more on these terms see M. M. Bakhtin, *The Dialogic Imagination*, ed. Michael Holquist, trans. Caryl Emerson and Michael Holquist, 13th ed. (Austin: University of Texas Press, 1981), 301-66.

18. *Preaching as Testimony* (note 11), 168.

19. Florence, following Mary Fulkerson, chooses this word which signals "a new kind of hospitality for the stranger" that "resists domination of the other and even acknowledges love's inability to know the other." *Preaching as Testimony*, 161. For more on the concept of "being with" see Jean-Luc Nancy, *Being Singular Plural* (Palo Alto: Stanford University Press, 2000).

20. *The Recovery of Preaching* (San Francisco: Harper and Row, 1977), 37.

21. *Interpreting God's Word in Black Preaching* (Valley Forge, Pa., Judson Press, 1984), 47.

22. *The Sacred Art: Preaching and Theology in the African-American Tradition* (Cleveland: Judson Press, 1995), 106.

23. For a good overview of the biblical concept of jubilee, see Maria Harris, *Proclaim Jubilee!: A Spirituality for the 21st Century* (Louisville: Westminster John Knox Press, 1996).

24. Perhaps this is why the kiss of peace — signing the peace — is one of the most ancient and fundamental liturgical practices in the church.

25. It is the testimony of love that ultimately distinguishes homiletical testimony from courtroom testimony or testimony as a form of forensic disputation. It moves preaching beyond the oppositional rhythm between testimony and counter-testimony, which in ways similar to those just discussed can once again keep us from the other. For more on this see my essay "The Way of Love: Loder, Levinas, and Ethical Transformation through Preaching" in *Redemptive Transformation in Practical Theology*, ed. Dana R. Wright and John D. Kuentzel (Grand Rapids: Eerdmans, 2004).

26. Ronald J. Allen and William E. Dorman, "Preaching as Hospitality," *Quarterly Review 14* (1994); Ronald J. Allen, *Interpreting the Gospel: An Introduction to Preaching* (St. Louis: Chalice Press, 1998); Lucy Atkinson Rose, *Sharing the Word: Preaching in the Roundtable Church* (Louisville: Westminster John Knox Press, 1997).

27. *Preaching as Local Theology and Folk Art* (Minneapolis: Fortress Press, 1997).

28. Charles L. Campbell and Stanley P. Saunders, *The Word on the Street: Performing the Scriptures in the Urban Context* (Grand Rapids: Eerdmans, 1997).

29. *A Healing Homiletic* (note 2).

30. Christine M. Smith, *Preaching as Weeping* (note 2), and *Weaving the Sermon: Preaching in Feminist Perspective* (Louisville: Westminster John Knox Press, 1989).

31. *The Roundtable Pulpit: Where Preaching and Leadership Meet* (Nashville: Abingdon Press, 1996).

John S. McClure is the Charles G. Finney Professor of Homiletics and Chair of the Graduate Department of Religion at Vanderbilt University, where he is also a Fellow in the Center for the Study of Religion and Culture. His publications include The Four Codes of Preaching: Rhetorical Strategies *(Fortress, 1991, 2nd ed. 2004),* The Roundtable Pulpit: Where Preaching and Leadership Meet *(Abingdon, 1995),* Telling the Truth: Preaching About Sexual and Domestic Violence *(co-edited with Nancy Ramsay, United Church Press, 1998),* Other-wise Preaching: A Postmodern Ethic for Homiletics *(Chalice, 2001), and* Claiming Theology in the Pulpit, *co-authored with Burton Z. Cooper (Westminster John Knox Press, 2003).*

The Trinitarian DNA of Christian Worship:
Perenniel Themes in Recent Theological Literature

JOHN D. WITVLIET

ONE OF THE REMARKABLE FEATURES OF CHRISTIAN theology in recent years is the resurgence of interest in the doctrine of the Trinity. One of the persistent features of this literature is the observation that Trinitarian theology has considerable implications for Christian worship — an observation that is often made, but less often developed.[1] On the assumption that doctrine and liturgy are inextricably intertwined, my interest is to isolate and clarify the links between the doctrine of the Trinity and the theology and practice of worship, and thereby to explore the basic "grammar" or "DNA" of Trinitarian worship.

Because my purposes are not primarily historical, but constructive, I will approach the recent body of Trinitarian theology thematically. This literature features what Robert Jenson describes as "several kinds of Trinitarian discourse."[2] It puts the doctrine of the Trinity to different uses, each of which arises out of a different motivation, aims at a different target, and speaks to a different antagonist. My procedure will be to identify briefly five unique though inter-related themes, five "kinds of Trinitarian discourse," and to explore the resonances or corollaries of those themes in work on the theology and practice of liturgy. By choosing to offer an overview, my goal is to present this material at a level of specificity that can best inform the work of musicians, artists, poets, preachers, and liturgists.[3]

1. *Imago Trinitatis: Divine and Human Relationality*

Arguably the most pervasive theme in recent Trinitarian literature is an emphasis on relationality as essential for understanding divine being and human personhood. The doctrine of the Trinity, the argument runs, depicts divine life as supremely relational, where "love-for-another" is seen to be the essential aspect of divine life and, consequently, the source and goal of human existence. Typical works feature rhapsodic descriptions of the "agapic other-regard, that divine reciprocity, the supreme mutuality that lies at the heart of the universe."[4] Many of the works in the field argue, with John Zizioulas, that Being itself is communion. This is a vision that accentuates *koinonia* as a primary attribute of divine life, and contends that human communal life should model, embody, mirror, or be analogous to that deep communion. This vision nearly always draws on the metaphor of *perichoresis* or "indwelling" — an "in-ness" relationship among divine persons intimated in the Gospel according to John and developed by John of Damascus[5] — that envisions divine life as a dynamic dance, where God's unity is a function of active relations. When seen as a vision for human life, this vision protests any form of either ecclesiastical or societal individualism. Here the term "Trinitarian" is used as an antonym to the terms "individualistic" and "isolated."

Broadly speaking, there are two basic ways of conceptualizing and highlighting relationality in Trinitarian terms. One way follows Augustine and Barth, drawing on psychological analogies of the Trinity to conceptualize the divine being as unipersonal, but nevertheless self-giving. God is relational toward us: Christ is a perfect sign of God's essential self-giving posture. This Trinitarian vision is deeply relational, in contrast with deist views of a pristine and remote God, but it shies away from speaking of an interpersonal exchange within divine life.

A second way of conceptualizing divine relationality, much discussed in recent literature, draws on the Cappadocian fathers (or at least the traditional understanding of them), and thinks tripersonally of Father, Son, and Holy Spirit as a communion, or even a community, of divine persons. This theme has seen sounded most aggressively by proponents of the so-called social doctrine of the Trinity, influenced by the work of Jürgen Moltmann. A tripersonal or social view of God posits that God is best conceived as a community of divine persons, where "God is three persons, Father, Son, and Holy Spirit, who exist in perichoretic union as one God."[6] The accent falls on the threeness over against the oneness of God, in ways that favor not unipersonal, but tripersonal descriptions, metaphors, and images of divine life. This is a vision that corresponds visually with the famous Rublev icon of the Trinity. Musically, it is a vision perhaps best expressed in Messiaen's "Meditations on the Holy Trinity," with three unique musical motifs that weave together in profound polyphony.

Underneath these two approaches are complex discussions about the nature of personhood, and terminological nuances of the meaning of key Greek, Latin, German, and English terms for divine unity and personhood. Both ways, however, work up a robust enthusiasm for a view of God that protests any intimation of isolation.

And both find complementary allies in anthropological concepts developed in nontheological contexts, including philosophical anthropology and social psychology, which favor ecstatic and relational accounts of human personhood.[7] This relational vision of divine life is transmuted to human, communal life through one out of several of what Christoph Schwöbel calls "bridging concepts" that span the doctrine of God and a socio-ethical vision. Two bridging concepts are especially prominent.[8] The first is a notion that the doctrine of God describes something that human beings are challenged to mirror, model, imitate, or image. This set of metaphors emphasizes the perfection of divine life and the distinction between God

and humanity. The second is the notion that the doctrine of God describes a reality that humans are called to embody or in which they are called to participate. This metaphor emphasizes the closeness, even the intimacy, of divine and human life. Either way, Trinitarian relationality is taken to provide a foundation for ethics, ecclesiology, political theology, and social theory—that is, for any area of discourse concerned with the ordering of human communal life, including its common worship.

This relational vision touches most closely on liturgy through work in ecclesiology. The church, to use a phrase of Jürgen Moltmann, is an "icon of the Trinity."[9] Among recent theorists, one of the first to draw the connection between the doctrine of God and the doctrine of the church was the missiologist, bishop, and teacher Lesslie Newbigin: "The Church is called to be a union of [those] with Christ in the love of the Father whereby their separate beings are made one with that perfect mutual interpenetration in love, that perfect community which is the glory of God."[10] Likewise, Letty Russell grounds her notion of "The Church in the Round" in the doctrine of the Trinity: "the partnership of God in the persons of the Trinity also provides an image of mutuality, reciprocity, and a totally shared life. The characteristics of partnership, or *koinonia*, may be discovered in their perfection in the Trinity, where there is a focus of relationship in mutual love between the persons and toward creation."[11]

To see the implications here for Christian worship is not hard. Christian worship is one arena where a Trinitarian ecclesiology is most tangibly expressed. As Jean-Jacques von Allmen argued, worship is "pre-eminently the moment of true community. . . . Christian worship is the most emphatic contradiction of human solitude and abandonment."[12] At its best, Christian liturgy embodies the mutuality and *koinonia* of a Trinitarian ecclesiology and thus prefigures the coming kingdom. In a public, concrete way, Christian worship is an icon of our union with

Christ through the work of the Holy Spirit. In a public, concrete way, Christian worship is an icon of the web of relationships that make up the Christian church, particularly in the sacraments, which are supreme moments for enacting gospel-shaped relationships.

In all of these discussions several temptations are to be avoided: the temptation to rethink the Trinity in light of prior social or political commitments; the temptation to apply our vision for relationality selectively to those liturgical practices we happen to like or that are politically expedient; and—perhaps most significantly—the temptation to think of divine life as only a model, and not also the source, for rightly ordered human relationships.

Nevertheless, this vision of corporate worship as a locus for *koinonia* calls for realization in tangible ways, in particular forms, institutions, rites, texts, and other liturgical practices. Recent literature has sought to ground any number of liturgical practices in a theology of Trinitarian relationality. Thus, the doctrine of the Trinity is often the lead doctrine that introduces discussions of architecture emphasizing human relationality, more egalitarian visions of Christian leadership, a greater liturgical ecumenism and unity, the corporate nature of Christian prayer, more communal ways of receiving the sacraments, sermons that aim at restoration of community, corporate almsgiving as a basic for another action of Christian *diakonia*, corporate processes for the creation of liturgical art forms (over against treating liturgical artists as solitary geniuses who work independently from worshiping communities), greater inclusion of children and persons with disabilities, language that is inclusive and accessible, to say nothing of ideas for deepening the practice of the passing of the peace. Concern for Trinity-like relationality thus grounds and inspires several community-building worship practices.

2. The "Divine Mediation" Theme

A second primary theme in recent Trinitarian literature is a recovery of active awareness of the action of Christ and the Spirit as fully divine persons who prompt and mediate human acts of prayer, praise, and sacramental participation. Here the term Trinitarian is used as an antonym of "Pelagian" or any other term that implies that human instrumentality brings about a divine-human encounter. Note that the use of the term "Trinitarian" brings a different, though not incompatible, emphasis from the relational theme described above (theme 1).

Consider this Trinitarian definition of Christian worship by Thomas F. Torrance: "In our worship the Holy Spirit comes forth from God, uniting us to the response and obedience and faith and prayer of Jesus, and returns to God, raising us up in Jesus to participate in the worship of heaven and in the eternal communion of the Holy Trinity."[13] For Torrance (and for Moltmann, Colin Gunton, and dozens of other theologians) worship involves two directional movements—God's coming to the church and the church's reponse to God—both of which involve the action of each member of the Trinity. When Colin Gunton calls Ephesians 2:18 "a Trinitarian way of speaking," and when Vincent Brümmer speaks about the Holy Spirit's work of enabling the human response to God by saying that "God motivates us in a Trinitarian way to turn to him,"[14] they refer not primarily to a notion of ecstatic relationality (theme 1), but to the divinity of the Son and Spirit as agents and mediators who act on or through us to make divine-human communication possible. The point here is that the agents that enable both God's coming to us and our response to God are not less than divine persons—whose work, as such, can be trusted to be efficacious. As Gunton concludes: "the first and last thing we have to say about God the Trinity is that he is a God who enables us to worship him."[15]

Any number of theologians could be quoted to illustrate this conceptualization. One is J.-J. von Allmen, who argues that the first, initiatory movement in the divine-human relationship enacted in liturgy is God's. In preaching, von Allmen concluded, "Christian preaching cannot therefore be understood apart from the doctrine of the Trinity: on the basis of the past work of His Son, and in the perspective of the work He is yet to do, God the Father gives us today, through the Holy Spirit, faith in the salvation which has been accomplished and hope in the salvation yet to be revealed." [16] Likewise, the sacramental movement of worship is neatly summed up in a Trinitarian formulation. "The sacrament is the means which the Holy Spirit uses to convey Christ and His salvation to us. . . . By the *sacrament*, the Holy Spirit binds the Christ to us"; and again, "The Christian place of worship is the assembly in which Jesus Christ, God's temple, is present, in the power of the Spirit."[17] In short, in liturgy God comes to the worshiping community "in Christ, through the Spirit." These formulations suggest why the doctrine of the Trinity is so crucial: it ensures that both the content of Christian proclamation and the source for perceiving that content are not less than God.

The God-humanward movement is complemented by a movement from human beings to God, a movement of faith, prayer, worship, and sacrifice. This movement, too, is frequently conceptualized in a Trinitarian way. Worship, praise, and prayer are offered "to the Father, in Christ, through the Spirit." Von Allmen's Trinitarian description of this human response begins with his analysis of the "messianic cult": the worship of God offered by Jesus Christ. He emphasized that Jesus' whole life was an act of priestly worship to God: "the true glorification of God on earth, which is the perfect worship, has been fulfilled by Jesus Christ in his ministry." He also insisted that this act of worship is ongoing, and is now rendered by Jesus to God in heaven: "the present of the history of

salvation is the heavenly offering which Jesus Christ renders to His Father in the glory of the Ascension."[18] Both Jesus' earthly life and Jesus' ongoing life in heaven are priestly. Our participation in Christ's worship is only possible because of the work of the Holy Spirit. The Holy Spirit is a "liturgical agent" who makes possible and effects the worship of God. Christian worship "is born of the outpouring of the Holy Spirit." The Lord's Supper is only effectual because of the "quickening by the Holy Spirit" — "the presence of the Holy Spirit in the Church means that worship is induced and brought into being." In sum, "the Holy Spirit brings us into communion with Christ."

Whether in von Allmen's writings or elsewhere, such Trinitarian descriptions of the inner workings of worship are marked with a certain rhetorical symmetry: worship consists in proclamation from the Father in Christ through the Spirit, and response in the Spirit through Christ to the Father — patterns that have been called the "chiastic meta-narrative of scripture" and "doxological summaries of the history of salvation."[19] Yet to get lost in the symmetry of such formulations and to miss their main point is easy. The point is to accent the way in which both revelation and response, both sacrament and sacrifice, are gifts of divine grace. The point is to preserve and make luminous the patristic instinct that both God's revelation and our human response are gifts to be received rather than accomplishments to be sought.

The target of this assertion is a perennial temptation toward a kind of liturgical Pelagianism. So James B. Torrance, for example, is particularly concerned with theological schemes that correctly stress "God-humanward movement in Christ" but wrongly imply that "the human-Godward movement is still ours." He contends that this tendency ignores the priesthood of Christ, so that "the only priesthood is our priesthood, the only offering our offering, the only intercessions our intercessions." Torrance maintains that this vision implies that "God throws us back upon ourselves to make our response" and ignores that "God has already provided for us that Response which alone is acceptable to him — the offering made for the whole human race in the life, obedience and passion of Jesus Christ." Torrance argues that this distorted view of worship is functionally unitarian, operating apart from the work of the Holy Spirit and the mediatorship of Christ. Even though we sing Trinitarian hymns and observe Trinity Sunday, we approach God more like the pristine, isolated God of deism than like an active, mediating Presence. For Torrance the key thesis is that *both* "the God-humanward movement and human-Godward relationship" are "freely given to us in Jesus Christ."[20]

A theology of worship that emphasizes that worship is a gift of divine grace has inevitable consequences for how liturgy is celebrated.[21] First, Christian worshipers acknowledge the giftedness of worship by means of epicletic prayers, prayers that express our longing for the Holy Spirit to work through liturgical actions to nurture and inspire faith; these are prayers typically offered at baptism and at the Lord's Supper, prayers for illumination prior to proclamation, and even prayers prior to our acts of praise, or in hymns like "Lord Jesus Christ, be present now." The epiclesis, concludes Hughes Oliphant Old, "is one of the basic acts of worship."[22] It is a prayer, says Lukas Vischer, that "shows that the church must always appear before God with empty hands, even when she prepares and performs her worship in obedience to God."[23]

Second, a theology of worship as a graced event calls for liturgical proclamation that is explicitly rooted in God's revelation in Jesus Christ through the Spirit. Just as the praise and prayer of the church is an act of acknowledgment, recognition, reception, and participation in the mediation of Jesus Christ and the Holy Spirit, so too liturgical proclamation is best conceived as participation

in, and grateful reception of, the gift of the Word of God. Liturgical proclamation does not require generating a new message, a new Word, a new gospel; it simply requires rehearsing the gospel given in Christ. As von Allmen argued, "We do not have to invent what we are to say, we have only to listen and pass it on." This occurs, he contended, through preaching that calls attention to God's work in Christ: "Preaching is none other than the preaching of Jesus Christ." Preaching that ignores what God has done in Christ elicits "an existential despair in which everything must be started afresh."[24]

Third, a theology of worship as a graced event calls for acts that acknowledge the mediation of Jesus Christ and the Holy Spirit. This occurs explicitly in Trinitarian formulas at the end of sung psalms or spoken prayers — and especially prayers offered *to* God *in* the name of Jesus *through* the Spirit, or *through* Jesus *in* the Spirit, a practice more thoroughly appreciated since Josef A. Jungmann's classic study *The Place of Christ in Liturgical Prayer* appeared. As Donald Bloesch argues: "To pray in the name of Christ . . . means that we recognize that our prayers cannot penetrate the tribunal of God unless they are presented to the Father by the Son."[25] Trinitarian doxologies at the end of prayers, sermons, absolutions, and benedictions all attest that the action being completed is accomplished only as a gift of grace.[26] They emphasize, concluded von Allmen, that "the whole service is taking place in the presence, under the authority, and with the power of the Holy Trinity."[27] Such liturgical formulas are acts of recognition, reception, and participation; they are the explicit acknowledgment of a Trinitarian theology of worship as a graced event.

The challenge here is enacting these elements of liturgy in ways that bring the mediation of Son and Spirit into the consciousness of ordinary worshipers — who may otherwise live with the implicit feeling that the success of a worship service depends either on the prowess of the local preacher or musician or on their own mental efforts to make worship work. We who preach or lead music violate this principle every time we unwittingly promote a rather sacramental view of ourselves as the ones who engineer a spiritual experience for people. Rather, our goal should be, in the words of a well-known John Bell hymn, to help people sense the Trinity "round me, above and beneath, before and behind" in worship and in life.[28] Offering the faithful such an all-encompassing and grace-filled vision to supplant the rather vague and impersonal notions of deity that our culture perpetuates is an act of profound pastoral care.

3. The Divine Economy Theme

The third theme in recent literature is a renewed emphasis on the divine economy as the basis for our knowledge of God—a theme established by Karl Barth's claim "God is as God revealed himself to be" and Karl Rahner's rule that the "immanent Trinity is the economic Trinity," and vice versa. The Princeton theologian Daniel Migliore articulates the pay-off of these basic assertations in observing: "Classical Trinitarian doctrine . . . wants to say that there is no sinister or even demonic side of God altogether different from what we know in the story of Jesus who befriended the poor and forgave sinners. God *is* self-expanding, other-affirming, community-building love."[29] Here the term "Trinitarian" is being used as an antonym to theology that is speculative, abstract, ethereal, or vague.

From the start, the doctrine of the Trinity has rested on the high Christological claims of Colossians and Hebrews that Christ is the "image [or icon] of the invisible God" (Col 1:15), the "exact imprint of God's being" (Heb 1:3). In contrast to the Greek inclination to define the concept of God on the basis of philosophically-derived ideals, the doctrine of the Trinity implies that human beings have a better, more direct and immediate source for knowledge of God in the person of Christ. And so, in contrast to

Arianism, the doctrine of the Trinity argued that the real God was not a pristine higher power disconnected from the actions of Jesus Christ and the Holy Spirit. In contrast to Sabellianism, the doctrine of the Trinity contended that God's actions in history are not mere shadows or masks of divine being, but are rather a reliable indicator of God's very nature. No—the doctrine of the Trinity boldly asserted that Christ and the Spirit are reliable signs of God's nature, for they themselves are truly divine. In Colin Gunton's words, the doctrine of the Trinity ensures that our thinking about God does not "float off into abstraction from the concrete history of salvation."[30] As Gunton concludes, this line of thinking "is based upon an insight of blinding simplicity: if Jesus Christ is God, then God is really given in him, and does not have to be sought behind or apart from him."[31]

Typically, extrapolations of this theme come with three large complaints: (a) that a lot of theological discourse historically has featured separate rather than integrated treatments of the oneness and threeness of God; (b) that a lot of theological discourse historically has featured separate rather than integrated treatments of the economic and immanent Trinity; and (c) that in all of this the influence of Plato and Hellenic thought patterns is vast and damaging. Extrapolations of this theme usually feature forthright methodological prescriptions, which aim at what Moltmann called "the theological remoulding of philosophical terms."[32] The goal is that whenever we speak of God, describe God, invoke God, or call God to mind, we do so in terms of the concrete ways in which God has been made known rather than through abstract concepts that are especially susceptible to being reshaped by culture's shfting intellectual climate. Thus this theme is a campaign against idolatry, whereby our worship is mistargeted toward a god of our own imaginations.

The liturgical corollary of this theme is simply that just as the Christian doctrine of God should be rooted in the divine economy, so too Christian worship should rehearse the divine economy. God's actions in history are the basis for *both* the knowledge and worship of the triune God. Liturgy, like theology, must not "float off into abstractions" about God. In other words, Christian liturgy is fundamentally an act of *anamnesis*, an act of rehearsing God's actions in history: past and future, realized and promised. Christians identify the God they worship by naming God as the agent of particular actions in history. Worship proceeds better by rehearsing eventful narratives of divine action — viewed iconically as reliable windows into divine life — than by re-stating rational deductions or abstract ideas. It is more like Masaccio's Trinity — in which we perceive God through the iconic cross.

This emphasis on God's actions in history is reflected in several theological definitions of worship. Jean-Jacques von Allmen insisted that "liturgy connects the Church with the history of salvation…it unites the Church of all places and times around the permanently decisive *magnalia Dei*."[33] John Burkhart posits that "true worship celebrates the most definite God of the covenant in Moses and Jesus, the God of Abraham, Isaac, and Jacob, of Sarah, Rebekah, and Rachel, and of countless others. Fundamentally, worship is the celebrative response to what God has done, is doing, and promises to do."[34] E. H. van Olst contends that in liturgy "people come together to celebrate the mighty acts of God . . . the basic structure of the saving acts of God [in which] the remembrance of Israel as well as the liturgical celebration of the church is rooted."[35]

In this view, worship is not primarily ahistorical mystical introspection.[36] Donald Bloesch, for example, links ahistorical mysticism with an attempt "to transcend the Trinity by positing a 'God above God,' an infinite abyss that lies beyond personality and diversity," which he identifies as "incontestably other than the God of Abraham, Isaac, and Jacob."[37] Neither is Christian liturgy merely a celebration of nature and natural cycles. Echoing an idea of

Abraham Heschel, among others, Adrio König places great emphasis on the fact that ancient Israel changed its calendar of feasts from one "linked with nature, into one which was tied to history," and thus transformed what had been celebrations of natural cycles into celebrations of historical events. König argues that this shift in cultic practice corresponded to the theological commitment to conceive of God on the basis of God's action in history,[38] a pattern inherited by Christian worshipers, appropriate for a faith that adores a God who acts in history, especially in the incarnation.

This historical orientation is expressed concretely through several particular liturgical actions. First, Christian worship features the reading and preaching of scripture as a prominent liturgical action. It is, A. C. Honders argues, "the most direct way of testifying to God's great acts."[39] William Placher claims that "only in regularly reading scripture and reflecting on it in the gathered community can there develop a common language and a framework of shared stories and understandings of those stories within which we can live our lives together as Christians. . . . Sermons provide the space for inviting the community to reflect together in the context of the language of the scriptural texts, thereby at once learning to use that language and learning to think about the world in its terms."

He concludes, "The preaching of the Word, the telling of the stories of God's work with Israel and of the crucified Jesus, plays its part in making a Christian community by issuing reminders of the sort of God Christians worship."[40] Just as needless speculation and untethered technical philosophical discourse must be rooted out from theology, so too they must be rooted out from liturgical language about God.

Second, in praise and prayer we identify God and specify God's character in terms of specific actions. Direct address *to* God in liturgical prayer proceeds best by identifying

God in terms of God's actions in history. Large portions of Hebrew prayer, and especially the Psalms, are devoted to telling God what God presumably already knows, what God has done in history. In Christian euchology this pattern is preserved, for example in the structure of the collect. Before any petition that asks God to act in a particular way in the present and future, the collect form often (though not always) names a specific way in which God has acted in the past,[41] for example, "O God, who by the leading of a star…" This pattern is also prominent in eucharistic and baptismal prayers, and in many hymn texts. A fitting example from the early church is the *Te Deum laudamus*. In the culture of the ancient world from which this text comes, it is not remarkable that God is praised as almighty and powerful. What *is* remarkable— and what makes it incipiently Trinitarian (or at least Binitarian)—is that praise is offered also for Jesus' birth and death, events that seem at first to be un-godlike. This orthodox prayer, which closely mirrors the Apostles' and Nicene creeds that were shaped during the same period, protests the picture of God as merely an Unmoved Mover, a solitary figure of power, and professes that Jesus' birth, life, death, resurrection, and coming again are "the radiance of God's glory and the exact representation of his being" (Heb 1:1).

Third, the large structures that guide Christian worship over the course of the year call attention to God's action in history. This is why N. T. Wright, in a sermon at Lichfield Cathedral, could argue that the events of the Christian year "function as a sequence of well-aimed hammerblows which knock at the clay jars of the gods we want, the gods who reinforce our own pride and prejudice, until they fall away and reveal instead a very different god, a dangerous god, a subversive god, a god who comes to us like a blind beggar with wounds in his hands, a god who comes to us in wind and fire, in bread and wine, in flesh and blood: a god who says to us, 'You did not choose me; I chose you.'"[42] This

point underscores not just why the Christian year should be observed, but also suggests how. If the Christian year is valuable in its rehearsal of God's actions in history, then it should be celebrated in such a way as to make this point clear. A celebration of Christmas will have little "anamnetic value" if it merely celebrates the importance of gift-giving. A celebration of Easter will have little "anamnetic value" if it merely highlights the endless cycle of death and rebirth. These celebrations aim at recalling the ways in which God has acted in history, and to contemplating what these actions imply iconically about God's character.

Fourth, the *anamnesis* of God's actions in history is realized in the liturgy of the Lord's Supper. Anchored in Jesus' words, "This do in remembrance of me," the function of memorializing is arguably the most universal feature of the dominical feast (though it is only one of many key themes associated with the Lord's Supper). Every Christian theologian, from the most sacramental to the least, understands the Lord's Supper as an act of memory, an act that rehearses the decisive events of Jesus' passion and triumph. Von Allmen argues that "the Christian supper offers to those who participate in it, not the experience of being in communion with a myth, but participation in historical events."[43] That is why traditional eucharistic prayers, like many biblical Psalms, are shaped as bard-like, doxological history lessons—recounting the history of God's actions from creation to new creation.

In all of these areas, of course, the challenge is not only to restore narrative recital but to look at narrative iconically, as a window into divine life. At Christmas we need not only Luther's narrative hymn "While Shepherds Watched Their Flocks," which tells the story, but also Wesley's "Hark! The Herald Angels Sing," which interprets what the nativity narrative means for our understanding of God and the salvation God provides. In the Eucharist we need not only historically-oriented eucharistic prayers, but also the adoration of the *Sanctus* and the strong petition of the *epiclesis*, which draw on this history to inform and deepen our vision for God.

In sum, in contrast with a deistic world in which praise is rooted in timeless attributes of pristine divine perfection, Trinitarian worship identifies God in terms of God's action in history. We constantly hone our ideas of God on the basis of meditation on the divine economy, and thus confront the inevitable idols that our culture may fabricate.

4. The Theme Of Balance And Integration

The fourth theme in recent literature is that of balance and integration. Consider Richard Mouw's quip, at the beginning of a recent chapter on Trinitarian ethics, that "Christians play favorites with the members of the Trinity."[44] Similary, H. Richard Niebuhr contended, only slightly whimsically, that Christianity might well be characterized as "an association, loosely held together, of three Unitarian religions."[45] Niebuhr's point is that Christians have a persistent tendency to narrow their view of God's actions, and to separate, rank, order, and pit against each other aspects of the divine economy. In contrast, the doctrine of the Trinity calls for viewing God's actions as a comprehensive and unified whole. As Niebuhr argued, part of the value of the doctrine of the Trinity is that it serves as "a formulation of the *whole* Church's faith in God in distinction from the partial faiths and partial formulations of parts of the Church and of individuals in the Church." The doctrine, he continues, is valuable "to correct the over-emphases and partialities of the members of the whole not by means of a new over-emphasis but by means of a synthesized formula in which all the partial insights and convictions are combined."[46]

Here "Trinitarian theology" is offered in contrast with a "christomonistic" or other partial or disintegrated approaches. Here "Trinitarian"

becomes a formal construct, resulting in books with chapters on each divine person, or hymns with each divine person getting a stanza—a formal construct much more interested in symmetry than the New Testament, in which the Holy Spirit is always the shy member of the Trinity. Interestingly, in the popular Christian imagination this is what Trinitarian worship is assumed to be: worship in which each of the persons of the Trinity gets some airtime.

The theme is, of course, more nuanced and sophisticated than this. A representative theologian to illustrate this is Arnold van Ruler, who called for a theological worldview informed by the full scope of divine activity, advocating a "more catholic, that is to say, purely Trinitarian way" of interpreting the divine economy, which would examine much more than God's actions in Christ. Van Ruler noted that "God did not, after all, *only* become man in Jesus Christ, he also created a world. And he is not only present in the cross and resurrection of Jesus Christ in a veiled way but will once again reveal himself definitively in the full and great theophany of the eschaton." Van Ruler concluded that "God's presence in Jesus Christ is only an element, albeit a decisive element, in his total activity in the world," and called for theology and spirituality that are aware of the full scope of the divine economy, from creation to eschatological fulfillment.[47] Van Ruler was most concerned to re-emphasize the work of the Holy Spirit, the "absolute necessity" of a vibrant and full pneumatology, in order that "the imperative of a Trinitarian theology would become apparent anew." He was especially critical of Barth's christocentrism, and lamented that pneumatology "remains impoverished" in twentieth-century theology.[48] Van Ruler stressed that a pneumatological framework makes two fundamental contributions to the structure of Christian theology. For one, it keeps our attention focused eschatologically, on the coming kingdom of God as the end or goal of creation and redemption. For another, it compels theologians to consider the full scope of the Spirit's work inside and outside of the church. An adequate pneumatic theology, he argued, points toward God's activity in all of creation. In this context "Trinitarian theology" means "a more comprehensive view than we otherwise might be tempted to take."

Yet this call for comprehensiveness is only one half of the argument. Recent work has argued that a fully Trinitarian theology is not only comprehensive but is also unified and integrated. The Augustinian formulation of the doctrine of the Trinity not only confesses that "the Father is God, the Son is God, and the Holy Spirit is God," but also that "there are not three gods, but one God"—a confession of divine *unity*. The central claim here is that the works of God, attributed as they are in scriptural narrative and the Christian tradition to Father, Son, and Holy Spirit, are not in any way disjointed or at cross purposes. The divine economy is not only unimaginably full, but wondrously interrelated. Thus, van Ruler argued that a fully Trinitarian theology should be characterized by two movements: first, "Trinitarian thought is typified by the movement of mutually inter-relating the various aspects of theology"; second, this is followed by "the movement of distinguishing these aspects." Van Ruler argued that the various topics in theological discourse, such as soteriology or missiology, should be approached from both a "christological" and "pneumatological" point of view,[49] positing that a fully synthetic or complete theology "will be possible only within the framework of a Trinitarian perspective."[50]

This calls for theological discourse that considers apparently paradoxical attributes together—thus Daniel Migliore: "In a Trinitarian context, the attributes of God are held together as mutually qualifying descriptions of the living God."[51] And it calls for the treatment of individual theological questions in terms of each person of the Trinity. Thus, following Moltmann, Paul Jewett argues that "the cross

must be understood not only in terms of the person and work of Christ but in terms of the God who is revealed in Christ, namely, the God who is a Trinity-in-Unity. While it is essential to view what happened at Calvary in terms of the Son who became incarnate, it is also essential to understand what happened there in terms of all members of the Godhead."[52]

Typical markers of this Trinitarian integration are calls for a pneumatological christology and a christological pneumatology. A century ago Abraham Kuyper had already argued that "the Church has never sufficiently confessed the influence the Holy Spirit exerted upon the work of Christ."[53] Kuyper's assertion could well be the thesis statement of the last generation of work on Christology in several traditions. Jürgen Moltmann for one, and Yves Congar for another, call for a complete integration of Christology and pneumatology.

Other typical markers of this integration theme are calls to restore a creation and eschatology as the bookends of our theological and spiritual consciousness. Thus van Ruler calls for the interrelation of God's action of creation, redemption in Christ, and eschatological fulfillment, arguing that these are "*the* questions that arise in a Trinitarian theology," and that "it is only in a fully Trinitarian framework that one is able to determine the meaning of reason, history, the state, art, and what it is to be human. To accomplish this, the doctrines of the creation and eschatology need to provide their own accents."[54] For van Ruler the pay-off is that redemption must be understood as the salvation *for* creation, not *from* it: "Regeneration is not a new creation (*nova creatio*) but a renewal of creation (*recreatio*)." Thus, every aspect of economy after creation refers back to it: "God does not create himself anew in Israel or in Jesus Christ. He [Jesus Christ] is not a new, strange God but the one who created the world. He is, thus, not estranged from the essence of things or from the depths of the human heart."[55]

A commitment to a comprehensive and

integrated view of the divine economy has inevitable corollaries for liturgical practice. First, it calls for liturgical practices that depict the divine economy as a comprehensive and integrated whole. Thus, Otto Weber argued that a deficient appropriation of the doctrine of the Trinity and an incomplete or unintegrated view of the divine economy has inevitable repercussions in prayer and spirituality: "It is only when we constantly keep the unity of God in his work in view that we can avoid an isolated 'theology of the first article,' or an isolated 'Christocentrism,' or an isolated 'Spiritualization' of theology." In fact, said Weber, "It can be said that at this point the Doctrine of the Trinity gains its most direct relationship to 'piety' . . . when the Doctrine of the Trinity falls apart or retreats in the consciousness of the Community, then piety becomes one-sided and, measured by the liveliness and the wealth of the biblical witness, is impoverished."[56]

Weber's lament about "one-sided piety" easily translates into a central criterion for liturgical celebration: Christian worship and spirituality must rehearse the full scope and unity of God's actions. Many liturgical elements accomplish this: the grand hymns of the Christian tradition like the *Gloria*, the *Te Deum*, the liturgical creeds, the more comprehensive eucharistic and baptismal prayers, the (unabridged) Easter Vigil service, the Christian year. While most sermons, scripture readings, and anthems isolate one important narrative or theme, creeds, eucharistic prayers, and Easter Vigil services provide the entire context that helps us identify their significance.

Second, this vision calls for looking at each part of the divine economy in light of the whole. Each element in the gospel drama can be viewed through a Trinitarian lens. Take the festival of Christmas as one example. Despite significant references to the Holy Spirit in several appointed readings for the Christmas season, the Holy Spirit is the forgotten participant in the Christmas drama. We see this omission not

only in the Christmas card selection at Hallmark but also in music for the season. Yet the juxtaposition of "Christmas" and "Holy Spirit" challenges our understanding of each. First, it anchors our understanding of the Spirit's work in the person of Jesus Christ: the Holy Spirit is not just any spirit we feel, it is the Spirit of Jesus Christ. Second, it makes our understanding of Christmas more dynamic and personal: the Spirit that came upon Mary is the same Spirit that anointed Jesus to preach good news to the poor and raised him from the dead, and that has now been poured into *our* hearts. The Spirit makes *us* participants in the Christmas drama. A fully Trinitarian approach to Christmas will work to highlight and probe these themes.

Third and finally, an integrated view of the divine economy provides the logic that makes prayers of thanksgiving and intercession plausible. It commends prayer that explicitly confesses the unity of divine action. Intercessory prayer, for example, depends upon a confidence that God will act faithfully in the future, that God's past works are a clue or sign about the way God will act. The past actions of God, says Colin Gunton, provide "the ground for believing that there are further divine acts to come, or that the ascended Christ is a living and active advocate with the Father, or that the Spirit works to perfect the creation." These past actions not only teach that God will act, but also point to what kind of divine actions the future is likely to hold. Gunton continues, "If God is the one who creates and redeems through Christ and the Spirit, and is made known as such by the incarnate, crucified, risen, and ascended Jesus, then that is the one he always is. Any new action, therefore, can be expected within the framework of this eternal revelation."[57]

This logic commends liturgical prayers that seek the apt pairing of praise and intercession, as can be found in any good collect. For example, consider the collect "Eternal God, you have called us to be members of one body. Join us with those who in all times and places have praised your name, that, with one heart and mind, we may show the unity of your church and bring honor to our Lord and Savior, Jesus Christ. Amen." Here, the acknowledgment of God's act of gathering the church is the ground for a petition concerning the unity of the church. The tight logical structure of the collect is a liturgical outworking of the confession of the unity of the divine economy.

In sum, the doctrine of the Trinity is a doctrine that calls for presenting the themes of the gospel and the teaching of the church in balanced and integrated ways. It militates against partial and incomplete treatments of Christian teaching in preaching, hymnody, and prayer.

5. The Redefinition Theme

Suppose that we take the divine economy as the source of our knowledge of God (theme 3), and then provide a comprehensive and integrated interpretation of it (theme 4). If that is our methodological claim, then what is the material pay-off? A fifth theme in recent work has been to engage in Trinitarian redefinitions of the images and attributes used in theology proper.

The primary targets of this work are (a) vague, impersonal notions of distant deity, especially in popular piety, and a corresponding notion of worship as detached, disinterested, aloof contemplation; (b) unwittingly fearsome, tyrannical depictions of God's power, and corresponding notions of worship as fearful obeisance; (c) any unwitting depiction of God as a contractual deity of obligations (certainly a primary worry when it comes to liturgical piety); and (d) any view of God that is especially sentimental, a liturgical worry any time we get near Christmas. Arguably, the central thrust of this work is summed up by Jan Lochman when he argues that "the central intention of the Trinitarian dogma" is to convey "the personal, social, and compassionate character of God."[58]

Recent work on the doctrine of the Trinity features five key metaphors, metaphors that depict divine life as personal, agential, relational, self-giving, and speaking. These fundamental images or root metaphors, in turn, influence every other adjective, attribute, characteristic, property, virtue, perfection, and predicate that is used to speak of God. As Daniel Migliore argues, "Our reflections on the triune reality of God point to the need for a thorough rethinking of the doctrine of the attributes of God, which have all too often been presented and debated without any reference to the life, death, and resurrection of Jesus Christ or to the doctrine of the Trinity."[59] As Paul Jewett suggests, the divine economy should be the "yardstick" against which any divine attribute is measured, so that, in Hendrikus Berkhof's words, theologians may "pour biblical content into these abstract concepts."[60]

A representative effort at redefinition along these lines, the Trinitarian refashioning of the attribute of divine omnipotence, is a central aspect of the work of Daniel Migliore. Migliore argues that concepts of God's power must be revised in light of Jesus Christ, the "power of God" (I Cor 1:24):

> The doctrine of the Trinity represents a revolution in the understanding of the power of God. . . . Christians do not worship absolute power. They worship that divine power narrated in the gospel story and symbolized in the doctrine of the Trinity. The power of God is shared power, power that makes for just and inclusive community. Here is a radically new beginning in our understanding of God and especially of God's power.[61]

The doctrine of the Trinity, Migliore concludes, provides the over-arching framework in which conceptions of divine power can be refined. It points to the work of Jesus Christ and the Holy Spirit as revelatory of God's very being:

> The doctrine of the Trinity identifies God and the coming kingdom of his liberating,

life-giving Spirit. It redefines the power of God and the presence of God. The power of God is defined as the self-imparting love of the crucified Christ and the presence of God is understood as the re-creating, liberating, reconciling Spirit of Christ at work in the world as the "first fruits" (Rom 8:23) of God's coming kingdom. . . . The primary function of the doctrine of the Trinity is to speak of God not as a lifeless absolute but as a living history which must be narrated.

In this way, Migliore concludes, the doctrine of the Trinity "safeguards against oppressive, sub-Christian conceptions of God."[62]

Migliore's work clarifies the concept of divine omnipotence. God's power certainly entails the ability to accomplish unfathomable activity: to create a cosmos or to raise someone from the dead. The category of power is not to be abandoned altogether. What is crucial for Migliore is that God's power is not unleashed capriciously. This power is revealed on a cross. This power is directed toward particular ends: toward the establishment of right relationships and cosmic redemption. And it is power engaged through particular means: not through "terror, torture, destruction, or threat" (to use a phrase from John Bell's hymn quoted below). This power is worthy of praise *both* because of its magnitude *and* the way in which it is deployed.

The resonances of this Trinitarian redefinition effort in the area of worship lie primarily in the central concepts, images, and metaphors that describe and shape liturgical events. Central images and root metaphors in theology proper are inevitably linked with central images and root metaphors in the theology of liturgy. Metaphors of divine identity generate and ground metaphors for liturgical activity.

A Trinitarian doctrine of God posits that God is a personal, relational being who acts in self-giving love. This paradigm, root metaphor, or key conceptual model suggests that the worship of this God, as enacted in public liturgy, should be construed as a series of personal, relational actions. In this view, liturgy is not the contemplation of an impersonal, ubiquitous higher power, nor is it primarily an act of obeisance to a divine tyrant, nor an act of propitiation to a divine judge, nor, to use a phrase of Hughes Oliphant Old, "a sacred drama unfolding some sort of Neoplatonic ascent to divine reality."[63] As Colin Gunton suggests, "Worship is not an activity in which we contemplate or observe a being who is over against us — though in a sense God is that also — but it is relational, something that happens between persons."[64] If the Christian God is best described by personal, relational, and dynamic metaphors, then so too is the liturgy of the Christian church.

This, too, has concrete corollaries in practice. First, these root metaphors suggest viewing each liturgical act as personal and relational. In this view, hymns of praise, sermons, sacramental celebrations, and corporate prayer do not exist for their own sake, but for the larger purpose of enacting a personal, relational encounter. They are means by which God speaks, and by which the gathered community responds. The various elements of worship are all functional; or, to use the language of speech-action theory, they are "illocutionary." We do things, interpersonal things, with the words and sounds of worship: namely, we enact the divine-human relationship.[65]

Second, a theology of worship as a personal, relational encounter suggests a natural criterion for the form or deep structure of liturgy. As Hendrikus Berkhof suggests: "The point [of liturgy] is always the encounter with the same God whom we come to know in Christ through the Spirit. The liturgy is to structure the encounter and therefore must itself be structured as encounter."[66]

Third, this calls for music and liturgical texts that are winsomely *subversive*. Consider John Bell's Advent hymn, with its nuanced treatment of the militaristic image of "Lord of hosts."

Lift up your heads, eternal gates, Alleluia!
See how the King of glory waits, Alleluia!
The Lord of Hosts in drawing near,
the Savior of the world is here. Alleluia!

But not in arms or battle dress, Alleluia!
God comes, a child, admist distress,
    Alleluia!
No mighty armies shield the way,
only coarse linen, wool, and hay, Alleluia!

God brings a new face to the brave,
    Alleluia!
God redefines who best can save, Alleluia!
Not those whose power relies on threat,
terror or torture, destruction or debt,
    Alleluia!

God's matchless and majestic strength,
    Alleluia!
In all its height, depth, breadth, and length,
    Alleluia!
Now is revealed, its power to prove,
by Christ protesting, "God is love,"
    Alleluia![67]

Here is a text concerned with refining common assumptions about divine attributes. It uses the life of Jesus to reinterpret how we understand divine life, illustrating one of the main concerns in much of recent systematic theology.

Concluding Analysis

With respect to the doctrine of the Trinity, distinguishing these five themes highlights the ways in which this single doctrine has been used to make so many different points. One way of sensing the breadth of the use of the doctrine of the Trinity would be to imagine a hypothetical entry for the term "Trinitarian" in a lexicon of modern theological terminology. Such an entry would require at least five distinct definitions.

Perhaps that entry would read:

Trinitarian (adj.):
1. a communitarian approach to ordering human relationships in the church and in society as a mirror or icon of divine life; antonym: individualistic;
2. a formulation of the divine-human relationship that stresses that divine revelation as well as human faith, prayer, and worship are actions of divine agents, and as such are gifts of divine grace; antonym: Pelagian;
3. a theological system based on reflection on the historical actions of Jesus of Nazareth and the Holy Spirit as recorded in Scripture; antonym: speculative, abstract;
4. a self-consciously comprehensive, unified, and synthetic approach to theology; antonym: christomonistic, Unitarian;
5. a doctrine of God that insists that God is a transcendently and immanently personal, acting, relational, and self-giving Being; antonym: deistic, pantheistic.

In this way, the doctrine of the Trinity is directly linked with many doctrinal loci: theological methodology, hermeneutics, theology proper, soteriology, and ecclesiology. Trinitarian worship is about much more than appending a *Gloria Patri* at the end of a Psalm, singing the *Te Deum*, or not beginning a sermon on Trinity Sunday with an apologetic statement of regret. It is about reconceiving the purpose and meaning of the entire grammar of the liturgical event, reconsidering how we approach God, constitute communities, and imagine God and these communities interacting.

Further, these five themes travel rather well ecumenically (though this short paper can't adequately demonstrate this). Each of the five could be illustrated with phrases from the *Constitution on the Sacred Liturgy* or *Baptism, Eucharist, Ministry*, or (as in this paper) primarily with theological voices from the Reformed-Presbyterian tradition. At least at this level of detail, these five themes appear in Barth, Balthasar, and Rahner; Calvin, Luther, and Wesley; Irenaeus, Augustine, and Gregory of Nyssa (albeit with instructive nuances in each case) — a very healthy sign that we are getting near themes that are fundamental to Christian practice.

This paper also provides a window into the relationship of theology and practice. First, it has established that a Trinitarian theology of liturgy has several concrete corollaries. Any observant cultural anthropologist who might attend a Christian assembly would notice the practices this paper has mentioned. Immanuel Kant was simply wrong when he lampooned the doctrine of the Trinity as entirely impractical. Second, it suggests that the rationale for a given liturgical action makes a big difference in how we practice it. Along the way I have described many traditional practices (traditional eucharistic prayers, epicletic prayers, collects), but suggested explicitly theological motivations or rationale for their adoption — which in turns affects how we practice them. If the Christian year is valuable in part because it at once concretizes and opens up our view of God, then it does little good to eliminate biblical historical narratives from these observances (or, conversely, to focus exclusively on narrative).

The doctrine of the Trinity is not a liturgical constitution that generates a host of minor liturgical ordinances and statutes. It does not produce neat formulas and tidy liturgical recipes that are universally applicable. This paper has called for liturgy that rehearses the divine economy, but it does not say that regular adherence to the Christian year is the *only* way to accomplish it. This paper has described the logic that undergirds the collect form for Christian prayer, but it in no way justifies the *exclusive* use of the collect. Typically, particular doctrines invite a range of practices with which they cohere. This is why the doctrine is just as important — perhaps even more important — for a free, evangelical church without a significant

liturgical tradition, as it is for an Eastern Orthodox congregation that is not likely to abandon Trinitarian worship any time in the next several centuries.

Another way to say it is that the doctrine of the Trinity is the foundation for several criteria that can be used to evaluate and prescribe liturgical practices in many contexts. These criteria can be phrased as simple questions: Does liturgy speak of God with reference to particular actions in history recorded in Scripture? Does corporate worship in a particular congregation rehearse the whole of the divine economy? Are its liturgical actions carried out as means for a personal relationship and encounter with God? Do these actions acknowledge the example and mediation of Jesus Christ and the inspiration of the Holy Spirit? Does the community itself model the kind of intimate fellowship or *koinonia* that is central both to divine life and the Christian life?

One strength of these criteria is that they are not applicable only in rarified or culturally specific settings. These criteria have as much to say about corporate worship offered in a Central American barrio as in a wealthy, suburban congregation in North America or in a majestic European cathedral. They are as applicable to a worship service offered at a summer camp or in a mission congregation as in a denominational or ecumenical assembly or at a gathering of the North American Academy of Liturgy. While they are certainly formulated in a very culturally specific way, they are the kind of transcultural criteria that are useful for contextual ministry on any continent.

Another virtue of these criteria is that they are *theological* criteria. These criteria emerge not only out of historical study and aesthetic preference but out of reflection on the mystery of the gospel that Christians proclaim. The Christian church is deeply divided into communities that rehearse different histories and embody divergent aesthetic preferences. Any lasting cease-fire in these worship wars is not likely to emerge from a resolution of the so-called culture wars which feed them, or from large-scale conversions of taste, or from carefully buttressed historical arguments about ancient liturgical precedents. Finally, such a cease-fire can only issue from the depth and mystery of the gospel which Christians proclaim. Christian worship is strongest when it is integrally and self-consciously related to the person and work of Jesus Christ and the power of the Holy Spirit. The study of Christian worship is most helpful to Christian communities when it demonstrates how this has happened in the past and how it might happen in the future in more profound ways.

Another virtue of these themes is that they are pastoral. Though recent Trinitarian theology often feature soaring, rhapsodic passages on the beauty of Trinitarian life, and stirring summons to mirror this life in Christian community, such passages typically occur only after wringing indictments of how the doctrine of the Trinity has been disregarded by the vast majority of contemporary Christians. Perhaps Karl Rahner said it best: "despite their orthodox confession of the Trinity, Christians are, in their practical life, almost mere 'monotheists.'"[68] Or consider this stinging indictment by William Placher: "In contemporary American society the dominant images of divinity and success and community are in some respects radically un-Christian. It cannot be taken for granted that Christians generally remember or ever understood the sort of God in whom we believe and the sort of people we are therefore called to be."[69] Even a good deal of popular Christian piety is characterized by an interest in the historical Jesus and in a vague, abstract notion of an invisible creator god. Who knows how many people stay away from church, or avoid participation in Christian worship, because they have no idea how compelling and beautiful a Trinitarian vision of God really is.

Beyond any other virtue these Trinitarian criteria have, the primary value that we find in

the doctrine of the Trinity is the compelling picture it paints of the God Christians worship, the community that renders this worship, and the actions used to do so. Finally, this Trinitarian vision is a summons to worship the triune God of Jesus Christ. It invites artists, hymn writers, musicians, liturgists, and poets to create art works, music, and texts that convey more fully the wonder and mystery of the gospel of Jesus Christ. It invites liturgists and pastors to plan and lead worship that portrays the privilege of Christian corporate worship, and to teach and nurture their congregations regarding what this privilege is all about. It invites worshipers to experience the grace of a self-giving God, and to join with all the faithful of every time and place who forever sing to the glory of God's name: *Te Deum laudamus.*

ENDNOTES

1. The links between the doctrine of the Trinity and the theology and practice of worship have been the subject of a number of recent articles. See Philip Butin, "Constructive Iconoclasm: Trinitarian Concern in Reformed Worship," *Studia Liturgica* 19 (1989): 133-142; Daniel Meeter, "The Trinity and Liturgical Renewal," in *The Trinity: An Essential Faith in Our Time*, ed. Andrew Stirling (Nappanee, Ind.: Evangel Publishing House, 2002), 207-232; Bruce V. Rigdon, "Worship and the Trinity in the Reformed Tradition," in *Theological Dialogue Between Orthodox and Reformed Churches*, ed. Thomas F. Torrance (Edinburgh: Scottish Academic Press, 1985-), 2:211-18; George W. Stroup, "The Worship of the Triune God," *Reformed Liturgy and Music* 17 (1983): 160-65; James B. Torrance, *Worship, Community, and the Triune God of Grace* (Carlisle, Great Britain: Paternoster Press, 1996); Christopher Cocksworth, "The Trinity Today: Opportunities and Challenges for Liturgical Study," *Studia Liturgica* 27 (1997): 61-78; Catherine Mowry LaCugna, "Making the Most of Trinity Sunday," *Worship* 60 (1986): 210-24, and "Trinity and Liturgy," in *The New Dictionary of Sacramental Worship*, ed. Peter E. Fink (Collegeville: Liturgical Press, 1990), 1293-96; H. B. Meyer, "Eine trinitärische Theologie der Liturgie und der Sakramente," *Zeitschrift für Katholische Theologie* 113 (1991): 23-48; Frank C. Senn, "Trinity Sunday, Trinitarian Worship and the Trinity in the Church's Life and Mission," *Lutheran*

Forum 28 (1994): 14-16; Bryan D. Spinks, "Trinitarian Theology and the Eucharistic Prayer," *Studia Liturgica* 26 (1996): 209-24; Geoffrey Wainwright, "Trinitarian Worship," *The New Mercersburg Review* 2 (1986): 3-11, and "Trinitarian Worship," in *Speaking of the Christian God: The Holy Trinity and the Challenge of Feminism*, ed. Alvin F. Kimel, Jr. (Grand Rapids: Eerdmans, 1992); and Jonathan Wilson, "Toward a Trinitarian Rule of Worship," *Crux* 29 (1993): 35-39.

2. *The Triune Identity: God According to the Gospel* (Philadelphia: Fortress Press, 1982), xii. A similar topical approach is followed by John Thompson in *Modern Trinitarian Perspectives* (New York: Oxford University Press, 1994), and by Ted Peters in chapter 2 of *God as Trinity: Relationality and Temporality in Divine Life* (Louisville: Westminster/John Knox Press, 1993). These five themes or kinds of discourse are a useful way of keeping track of how the doctrine of the Trinity functions in a given theologian's work. Many theologians will focus on some but not all of these themes. This paper will, then, give preference to articulating broad themes, rather than identifying the social location and conceptual angularities of particular theologians, and will isolate themes at a "landscape" level of detail that tends to ride above several areas of persistent tension, such us important discussions about inclusive language. I do not intend to suggest that these are unimportant tasks.

3. Several of the themes of this paper are developed further in my chapter "The Opening of Worship/ Trinity," in *A More Profound Alleluia: Worship and Theology in Harmony*, ed. Leanne Van Dyk (Grand Rapids: Eerdmans, 2005).

4. Ronald J. Feenstra and Cornelius Plantinga, Jr., "Introduction," in *Trinity, Incarnation, and Atonement: Philosophical Essays* (Notre Dame: University of Notre Dame Press, 1989), 4. The prominence of this theme in recent Trinitarian theology has been analyzed in Faye E. Schott, "God is Love: The Contemporary Theological Movement of Interpreting the Trinity as God's Relational Being" (Ph.D. diss., Lutheran School of Theology at Chicago, 1990).

5. See, for example, Cynthia Campbell, "*Imago Trinitatis*: An Appraisal of Karl Barth's Doctrine of the 'Imago Dei' in Light of His Doctrine of the Trinity" (Ph.D. diss., Southern Methodist University, 1981), 255-59; Colin Gunton, *The One, the Three, the Many: God, Creation, and the Culture of Modernity* (Cambridge: Cambridge University Press, 1993), 13-166;

Shirley Guthrie, *Always Being Reformed: Faith for a Fragmented World* (Louisville: Westminster/John Knox Press, 1996), 40-42; Jürgen Moltmann, *The Trinity and the Kingdom*, trans. Margeret Kohl (San Fransisco: Harper & Row, 1981), 104, 150, 174; Thomas Torrance, *The Christian Doctrine of God, One Being Three Persons* (Edinburgh: T. & T. Clark, 1996), chapter 7.

6. Thomas R. Thompson, "*Imitatio Trinitatis*: The Trinity as a Social Model in the Theologies of Jürgen Moltmann and Leonardo Boff" (Ph.D. diss., Princeton Theological Seminary, 1996), 26.

7. Henry Jansen, *Relationality and the Concept of God* (Amsterdam-Atlanta: Rodopi, 1995), 15; also 62.

8. Christoph Schwöbel, ed., *Trinitarian Theology Today: Essays on Divine Being and Action* (Edinburgh: T. & T. Clark, 1995), 10.

9. *History and the Triune God: Contributions to Trinitarian Theology*, trans. J. Bowden (New York: Crossroad, 1992), xii.

10. *The Household of God* (New York: Friendship Press, 1953), 140, 145.

11. *The Future of Partnership* (Philadelphia: Westminster Press, 1979), 35. It is important to acknowledge that while concern with relationality proceeds with great enthusiasm and is often simply assumed, work in this vein also features vigorous ongoing debates over the proper grounding and articulation of this relational vision: debates over the propriety of the social Trinitarianism, over the definition of divine personhood, over appropriate exercises of human authority in light of worries about subordinationism, over how specific formulations of Trinity doctrine are translated into ecclesiastical structures, and over correct interpretations of both the Gospel according to John and Gregory of Nyssa. What seems universal, despite these areas of disagreements, is enthusiasm for ensuring that self-giving relationality is built into our fundamental idea of divine and human identity.

12. *Worship: Its Theology and Practice* (New York: Oxford University Press, 1965), 198.

13. *Theology in Reconstruction* (Grand Rapids: Eerdmans, 1965), 250.

14. Colin Gunton, *Theology Through Preaching* (Edinburgh: T.&T. Clark, 2001), 56, and Vincent Brümmer, *The Model of Love: A Study in Philosophical*

Theology (Cambridge: Cambridge University Press, 1993), 223, 178. This formulation of the divine-human relationship is also central in Stephen Pickard, "The Trinitarian Dynamics of Belief," in *Essentials of Christian Community: Essays for Daniel W. Hardy*, ed. David F. Ford and Dennis L. Stamps (Edinburgh: T. & T. Clark, 1996), 67.

15. *Theology Through Preaching*, 60.

16. *Preaching and Congregation* (Richmond: John Knox Press, 1962),8.

17. Von Allmen, *Worship*, 180, 242, 40.

18. Ibid., 21, 35. Von Allmen continues, "the New Testament shows us the historical ministry of Jesus and hence His whole life, as a liturgical process and in fact as *the* liturgy, *the* life of worship, accepted by God" (23).

19. Thomas R. Thompson, "*Imitatio Trinitatis*," 293, and Benjamin Leslie, *Trinitarian Hermeneutics: The Hermeneutical Significance of Karl Barth's Doctrine of the Trinity* (New York: Peter Lang, 1991), 36.

20. James B. Torrance, *Worship, Community, and the Triune God of Grace* (Downer's Grove: Intervarsity, 1996), 18, 7, 43, also 50.

21. Ibid., 72.

22. *Themes and Variations for a Christian Doxology: Some Thoughts on the Theology of Worship* (Grand Rapids: Eerdmans, 1992), 17, see 17-40.

23. "The Epiclesis: Sign of Unity and Renewal," *Studia Liturgica* 6 (1969): 35.

24. *Preaching and Congregation*, 7, 5, 10-11.

25. *The Struggle of Prayer* (San Fransisco: Harper & Row, 1980), 36-37.

26. The mediation of Christ is also acknowledged in the phrase "pleading his eternal sacrifice" in a number of Reformed eucharistic rites, particularly in Scotland. See John M. Barkley, " 'Pleading His Eternal Sacrifice' in the Reformed Liturgy," and Bryan D. Spinks, "The Ascension and the Vicarious Humanity of Christ: The Christology and Soteriology Behind the Church of Scotland's Anamnesis and Epiklesis," in *The Sacrifice of Praise: Studies on the Themes of Thanksgiving and Redemption in the Central Prayers of the Eucharistic and Baptismal Liturgies*, ed. Bryan D. Spinks (Rome: Edizioni Liturgiche, 1981), 185-201.

27. *Worship*, 139; and H. O. Old, *Leading in Prayer: A Workbook for Ministers* (Grand Rapids: Eerdmans, 1995), 182.

28. "Lift Up Your Heads" (Chicago: GIA Publications, 2001).

29. *Faith Seeking Understanding: An Introduction to Christian Theology* (Grand Rapids: Eerdmans, 1991), 63.

30. *The Promise of Trinitarian Theology* (Edinburgh: T. & T. Clark, 1991), 34.

31. *Being and Becoming: The Doctrine of God in Charles Hartshorne and Karl Barth* (Oxford: Oxford University Press, 1978), 129.

32. *The Trinity and the Kingdom*, 148; and John W. de Gruchy, *Liberating Reformed Theology: A South African Contribution to an Ecumenical Debate* (Grand Rapids: Eerdmans, 1991), 75.

33. *Preaching and Congregation*, 36.

34. *Worship* (Philadelphia: The Westminster Press, 1982), 17; also 31-33.

35. *The Bible and Liturgy*, trans. John Vriend (Grand Rapids: Eerdmans, 1991), viii, 6.

36. The following criticism of mysticism is directed specifically against ahistorical forms of mysticism that seek an experience of God apart from historical time, and often posit a God beyond the divine economy. Commenting on mysticism in the interpretation of Paul, Lewis Smedes argues that "oriental mysticism could not tolerate dependence on specific historical events or concrete historical personalities. The one thing people need is to escape the concrete things of history and to be immersed into the divine life. . . . Mysticism and history were incompatible as foundations of religion" (*Union with Christ: A Biblical View of New Life in Christ* [Grand Rapids: Eerdmans, 1983], 28). Donald Bloesch distinguishes ahistorical mysticism from acts of meditation that are "centered on the works and acts of God not only in creation but also and preeminently in Jesus Christ" (*The Struggle of Prayer*, 21).

37. *The Struggle of Prayer*, 21, 27. This is not to say that contemplative prayer has no place in Christian worship, but that contemplation is focused on historical events. Thus, Moltmann argues that "Christian meditation and contemplation are . . . at their very heart *meditatio crucis*," i.e., meditations on an historical event (*The Trinity and the Kingdom*, 8).

38. *Here Am I: A Believer's Reflections on God* (Grand Rapids: Eerdmans, 1982), 124; also 171.

39. "Remarks on the Postcommunio in Some Reformed Liturgies," in *The Sacrifice of Praise: Studies on the Themes of Thanksgiving and Redemption in the Central Prayers of the Eucharistic and Baptismal Liturgies*, ed. Bryan D. Spinks (Rome: Edizioni Liturgiche, 1981), 154.

40. *Narratives of a Vulnerable God: Christ, Theology, and Scripture* (Louisville: Westminster John Knox Press, 1994), 137, 139, 142.

41. See, for example, the prayer in Acts 4, and David Buttrick, "The Praise of Ordinary People," *Liturgy* 4 (1985): 22-23.

42. *For All God's Worth* (Grand Rapids: Eerdmans, 1997), 24.

43. *The Lord's Supper*, trans. W. Fletcher Fleet (Richmond: John Knox Press, 1969), 23.

44. *The God Who Commands* (Notre Dame: University of Notre Dame Press, 1991), 150.

45. "The Doctrine of the Trinity and the Unity of the Church," *Theology Today* 3 (1946): 372, 374, 376.

46. Ibid., 372, 383. In fact, Niebuhr argues that regardless of any other merits, the doctrine of the Trinity is valuable if only as a heuristic device for maintaining a balanced theological vision: "Apart from any other considerations which may lead the church to the formulation of a Trinitarian doctrine, it must endeavor to do so because it must set forth the faith which is not the realized conviction of any of its parts but rather the common faith" (383).

47. *Calvinist Trinitarianism and Theocentric Politics*, trans. John Bolt (Lewiston: Edwin Mellen Press, 1989), 107.

48. Ibid., 1, 11, 6, 60.

49. See especially the essay, "Structural Differences Between Christological and Pneumatological Perspectives" in *Calvinist Trinitarianism*, 27-46.

50. *Calvinist Trinitarianism*, 1-2, 11, 14, 16.

51. *Faith Seeking Understanding*, 74.

52. *God, Creation, & Revelation: A Neo-Evangelical Theology* (Grand Rapids: Eerdmans, 1991), 410.

53. *The Work of the Holy Spirit*, trans. Henry De Vries (Grand Rapids: Eerdmans, 1941), 37.

54. *Calvinist Trinitarianism*, 1-3, 19.

55. *Calvinist Trinitarianism*, 32, 181; also 82.

56. *Foundations of Dogmatics*, trans. Darrell L. Guder (Grand Rapids: Eerdmans, 1981), 1:393.

57. *A Brief Theology of Revelation* (Edinburgh: T. & T. Clark, 1995), , 80.

58. "The Trinity and Human Life," *Theology* 78 (1975): 183.

59. *Faith Seeking Understanding*, 72.

60. Jewett, *God, Creation & Revelation*, 412; Hendrikus Berkhof, *Christian Faith: An Introduction to the Study of the Faith*, trans. Sierd Woudstra (Grand Rapids: Eerdmans, 1979), 141.

61. *The Power of God* (Philadelphia: Westminster Press, 1983), 77.

62. *The Power of God*, 66, 68.

63. *Leading in Prayer*, 362.

64. *The Promise of Trinitarian Theology*, 5.

65. Nicholas Wolterstorff, *Art in Action* (Grand Rapids: Eerdmans, 1980), 3, 184-85, 116. Wolterstorff develops this theory more comprehensively in his *Works and Worlds of Art* (Oxford: Clarendon Press, 1980).

66. *Christian Faith*, 377.

67. "Lift Up Your Heads" (Chicago: GIA Publications, 2001).

68. *The Trinity*, trans. J. Donceel (New York: Herder and Herder, 1970), 10.

69. *Narratives of a Vulnerable God*, 140.

John D. Witvliet is Director of the Calvin Institute of Christian Worship and serves as Associate Professor of Worship, Theology, and Music at Calvin College and Calvin Theological Seminary. He is the author of Worship Seeking Understanding *(Baker Academic, 2003) and co-editor of* Worship in Medieval and Early Modern Europe *(University of Notre Dame Press, 2004). He also serves as the editor of book series for both Eerdmans and the Alban Institute.*

Two Views of Ritual and Inculturation

Singing with the Faithful of Every Time and Place:
Thoughts on Liturgical Inculturation and Cross-Cultural Liturgy

C. MICHAEL HAWN

Jesus shall reign where'er the sun
Does his successive journeys run;
His kingdom stretch from shore to shore,
Till moons shall wax and wane no more.

Isaac Watts, *Psalms of David Imitated*, 1719
(Stanza 1)

THE UNITED METHODIST BISHOP JOEL MARTÍNEZ noted at a conference in 1996 that "each generation must add its stanza to the great hymn of the church." I have found this a viable metaphor for understanding the range of congregational song available to us today. If we think of all Christian congregational song as comprising a grand hymn of the church throughout the ages, two thoughts come to mind immediately: (1) when singing a hymn, one does not begin on the final stanza but usually sings all of the stanzas, and furthermore, one does not usually stop on stanza three of a four- or five-stanza hymn; (2) the second point that this metaphor raises is a question: What does the stanza being shaped by Christians in this generation look and sound like? Looking at worship in general and congregational singing specifically through the lens of culture may open up some insight into this question.

The Dialogue between Cult and Culture

Culture has always been integral to cult. Since the Second Vatican Counsel (1962-65), this relationship has come to the forefront of liturgical discussions. Many of these discussions reflect the worship concerns of minority cultures within a dominant cultural environment. Ethnic minorities increasingly are seeking ways to embody in worship their language, customs and patterns of being-in-community. Africa,

in particular, has been a fertile trial region for contextual liturgies. Even before Vatican II, the Belgian missionary Guido Haazen notated the Congolese *Missa Luba* in 1956, sung in Latin from oral practice. Father Stephen Mbunga, whose doctoral thesis in 1963 supported in strong terms the development of African expressions of music,[1] composed *Missa Baba Yetu* (Mass of Our Father) in 1959 based on traditional music of the Lake Malawi region. These works, countless discussions among Africans, and the encouragement of forward-thinking missionaries paved the way for the recognition by Pope John Paul II of the "Zaïrian Rite" of the Mass in 1988. Many composers of African Christian music since the Second Vatican Council have been encouraged to continue their efforts toward musical inculturation.

In the United States discussions concerning the relationship between cult and culture have increased in frequency and intensity. The ten-year report of *The Milwaukee Symposium for Church Composers* (1992) includes a section on "Cross-Cultural Music Making."[2] According to Edward Foley, the primary drafter of the Milwaukee report, *The Snowbird Statement on Catholic Liturgical Music* (1995) represents in part a reaction to, and perhaps a retrenchment from, many of the ideas presented in it. Under the auspices of the Lutheran World Federation, *The Nairobi Statement on Worship and Culture* (1996) reflects a much broader ethnic consultation combining the efforts of many representatives, who include the liturgical theologian Gordon Lathrop from the United States, and the Benedictine liturgical scholar Anscar Chupungco from the Philippines.[3] One of the most systematic discussions of the relationship between worship and culture thus far, this document specifies four areas of interaction:

• Worship is *transcultural*. "The resurrected Christ whom we worship, and through whom by the power of the Holy Spirit we know the grace of the Triune God, transcends and indeed is beyond all cultures" (2.1). Transcultural elements extend to various aspects of worship as well as to the ordo or core liturgical structure of liturgy.

• Worship is *contextual*. "Jesus whom we worship was born into a specific culture of the world" (3.1). Borrowing from Chupungco's theories of liturgical inculturation, the contextual aspects of worship are derived from the principle of dynamic equivalence and creative assimilation. Dynamic equivalence involves "re-expressing components of Christian worship with something from a local culture that has an equal meaning, value, and function. Dynamic equivalence goes far beyond mere translation; it involves understanding the fundamental meanings both of elements of worship and of the local culture, and enabling the meanings and actions of worship to be 'encoded' and re-expressed in the language of local culture" (3.2). Creative assimilation requires "adding pertinent components of local culture to the liturgical ordo in order to enrich its original core" (3.4).

• Worship is also *counter-cultural*. Based on Romans 12:2, the Nairobi Statement suggests that "Jesus Christ came to transform all people and all cultures, and calls us not to conform to the world, but to be transformed with it" (4.1). Furthermore, a counter-cultural perspective "also involves the transformation of cultural patterns which idolize the self or the local group at the expense of a wider humanity, or which give central place to the acquisition of wealth at the expense of the care of the earth and its poor" (4.2).

• Finally, worship is *cross-cultural*. "Jesus came to be the Savior of all people. He welcomes the treasures of earthly cultures into the city of God" (5.1). The document states that "care should be taken that the music, art, architecture, gestures and postures, and other elements of different cultures are understood and respected when they are used by churches elsewhere in the world" (5.2).

These four criteria together provide insight into how liturgy and culture may be effectively woven together in the worship experience. While all are important and essential in any analysis, I will focus on contextual and cross-cultural aspects of congregational singing. What and how we sing in worship is a significant aspect of liturgical inculturation.

Aylward Shorter defines inculturation as "the on-going dialogue between faith and culture or cultures. More fully, it is the creative and dynamic relationship between the Christian message and a culture or cultures."[4] Anscar Chupungco enlarges on this definition: Inculturation is a "process of reciprocal assimilation between Christianity and culture and the resulting interior transformation of culture on the one hand and the rooting of Christianity in culture on the other.... [This] process of interaction and mutual assimilation brings progress to both [worship and culture]; it does not cause mutual extinction."[5] Using these definitions as a guide, I propose to look at inculturation through selected congregational songs.

Case Studies in Culture and Hymnody

Drawing on the Nairobi Statement, we can say that congregational singing is a *transcultural* activity in worship. Virtually all Christian traditions have and do participate in some form of congregational singing.[6] Hymns are also *contextual* artifacts. Analyzers of Western hymnody usually include literary, theological, and historical perspectives, but are less likely to look at hymns through a cultural lens. It may be that cultural knowledge is assumed. However, when songs beyond the Euro-North American context are sung, the cultural aspects of the experience come to the fore.

In an attempt to explore the benefits of a cultural analysis of hymns and hymn singing, we will examine more closely three well-known congregational songs that represent stanzas of what Bishop Martínez called "the great hymn of the church." Isaac Watts's "Jesus Shall Reign" serves as an object of contextual analysis. Prudentius's "Corde natus ex Parentis" illustrates a cross-cultural dimension of hymnody from a historical perspective. The South African freedom song "Siyahamba" is an example of a song, forged recently in a specific cultural and political context, that has spread around the world, and is used extensively across cultures. As the choice and popularity of "Siyahamba" indicates, many of the songs that make up the "stanza" of our generation come from the Southern hemisphere. Noting this reality, I will suggest an approach for understanding and incorporating in our worship the different structures that come to us through the use of songs from beyond the Euro-North American context.

"Jesus Shall Reign"— a contextual case study. As one of the best known hymns in the English language, "Jesus Shall Reign" (1719) has served as an expression of missionary vision for virtually all Protestant denominations for at least two hundred years. By the nineteenth century Watts's free paraphrase of selected verses from Psalm 72 had come to epitomize the emerging expansion of the missionary movement.[7] His words have shaped the thought and theology by which the Western church defined its understanding of missions during the period of its most dramatic growth.[8] The identity of Christian missions was nurtured in the milieu of European political monarchies, and developed during a time when Christians assumed not only a relationship between the kingdom of Christ and major European kingdoms, but also the divine right of kings. "Jesus Shall Reign" gives voice to an emerging movement devoted to spreading the Good News of salvation "throughout the world which was ignorant of this knowledge of God in Jesus Christ."[9]

This, and many of Watts's other hymns and psalm paraphrases, deserves to be sung in churches everywhere. Like all of our congregational song, "Jesus Shall Reign" reflects its culture, and may be seen as an artifact of liturgical inculturation. Watts understood the context of those who would sing his psalm-paraphrases and hymns; part of the process of hymnic inculturation was to compose texts in a manner that allowed them to be understood by the singers of his time, "working-class worshipers of England's Nonconformist congregations."[10] Furthermore, he adapted to the practice of lining out metrical psalms by following the principle of one line, one thought, so that precentors expressed a complete thought when speaking a line before the congregation was to sing it. This avoided the dreadful practice of singing only a partial idea and having to wait for the next phrase from the precentor to complete the thought.[11]

While I value this psalm paraphrase as representative of one stanza in the unfolding hymn of the church throughout the ages, our present context forces us to examine Watts's understanding of "kingdom" in light of increasingly cross-cultural societies. The image of kingdom in Watts's day was one of a consummate hierarchy in which the rulers of the nations represented, to varying degrees, the authority of God. Such an image crumbles under the weight of the current international reality. This old-world view of "kingdom" inherited from the eighteenth century provides at best an ambiguous model for Christ's realm on earth. In a world where the influence of multi-national corporations often supersedes that of national governmental structures, the concept of kingdom may come across as both archaic and irrelevant unless it is grounded theologically in an understanding of the eschatological realm of God.

As we shall see "Jesus Shall Reign" shows Watts as a patriot of the monarchy. Yet he and Dissenters in England were often in tension with this monarchy. The Schism Act of 1714 forbade independent congregations like Watts's to run schools, and foreshadowed the possibility of further persecution for those outside the Church of England. Queen Anne died providentially on the day the Act was to take force, and it was repealed by 1719, the year that Watts's *Psalms of David Imitated* was published.[12] Perhaps Watt's paraphrase of Psalm 90, "Man Frail and God Eternal" (better known as "Our God, Our Help in Ages Past"), written following the enactment of the Schism Act, reflects a tempering of his patriotic pride. In stanzas four and eight of the original text Watts notes the ephemeral nature of all nations:

> Thy word commands our flesh to dust,
> Return, ye sons of men:
> All nations rose from earth at first,
> And turn to earth again.

> Like flow'ry fields the nations stand
> Pleas'd with the morning light;
> The flowers beneath the Mower's hand
> Lie withering e'er 'tis night.[13]

Watts's habit of Christianizing the psalter, a hallmark of his psalm paraphrases,[14] was a major change from earlier metrical versions that attempted to stay as close as possible to the Hebrew. So, rather than follow the lead of Sternhold and Hopkins's *Whole Booke of Psalmes* in the mid-sixteenth century, or Tate and Brady's *New Version*, first published at the end of the seventeenth century, Watts set out on a new course, "[taking] the Hebrew and recast[ing] it, as if the psalmist were writing in the Christian era."[15] One result was "Jesus shall reign," the astonishing incipit for Psalm 72.[16] As Watts states in his "Preface; or An Inquiry into the right way of Fitting the Book of Psalms for Christian Worship," Christians sing the psalms from a

different perspective from the Hebrews, for we express nothing but the character, the concerns, and the religion of the Jewish king; while our own circumstances, and our own religion (which are so widely different from his) have little to do in the sacred song; and our affections want something of property or interest in the words, to awaken them at first, and to keep them lively.[17]

As Robin Leaver has noted, "In the older metrical versions there was a concern for a re-representation of the psalm, but in Watts the concern was for re-interpretation."[18] Re-interpretation of the psalter for worship is liturgical inculturation through congregational song. While Watts's approach to the psalter demonstrates a particular Christocentric inclination, there is both internal textual and external social evidence that the hymn "Jesus Shall Reign," though reflecting its culture well, suffers from an ethnocentric propensity by today's standards. One of the dangers of liturgical inculturation is that the regional appeal of a hymn may limit its universal application. As Watts Christianized the psalter to fit his own religion, he also particularized the psalter to fit his own region of the world. Hymnal editors have usually excised stanzas two and three of Watts's original hymn partly for their regional disposition:

> Behold the islands with their Kings,
> And *Europe* her best tribute brings;
> From *North* to *South* the princes meet
> To pay their homage at his feet.

> There *Persia* glorious to behold,
> There *India* shines in *Eastern* gold;
> And barbarous nations at his word
> Submit and bow and own their Lord.[19]

Psalm 72 specifically mentions Tarshish, Arabia, and Saba; Watts substituted locations where England was developing mission activity along with colonial and economic interests. The "barbarous nations" in the second stanza quoted above actually appear in a revised form in a twentieth-century American hymnal as "savage tribes."[20]

This substitution of contemporary locations for biblical or mythological ones represented a codified literary device of the time known as "imitation." Following the example of great eighteenth-century poets such as John Milton, Alexander Pope, and John Dryden, Watts was not only a master of this device, but also was in the vanguard of its use.[21] While freeing psalm-singing from a strict metrical approach that was often poetically stilted, he offered Dissenting congregations freer adaptations or paraphrases of the psalms. Indeed, the complete title of his primary psalm collection, *The Psalms of David Imitated in the Language of the New Testament, and Apply'd to the Christian State and Worship*, is a direct reference to the device of imitation.[22] Many followed Watts's lead by "imitating" the psalms in their own cultural context. The effective use of imitation depended on a thorough knowledge of the original psalm, usually in the 1611 translation commonly known as the King James Version.

Although Watts could identify with the "stranger in distress, the widow and the fatherless," as he did in his paraphrase of Psalm 146, "I'll Praise my Maker While I've Breath,"[23] issues of justice receive short shrift in "Jesus Shall Reign." Psalm 72 states that "He shall keep the simple folk by their right, defend the children of the poor, and punish the wrong doer. . . . For he shall deliver the poor when he crieth; the needy also, and him that hath no helper. He shall be favorable to the simple and needy, and shall preserve the souls of the poor" (verses 4, 12-13). The mandate of this prophetic passage is considerably obscured in Watts's paraphrase found in the original stanza six:

> Blessings abound where'er he reigns,
> The prisoner leaps to lose his chains,
> The weary find eternal rest,
> And all the sons of want are blest.

Watts freely adapted the psalms and omitted those ideas that he thought unworthy of a New Testament ethic.[24]

How can we know what the hymn meant in its time? Evidence comes from the colonial caste system in eighteenth-century India under British rule. The East India Company was chartered by Queen Elizabeth I in 1600, and by 1689 the directors of the Company resolved to "make us a nation in India."[25] By 1711, just a few years before the writing of Watts's hymn, Alexander Dalrymple noted that the "great endeavour of all commercial states, is to draw the production of other countries to its own center."[26] Because Western music of this era was philosophically based on certain "universal" laws that were as constant as "the circulation of the blood and the law of gravity,"[27] music not corresponding to these natural laws was by implication inferior. Music was one of the cultural props that allowed eighteenth-century British expatriates to maintain their role at the assumed pinnacle of society, separate from the local population. The arts "mask[ed] the image of *realpolitik* by erasing all evidence of that which had been subdued and of how the defeat was accomplished by trade and labor exploitation, racial separation, bureaucratization, and the brutality of military enforcement."[28]

In his discussion of the great missionary expansion of the eighteenth and nineteenth centuries, Jaroslav Pelikan refers to "Jesus Shall Reign" as a symbol of Christian growth. He notes that "the sun never sets on the empire of Jesus the King, the Man Who Belongs to the World."[29] God's purpose and Great Britain's ecclesiastical, political, and economic destiny seem to merge in "Jesus Shall Reign." Was the Dissenting British parishioner singing subconsciously:

> [Britain] shall reign where'er the sun
> Does [her] successive journeys run;
> [Her] kingdom stretch from shore to
>   shore,
> Till moons shall wax and wane no more.

Given that Watts was known to substitute "Britain" for "Israel" in some of the psalms, probably not.[30]

"Corde natus ex parentis"—a cross-cultural case study. The text of "Jesus Shall Reign" clearly reflects the culture of its time not only in its Christian updating of the psalter, but in the rhyming of its poetic couplets and its long meter structure. "Of the Father's Love Begotten" demonstrates a historical cross-cultural excursion of nearly sixteen centuries.

This Latin hymn is the work of the Spanish poet Marcus Aurelius Clemens Prudentius in the early fifth century of the Christian era. Prudentius was educated in law before turning to an ascetic spiritual life at age fifty-seven.[31] His devotional poetry was widely read, and was influential during the Middle Ages. Many hymns were derived from his long Latin poems, as was the case with "Corde natus ex parentis." Needless to say, early fifth century Spanish piety is far removed from a twenty-first century Christian. Prudentius' poetic reflections on the nature of Christ within the Trinity, however, growing out of the theological controversies of the fourth century, provide a transcultural content—that is, content that has relevance across cultures in time and in space—for the broader Christian community.

In 1851 John Mason Neale, a guiding light of the Oxford movement in worship, architecture, and hymnody, translated and versified the Latin text as "Of the Father's Love Begotten." Translation always modifies the original, especially in hymnody, where stringent rules of meter and rhyme must be observed. Even the opening line of the English translation departs significantly from the Latin, which is literally "born of the parent's heart." Neale's English text was revised by Henry Williams Baker for inclusion in the first edition of the monumental *Hymns Ancient and Modern* in 1861. A doxological stanza was added at a later date.

To the poem of a fifth-century Spanish

poet, and a tune found in medieval Italian and German trope collections (*Divinum mysterium*), the English translation added the imprint of mid-nineteenth-century Great Britain during a time when the Anglican Church was attempting to reclaim the glory of the medieval church. England also left other cultural marks on this text when the previously monophonic, unaccompanied melody was harmonized and accompanied on the organ, and when it was sung not by choirs at monastic gatherings but by congregations. The hymn comes to many of us in our hymnals more or less in the manner conceived by Neale and Baker in mid-nineteenth century England.

The story is not over, however. Federico Pagura, a bishop in the Argentine Methodist Church and a fine poet in his own right, translated the original Latin poem into Spanish, a language descended from Prudentius' proto-Catalonian native tongue. Though the Spanish of Pagura's Argentina is vastly removed in syntax, time, and space from Prudentius' Latin, the Spanish translation, "Fruto del amor divino" (1962), offers Spanish-speaking Christians a way to sing this great classic hymn in their own language. Furthermore, it is a way for contemporary descendants of folks from the Iberian peninsula to claim through song a sense of unity with a church dating back to the fifth century.[32] The incipit of the Spanish translation, literally "fruit of the divine love," once again departs from the original Latin. "Fruto del amor divino" appears in *Mil Voces Para Celebrar* (1996), the United Methodist Spanish-language hymnal, with an organ accompaniment from *Hymnal 1940*, an earlier hymnal of the Episcopal Church in the United States. With Pagura's translation and the new harmonization, this classic hymn is given a thoroughly American (South and North) treatment.

The spirit of Prudentius' original poem pervades the versions we sing today, although regrettably many current hymnals have omitted some of the most important stanzas.

After several translations and adaptations, however, this is not the original poem. Neither is the musical experience of singing this hymn today similar to that of the monastic world of Prudentius' day. The versions of "Corde natus ex parentis" offer a cross-cultural mosaic of fifth-century Spain, medieval Italy and Germany, nineteenth-century England, twentieth-century Argentina, and the United States. While this is a more complex example than some, whenever we sing Martin Luther's "A Mighty Fortress," Isaac Watts's "Our God, Our Help in Ages Past," Charles Wesley's "Hark, the Herald Angels Sing," Fanny Crosby's "Blessed Assurance," the anonymous American folk hymn "Wondrous Love," or Charles Tindley's "Stand by Me," we are entering into a cross-cultural experience that has countless permutations depending on translations, textual modifications, and musical arrangement.

"Siyahamba"—an African case study.[33] This well-known Zulu song has been incorporated into several recent hymnals and is widely sung in North America.[34] Rather than being composed for congregations, it emerged out of struggles in the streets and townships of South Africa, being conceived orally and only later written down. The South African ethnomusicologist David Dargie notes that "Siyahamba" originated as a freedom song with Amadodana, a Methodist young men's group, within the cultural context of apartheid political oppression.

Though the words are few, they are as pregnant with meaning as an African proverb—especially to those who live in the culture. Usually translated as "We are marching in the light of God," the simple text contains layers of meaning. "We" is a word of community, the community of those living, as well as the community of the living dead, the ancestors. "Marching" is an action that unifies the members of the community as they move physically and spiritually in the same direction. It is a physical, kinesthetic response

to the Spirit, not a passive acquiescence. "The light of God" has meaning on several levels. While light is a symbol of creation and of Jesus Christ, who is "the light of the world," it is also a common subject of songs of healing, or *ngoma*, throughout Southern and Central Africa. The refrain, "Let darkness be replaced with light," is coded language for "seeing clearly."[35] God is the source of clear sight in the midst of the struggle; that is, God is the source of discernment and truth. As we march we can see our way ahead— even though armed police may be in our way. Our path is clear. Where there is light, there is hope.

"Siyahamba" and many of the South African freedom songs available in current hymnals were forged in the fires of the anti-apartheid struggle. Out of defining events like the Sharpeville Massacre in 1960 a song emerged that when sung in the streets could convey hope in the face of oppression, maintain dignity in the face of violence, and unite people in the face of turmoil. When this message is sung, the words are embodied in the lives of the community that sings and dances it. The song's cyclic musical structure immediately draws in everyone present. As "Siyahamba" was conceived orally, and is performed without written music, its portability allows the song to be taken to places of darkness where its message can expose evil in its myriad forms, and offer the singers hope. It allows the performers/participants to add to the basic song a message that draws into it the existential reality of the situation. "We" grow in number as we "march," for there are those who join us literally on the way. The song accommodates and even facilitates a growing, evolving community of believers. "We are marching," knowing we are never alone in our struggle. The living dead are always singing with us. When this song is taken into the liturgy as a processional it brings with it the struggle of the streets, and it sanctifies this struggle in the liturgy. Singing "Siyahamba" says that liturgy is not hermetically sealed from daily life, but is a place to mend the wounds of oppression, and to receive a blessing to return to the streets in hope for freedom.

Three cross-cultural messages. As North American congregations sing these songs in worship in the twenty-first century, they receive not only their textual and musical content, but also aspects of their culture. "Jesus Shall Reign" is an icon of the English monarchy at the height of its missionary zeal and colonial expansion. Though hymnal editors have excised the stanzas that manifest its most parochial aspects, vestiges of eighteenth-century colonialism remain. Yet "Jesus Shall Reign" reflects for us, as much as for eighteenth-century Christians, a vision of a world where Christ is sung—in the words of "From All That Dwell Below the Skies," Watts's paraphrase of Psalm 117, "through every land, by every tongue." It is a cross-cultural expression whose "kingdom" images present a challenge to Christians living in a democratic, non-monarchial political system such as the United States. Yet its cross-cultural message is still relevant.

"Of the Father's Love Begotten" is a much more complex example which draws from several cultures through seventeen centuries. It is a historical cross-cultural masterpiece that caries with it vestiges of early Christian theology, medieval plainsong, the Oxford movement of the nineteenth century, with twentieth-century permutations. The essential Trinitarian theology that emerged from the councils of the early church is still relevant to Christians today.

"Siyahamba" differs from the other two in that it is a song growing out of a relatively recent struggle—against apartheid in South Africa, one of the most insidious forms of sustained institutionalized political oppression perpetrated by a dominant government on its people. Though the experience of oppressed South Africans may seem far removed from our lives, those who join in solidarity with them by singing "Siyahamba" sing of resistance to

all forms of oppression. Furthermore, singing "Siyahamba" may give voice to those who have experienced oppression within the United States and to others who wish to stand in solidarity with them.

As a concurrent cross-cultural experience, "Siyahamba" may offer particular challenges to congregations in the United States, challenges that may not be present in Western historical cross-cultural artifacts. "Siyahamba" originates in an oral culture and uses a cyclic musical form that differs from the stanzas of Western poetry. It is to this particular cross-cultural challenge that I wish to turn.

Sequential versus Cyclic Song Structures

Sequential songs. These maintain a train of thought over several stanzas, and develop an idea, bringing it to a climax or logical conclusion.[36] This may be achieved in several ways. A hymn on the Trinity may devote each of its first three stanzas to an aspect of the concept, and conclude with a doxological stanza of praise that lifts up all three facets in unity. "Come, Thou Almighty King" is a classic example. A more recent Trinitarian hymn is Jeffrey Rowthorn's "Creating God, Your Fingers Trace," which refers to the work of the members of the Trinity as "Creating God," "Sustaining God," "Redeeming God," "Indwelling God," omitting the classic formula, Father, Son, and Holy Spirit.

Or a hymn may follow the progress of a passage of Scripture. See the familiar setting of Psalm 23 from the *Scottish Psalter,* "The Lord's My Shepherd," or, for a New Testament example, "While Shepherds Watched Their Flocks by Night," based on Luke 2. Both of these follow the narrative as presented in the King James Version. A more recent example is Timothy Dudley-Smith's paraphrase of the *Magnificat* in Luke 1, "Tell Out My Soul," derived from the translation found in the *New Jerusalem Bible.*

A sequential hymn may tell a story. Hymns have always told part or all of the life of Christ as musical ballads. The medieval hymn, "O Love, How Deep, How Broad, How High," is a fine example. "O Sons and Daughters" takes the singer through the passion, resurrection, and post-resurrection events of Christ's life. The stanzas of the African American spiritual, "Were You There," focus on the progression of events during Christ's passion. Sydney Carter's "Lord of the Dance" is a more recent example of a hymn that tells the story of Christ's life in a ballad form around the metaphor of dance.

Some hymns describe an attribute of God, or praise God, but conclude with a final stanza of petition. Petitions often employ subjunctiv or imperative verbs — for example, note the petitions (italicized) in the final stanza of Charles Wesley's famous hymn, "Love Divine Loves Excelling":

> *Finish* then thy new creation;
> Pure and spotless *let us be.*
> *Let us find* thy great salvation
> Perfectly restored in thee.

A more recent example is the Japane hymn "Here, O Lord, Your Servants Gathe by Tokuo Yamaguchi, with a translation b Everett Stowe. The first three stanzas elab the theme of John 14:6, "I am the way, the and the life," while the final stanza is a seri of petitions with the imperative verbs "grant," "help," and "send." These petitions to God serve as a climactic conclusion to a sequential hymn.

Other hymns elaborate on a specific teaching of Christ, and then bring the idea home by applying it to the lives of persons today (a hermeneutic approach). The African American spiritual "When Israel Was in Egypt's Land (Go Down Moses)" concludes in some hymnals with a hermeneutical stanza:

> O let us all from bondage flee, (Let my
>   people go.)
> And let us all in Christ be free, (Let my
>   people go.)

The classic Christmas hymn "Once in Royal David's City," written for children by Cecil Frances Alexander, a children's educator and the wife of an Anglican minister, has a strong hermeneutical sense:

> Jesus is our childhood's pattern,
> Day by day like us he grew;
> He was little, weak and helpless,
> Tears and smiles like us he knew;
> And he feels for all our sadness,
> And he shares in all our gladness.

> Jesus, our only joy be thou,
> As thou our prize will be;
> Jesus, be thou our glory now,
> And through eternity.

Hymns about communion often do this, referring in the final stanza to the celestial banquet in which all Christians will share, with Christ at the head of the table. Cesareo Gabaraín's communion hymn "Sheaves of Summer" ("Una Espiga") captures this spirit beautifully in its final stanza:

> En la mesa de Dios de sentarán.
> (At God's table we will sit.)

Como hijos su pan compartirán.
(As God's children we will share his bread.)

Finally, the concluding stanzas of some hymns may call us to a commitment to Christ in response to what Christ has done for us. Isaac Watts's "When I Survey the Wondrous Cross" is a classic example:

Were the whole realm of nature mine,
That were a present far too small;
Love so amazing, so divine,
Demands my soul, my life, my all.

John Bell's recent hymn, "The Summons," asks the question, "Will you come and follow me?" in the first four stanzas. The final stanza responds to Christ's summons:

Lord, your summons echoes true when you but call my name.
Let me turn and follow you and never be the same.

Classic sequential hymns use endless variations. The list above is only illustrative.

Cyclic songs. These also have many possibilities for worship. They are usually more textually and musically compact. Unlike the literary approach of sequential structures, cyclic forms may be sung with little or no reference to printed text or music once the song has become familiar to the assembly. Their brevity, and the oral or aural means of transmission, allow worshipers to move their bodies without being encumbered by books, and to observe other ritual actions as they sing. Congregations may sing, for example, while the offering is being taken, while communion is being shared, as families and sponsors come forward for baptism, or as the people welcome a newly baptized person. I have noticed that the level of congregational participation is much greater when people participate in liturgical actions unencumbered with hymnals.

A common ritual action is bringing forward the congregation's offering, accompanied by a short, familiar song. In some traditions, the Bible, a symbol of the Word made flesh among us, is held high and carried in procession to the middle of the people before the reading of the Gospel. These are times when a brief cyclic song can gather the community around this important event to watch or participate as singers in the procession.

One common misunderstanding about cyclic structures is that they are repetitive. While this may appear to be the case, I have observed that creative leaders of cyclic songs vary nearly every cycle in some modest way. Those who use cyclic structures effectively approach them more as theme and variation. They may change the instrumentation slightly, or sing some cycles unaccompanied. They may vary the text slightly, changing only a word or two. For example, "Father, I Adore You" uses this approach, with successive cycles naming the remaining persons of the Trinity. Varying the dynamic level from cycle to cycle is another way to add variety. Cantors may improvise separate parts over the congregation's ongoing cycle.

Many Taizé chants use this technique. The cantor's part for the familiar Taizé song "Bless the Lord, My Soul" is based on verses from Psalm 103. This part adds variations to the basic cycle sung by the people. African songs in particular, though not all of them, use an additive approach to each cycle. A soloist may begin, followed by the choir, and finally all of the people. Through successive cycles the enlivener signals slight changes in the text, or sings with increasing energy a separate part above the congregation's cycle.

Percussion instruments may be added little by little. Movement may begin minimally, and increase in intensity as the musical experience "heats up." Variations may be planned to some degree, but groups that work together over time learn to vary cycles spontaneously. This applies to congregations as well as instrumental groups, whether a West African drum ensemble, a Taizé group, or a praise team preparing contemporary Christian music. Cultural groups whose traditional music is cyclic seem to understand instinctively how these forms work. Others can learn to lead cyclic songs effectively, however, by becoming sensitive to the possibilities of the form.

Refrain forms. The third musical structure combines aspects of both sequential and cyclic structures. The refrain reinforces the overall theme of a hymn. Recent hymns using refrains, many coming from Roman Catholic renewal music, have become popular. "I, the Lord of Sea and Sky" uses this form effectively: the stanzas speak from the perspective of God, and the refrain offers an opportunity for the people to respond, "Here I am, Lord," borrowing from Isaiah 6:8. A soloist or choir can sing the stanzas, while the congregation responds on the refrain. "Lord, You Have Come to the Lakeshore" ("Tu has venido") is similar. The refrain, beginning with "O Lord, with your eyes you have searched me," establishes a strong first-person perspective, drawing the singer into the story as participant.

Refrains may be helpful when teaching a congregation new hymns. Beginning with the refrain when introducing the hymn, and using choir or soloists on the stanzas, allows the congregation to participate quickly while learning parts of the song by listening. Brian Wren's "Woman in the Night" is an example of a hymn that can be taught effectively by this method. Each of the stanzas reflects the perspective of a different female biblical character, and having various women sing the stanzas solo not only personalizes the story but also creates contrast when the people all enter on the refrain, "Come and join the song, women, children, men."

Closely related to refrains are call-response forms. African American spirituals often use this approach. Not only does a call-response add variety to the musical presentation, it is a more authentic way of singing spirituals, as this pattern was used by African American during slavery. Here are some examples:

> "They Crucified My Lord"
> Call (Solo): They crucified my Lord;
> Response (All): And he never said a
>   mumbalin' word.

> "When Israel Was in Egypt's Land"
> Call (Solo): When Israel was in Egypt's
>   land;
> Response (All): Let my people go.
> Call (Solo): Oppressed so hard they could
>   not stand;
> Response (All): Let my people go.

In many hymnals the call-response patterns may not be indicated. The leader will need to decide how to achieve this effect after examining the song.

Choosing songs according to structure. Knowledge of underlying structures not only adds variety to the presentation of the music in worship but also may bring out the meaning of the text for the singers. Structural knowledge of congregational songs can also be helpful when placing songs within the liturgy. Three general principles emerge:

1. Sequential structures communicate theological content in an ample and carefully worded manner. Because of their literary form sequential hymns often work well to provide theological commentary, reinforcing the theme of the day, and anticipating or following ritual actions.

Sequential hymns are not generally effective during ritual activity in worship unless they are very familiar to the congregation (virtually memorized). If well known, sequential hymns may function in a cyclical manner. The selection of well-known hymns varies from congregation to congregation and by faith tradition. Even congregations that use sequential hymns for choir processionals usually sing only familiar songs when combined with ritual activity. Generally, ritual activity that demands the congregation's complete participation does not blend well with sequential hymn singing; for example, a processional during communion is not the best time to introduce a new sequential hymn and expect full and active singing by the congregation.

2. Cyclic structures focus on community-building and support ongoing ritual activity, especially since they may easily be sung without the aid of books. The essentially oral character of cyclic forms (even though appearing in hymnbooks or other media) calls for a physical response. This is obvious in African and African American cyclic music as well as many Contemporary Christian songs where an outward physical response is normative. The mantra-like cyclic structures of the Taizé chants also have a profound physical effect on the one who sings or prays the song. It is a response that relaxes the body and focuses the mind for centered prayer.

Congregations may benefit by having a variety of cyclic songs at their disposal, perhaps as many as thirty to forty at any one time. The assembly may sing memorized cyclic songs in liturgy on short notice, giving the order of worship an element of spontaneity. While a memorized sequential hymn may work spontaneously, the flow of the service may be lost if the people need to take time to look it up in the hymnal.

3. Refrain forms can be used in a variety of situations. When soloists or choir sing the stanzas, leaving only the refrain for the congregation, the congregation may be able to participate in a ritual activity as they sing. An example of a ritual activity in which cyclic songs or refrain forms are effective is receiving communion, especially if the congregation processes to receive the communion elements. Cyclic songs such as "Eat This Bread," or "Jesus, Remember Me" from the Taizé Community,

work well. Refrain hymns such as "One Bread, One Body," "You Satisfy the Hungry Heart," and "Alleluia, Alleluia, Give Thanks to the Risen Lord," are effective during this ritual activity, as the choir or a soloist sings the stanzas.

Conclusion

All congregational song structures have the potential for providing valid liturgical experiences. Community formation takes place, and theological content is provided, whenever a congregation sings. Using a variety of song structures at appropriate places in the liturgy recognizes the strength of each. One of the challenges of singing cross-culturally, using the music of the world church, is to understand the structures of the songs and how these structures may function most effectively within the liturgy. Music leaders will add energy to worship, and integrate music more completely into the fabric of liturgy, if their choices are not based only on textual themes or musical style, but also for integration into liturgical rituals. Choosing congregational music with an understanding of its structure allows the music to permeate liturgy without drawing attention to itself, while it provides more emphasis on the theological themes and ritual actions that enrich worship.

Spectrum of Congregational Song Structures

© *C. Michael Hawn, Perkins School of Theology, Southern Methodist University*

Refrain Forms
Response
Antiphon
Litany
Epimone

Sequential Structures	*Cyclic Structures*
Strophic	Theme and Variation
Textual orientation	Movement orientation
Eye oriented	Ear oriented
Literate tradition	Oral tradition
Predictable performance time	Open-ended performance time
Linear in structure	Episodic in experience
Verbose	Concise
Comments on ritual activity	Participates in ritual activity
Content oriented	Community oriented
Moves toward climax in content	Moves toward total participation and integration of participants

Musical Considerations for Sequential Song

- Includes strophic hymns where the same music is repeated for successive stanzas

- Includes through-composed music and texts where there is no repetition of the music

- May include texts with brief textual repetition (usually on the last line) or epimone

- The essence of the text is essentially monochronic (teleological)

- Harmonic variations, varying instrumentations, and descants may provide musical variety from stanza to stanza

Musical Considerations for Cyclic Song

- Maintains a steady beat once the song begins

- Each repetition of a cycle needs some small variation

- Often uses a soloist (cantor) to sing over the cycle

- Improvisations by soloist over ends of phrases

- Often accompanied by physical response

- Integration of choir and congregation as a unit

- Polychronic (vs. monochronic) sense of time

- Textual improvisations to fit ritual context

ENDNOTES

1. Stephen B. G. Mbunga, *Church Law and Bantu Music: Ecclesiastical Documents and Law in Sacred Music as Applied to Bantu Music* (Schieneck-Beckenried, Switzerland: Nouvelle Revue de Science Missionaire, Supplement 13, 1963).

2. *The Milwaukee Symposium for Church Composers* (Washington, D.C.: The Pastoral Press, 1992). See paragraphs 56-80.

3. "Nairobi Statement on Worship and Culture: Contemporary Challenges and Opportunities," in *Christian Worship: Unity in Cultural Diversity*, ed. S. Anita Stauffer (Geneva: Lutheran World Federation, 1996), 25-28.

4. *Toward a Theology of Inculturation* (Maryknoll, N.Y.: Orbis Books, 1988), 11.

5. *Liturgical Inculturation: Sacramentals, Religiosity, and Catechesis* (Collegeville, Minn.: Liturgical Press, 1992), 29. The term "inculturation" is derived from the Latin *inculturatio* and is currently used almost exclusively when referring to the relationship between liturgy and culture. "Enculturation" is a term reserved by anthropologists for the socialization of individuals. John E. Kaemmer, *Music in Human Life: Anthropological Perspectives on Music* (Austin: University of Texas Press, 1993), states that "a universal feature of human life is the replication in every generation of the techniques, values, and symbols that characterize a particular mode of human life. The instilling of these qualities in the young is called socialization or enculturation" (75).

6. By exception the reformer Ulrich Zwingli restricted congregational singing of any kind, though he was a music lover and performer himself. Even The Society of Friends, noted for gathering in silence, have a hymnbook in the United States: see *Worship in Song: A Friends Hymnal* (Philadelphia: A Publication of Friends General Conference, 1996).

7. See Robert A. Schneider, "Jesus Shall Reign: Hymns and Foreign Missions," in *Wonderful Words of Life: Hymns in American Protestant History and Theology*, ed. Richard J. Mouw and Mark A. Noll (Grand Rapids: Eerdmans, 2004), 83-84. Schneider notes that "Jesus Shall Reign" is the second most widely published mission hymn in the nineteenth century, after Reginald Heber's "From Greenland's Icy Mountains."

8. Kenneth Scott Latourette devotes three volumes out of seven of his *A History of the Expansion of Christianity* (New York: Harper and Brothers, 1939-1945) to the nineteenth century.

9. Robin A. Leaver, "Theological Dimensions of Mission Hymnody: The Counterpoint of Cult and Culture," in *The Hymnology Annual: An International Forum on the Hymn and Worship*, ed. Vernon Wicker (Berrien Springs, Mich.: Vande Vere Publishing, 1991), 1:38. See also Lionel Adey, *Class and Idol in the English Hymn* (Vancouver: University of British Columbia Press, 1988), 15, who refers to "Jesus Shall Reign" as an "idol" of the British nation, and describes how patriotism and the church have often functioned inseparably in hymns.

10. Esther Rothenbusch Crookshank, "'We're Marching to Zion,' Isaac Watts in Early America," in *Wonderful Words of Life* (note 7), 21.

11. Rothenbusch Crookshank, 23.

12. See Rochelle A. Stackhouse, "Hymnody and Politics," in *Wonderful Words of Life*, 47.

13. Ibid., 47-52. I am indebted to Rochelle Stackhouse for her insightful analysis of "Our God, Our Help in Ages Past" reflected in this portion of my essay.

14. Watts's free paraphrases of the psalter, including the addition of overtly New Testament references, caused a firestorm of controversy among Reformed groups and others who followed John Calvin's mandate of 1542: "No one can sing anything worthy of God, unless he has received it from God himself . . . we can find no better songs for this purpose than the Psalms of David, which the Holy Spirit himself has uttered and made" (quoted by Louis F. Benson, *The Hymnody of the Christian Church* [1927; Richmond: John Knox Press, 1956], 82-83, 86-87). For a detailed account of the clash between psalm singing and Watts's paraphrases in Reformed congregations in America, see William B. Bynum, "'The Genuine Presbyterian Whine': Presbyterian Worship in the Eighteenth Century," *American Presbyterian: Journal of Presbyterian History* 74:3 (1996): 160-65.

15. J. R. Watson, *The English Hymn: A Critical and Historical Study* (Oxford: Clarendon Press, 1997), 153.

16. For further examples see Watson, *The English Hymn*, 153-56.

17. George Burder, ed., *The Works of the Reverend and Learned Isaac Watts, D.D.* (London, 1810), 4:113, as cited in Watson, *The English Hymn*, 153.

18. Robin A. Leaver, "Isaac Watts's Hermeneutical Principles and the Decline of English Metrical Psalmody," *Churchman* 92 (1978), 58.

19. See Erik Routley, *A Panorama of Christian Hymnody* (Collegeville: The Liturgical Press, 1979), 20-21, for the complete text. Italics in original.

20. While most hymnals eliminate these two stanzas altogether, at least four hymnals published by Southern Baptists in the twentieth century combine parts of the two stanzas with some alterations. *The Baptist Hymnal* (1975, p. 282) provides the following conflation of Watts's original stanzas two and three: "From north to south the princes meet/To pay their homage at his feet;/While western empires own their Lord,/And savage tribes attend his word." I experienced the irony of this particular version of Watts's hymn when the students I was teaching in a Nigerian seminary sang it during a morning chapel service. In a hymnology class after chapel, the ensuing discussion allowed these capable Nigerian pastors to express their feelings not only about the issue of colonialism in hymnody, but the difficulties of singing many Western hymns in their worship.

21. Watson, *The English Hymn*, 104-05, cites a historical and literary precedent for substituting images of Great Britain for those in the Hebrew Bible in William Barton's Old Testament readings of seventeenth-century British history. Barton, a Puritan minister, gave the reader bracketed English alternatives to Israel in one case, or from Parliament to Deborah and Barak in another. His version of the psalter was preferred by the House of Lords during the Civil War.

22. I am grateful to my colleague, Kenneth Shields, a professor in the English Department of Southern Methodist University and a founding member of the Charles Wesley Society, for pointing out this particular literary trait of imitation in Watts's hymns and for placing it in the context of literary devices used at this time. Shields discusses imitation in his article, "Charles Wesley as Poet," in *Charles Wesley: Poet and Theologian*, ed. S T Kimbrough, Jr. (Nashville: Kingswood Books, 1992), 49-52. As Shields noted in a conversation with me on June 6, 1997, "In eighteenth-century poetic tradition of Milton, Pope and Dryden, imitation pays homage to the authenticity of the western literary tradition of Greece and Rome, appropriates those texts

and gives authority to the imitation, and provides pleasure to the sophisticated reader who knows what is going on." A similar process was employed in the case of biblical imitation. It is a hermeneutical device that is most effective if those who read it are thoroughly familiar with the original text. Since the singers of Watts's hymns were steeped in the tradition of the metrical psalms, it was most likely that they were able to appreciate his poetic commentary regardless of whether or not they approved of it. As Watts stated in a letter to Cotton Mather in 1717 concerning *The Psalms of David Imitated*, "Tis not a translation of David that I pretend, but an imitation of him, so nearly in Christian hymns that the Jewish Psalmist may plainly appear, and yet leave Judaism behind" (quoted in Albert E. Bailey, *The Gospel in Hymns* [New York: Charles Scribner's Sons, 1950], 52).

23. Isaac Watts, *Psalms of David Imitated in the Language of the New Testament*, 1719, alt. by John Wesley, 1737.

24. See Bynum, "'The Genuine Presbyterian Whine'," 163. As Albert Bailey states in *The Gospel in Hymns*, "Watts himself knew perfectly well that the Psalms were a veritable treasure of praise. What he objected to was the undiscriminating way in which this treasure was used: the failure of the Church to disregard the obsolete, the heathen, the un-Christian elements found therein, and so suffuse what was left with the spirit of the gospel" (52).

25. See Richard Leppert, "Music, Domestic Life and Cultural Chauvinism: Images of British Subjects at Home in India," in *Music and Society: The Politics of Composition, Performance and Reception*, ed. Richard Leppert and Susan McClary (New York: Cambridge University Press, 1987), 63-64.

26. Ibid., 63, as quoted by Leppert from Dalrymple's *Observations on the present state of the East India Company; and on the measures to be pursued for ensuring the permanency, and augmenting its commerce.*

27. *Music and Society*, 74.

28. Ibid., 68.

29. *Jesus Through the Centuries: His Place in the History of Culture* (New York: Harper & Row, 1985), 221.

30. Bynum, "'The Genuine Presbyterian Whine'," 163. One must also bear in mind that hymn singing was primarily the domain of Dissenting and Evangelical congregations during the early eighteenth century, and

not of the Church of England.

31. See *Hymns of Prudentius*, trans. David R. Slavitt (Baltimore: The Johns Hopkins University Press, 1996) for an orientation to Prudentius' hymns.

32. Pablo Sosa traces the development of Latin American liturgical music all the way back to Prudentius' hymn in "Spanish American Hymnody: A Global Perspective," *Hymnology Annual*, ed. Vernon Wicker (Berrien Springs, Mich.: Vande Vere Publishing Ltd., 1993), 3:57-70.

33. Portions of this section appeared in an earlier essay, "Siyahamba, South African Freedom Song," *The Chorister* 51:6 (December 1999), 23-27. David Dargie comments that the text is basically the same in Siswata (the Swazi people), Xhosa, and Zulu.

34. The collection and cassette, *Freedom Is Coming: Songs of Protest and Praise from South Africa*, ed. Anders Nyberg (Chapel Hill, N.C.: Walton Music Corporation, 1984), first brought these songs to a broader audience through the impetus of the Iona Community in Scotland. Selections from this book, originally published by Utryck for the Church of Sweden Mission, have appeared in at least seven North American hymnals since this time. For example, see *United Methodist Hymnal* (1989): "Thuma Mina" (497); *Hymnal: A Worship Book* (1992), "Asithi: Amen" (64), "Thuma Mina" (434); *Chalice Hymnal* (1995): "Masithi" (30), "Siyahamba" (442), "Thuma Mina" (447); *Covenant Hymnal* (1996): "Siyahamba" (424), "Hallelujah! Pelo Tso Rona" (499), "Thuma Mina" (626); *Voices United* (1996): "Sanna Sannanina" (128), "Thuma Mina" (572), "Siyahamba" (646); *The New Century Hymnal* (1995): "Masithi" (760), "Siyahamb'" (626), "Thuma Mina" (360), "We Shall Not Give Up the Fight" (437); *The Book of Praise* (1997): "Thuma Mina" (777), "Siyahamba" (639), "Asithi Amen" (264), "Freedom Is Coming" (725). Recent African American hymnals such as *This Far By Faith* (1999) from the Evangelical Lutheran Church of America (ELCA) make extensive use of South African sources. Current hymnal supplements continue to expand this literature into common usage: see *With One Voice* (1995) from the ELCA, *Wonder, Love and Praise* (1997; Episcopal Church, USA), and *The Faith We Sing* (2000; United Methodist), for more examples.

35. See John M. Janzen, *Ngoma: Discourses on Healing in Central and Southern Africa* (Berkeley: University of California Press, 1992), 111-18.

36. An expanded version of the following section is available in C. Michael Hawn, *Gather into One: Praying and Singing Globally* (Grand Rapids: Eerdmans, 2003), chapter 7.

C. Michael Hawn is Professor of Church Music at Perkins School of Theology and Director of the Master of Sacred Music Program at Southern Methodist University. He is also a student of global music, having received several fellowships for study of music around the world including Africa, Asia and Latin America. He is the author of Halle Halle: We Sing the World Round *(Choristers Guild, 1999),* Gather Into One: Praying and Singing Globally *(Wm. B. Eerdmans, 2003), and* One Bread, One Body: Exploring Cultural Diversity in Worship *(The Alban Institute, 2003), as well over 100 articles, reviews and curriculum materials.*

Contextualization versus Globalization:
A Glimpse of Sounds and Symbols in Asian Worship

I-TO LOH

LET ME TAKE THIS OPPORTUNITY TO THANK your Institute of Sacred Music, formerly my alma mater at Union Theological Seminary. My studies there, nearly forty years ago, laid the foundation for my long journey toward contextualization of church music and liturgy in Asia. My intention in this talk is to explore some of the struggles between contextualization and globalization, and to give you a glimpse of how some Asians are dealing with sounds, and to a lesser extent symbols, in worship. I will describe a framework that presents some of the relevant dimensions. In order to really understand and feel the musical issues I am talking about, we will look at some examples together

The General Asian Scene

Over fifteen years ago I gave a lecture in Hong Kong for the World Association of Chinese Church Music in which I pointed out the awkward situation of Chinese-speaking churches around the world. I said that Chinese churches:
  • were banana churches, because they looked yellow in their skin, but deep in their heart and mind they wanted to be as white as Caucasians;
  • translated and borrowed theologies, having no theologies of their own;
  • copied music – they copied Western styles of composition, and also illegally copied Western published anthems;
  • used liturgies that were all secondhand liturgies introduced and used by missionaries over a century ago.[1]
  I challenged these Chinese musicians and pastors: "Where is the rice?" Where is the staple food, the substance of their Chinese Christian expression? Unfortunately those observations and comments still to some extent reflect the general situation and attitude of most of the

churches in Asia today, with the exception of a few seminaries and institutions in India, Philippines, Taiwan, Thailand, and Indonesia.
  The central theme of my life's work has been this struggle between contextualization and Westernization or globalization. You may ask, what is wrong with globalization? Globalization is not inherently bad. But globalization, like Westernization, is problematic when it promotes the wholesale supplanting of local cultures by Western ideas. I frequently tell my Asian students and colleagues that modernization does not equal Westernization. If you copy others all the time, then you lose yourself. In regard to Christianity, this has occurred primarily in two ways: the initial wholesale transplantation of the Gospel by early missionaries without any regard for local context, and rapid globalization. As a result, local people have come to see their own culture as without value. Local culture is being thrown out in favor of Western ideas.
  Let me give you some examples of the impact of globalization on local culture in Taiwan and Asia.
  • The wholesale importation of Western praise choruses and pop style hymns is causing a host of problems. First, music is no longer placed in its liturgical context; it is only used as a warm-up for half-an-hour or longer without consideration for its relevance in the liturgy. Second, the people's musical ability has declined. Fewer people are interested in other types of music. Native traditions and newly composed songs in ethnic styles have little chance of survival. Third, the church is losing her historical and ecumenical links. The overall result is that Christians are becoming narrow-minded, and Christian doctrines of God and the Church are distorted.
  • Entertainment-oriented worship services and success-theology, formulated after

globalization, have become the primary mode of preaching and evangelism.

• Some Western editors/compilers have made recordings of songs from the Third World which they then published under their own names as arrangers, when in fact they had only transcribed, or at most changed a few notes, and then claimed ownership.

• Some Western composers have arranged simple Third World songs into larger Western-style choral works, altering the original styles so much that their uniqueness was lost. Even worse, the Western arrangers then copyrighted the songs for themselves, forcing the original developers to pay money for their own diluted music.

Ethical issues also emerge from this aspect of globalization. The rich West has the know-how and power to take over the works of the poor Third World. "Learned composers" randomly superimpose Western harmony in order to "globalize" Third World songs for Western consumption. Forcing these songs into Western style is like forcing people from hot climates to put on formal suits and ties before being allowed to worship God.

This is not a new problem. D. T. Niles, the cofounder of the Christian Conference of Asia and its first General Secretary, recognized this problem decades ago. In his writings he suggested an elegant metaphor for explaining the problem of transplanting the Gospel. Although he did not live long enough to experience the phenomenon of globalization, his observations and suggestions for solutions are still valid. He said:

> The Gospel is like a seed and you have to sow it. When you sow the seed of the Gospel in Palestine, a plant that can be called Palestinian Christianity grows.... The seed of the Gospel is later brought to America and a plant grows of American Christianity. Now when missionaries came to our lands they brought not only the

seed of the Gospel, but their own plant of Christianity, flower pot included! So, what we have to do is to break the flower pot, take out the seed of the Gospel, sow it in our own cultural soil, and let our own version of Christianity grow.[2]

Here Niles pinpoints the heart of the problem, not only of the Gospel but also of our music and worship. The major part of our effort in Asia today is still focused on translating, imitating, and copying Western ways of singing and worship, believing them to be the only authentic Christian expression. Instead, our efforts today should be focused not only on breaking the Western flowerpot, but also on taking out the seed of the Gospel and figuring out how to plant this new seed. We need to cultivate a version of Christianity that is appropriate to our own cultural soil.

Contextualization of Christian Musical Expression

Our basic challenge is this: How can we encourage an expression of Christian faith that is Asian in nature, and not merely a transplantation of Western Christianity? In my view, contextualization is the approach we need to take in order to plant this new seed of the Gospel. In my first attempt, in 1984, to define the meaning of contextualization, I concluded that contextualization is, above all, the manifestation of the Imago Dei in human kind. It is the revelation of the mystery of God's creative power as shown in his creation, including human minds that formulate various art forms. And it is our participation in God's continuous creation, letting God transform our culture and arts into dynamic media that will effectively communicate and express the meanings of the Gospel to our people.[3]

Today I would add that the ultimate goal of contextualization is the realization of incarnation in any given context, that is, God in Christ taking native forms and speaking native languages. The Gospel is no longer confined in any flowerpot, or in need of translation.

In the rest of this presentation I will give you examples of Asian music at different degrees of contextualization. I hope that you will appreciate both the challenge that we face in promoting contextualization, as well as the enormous potential for creative contextualization and insight into faith that can be gained by drawing upon the rich cultural diversity of Asia. I am going to begin by characterizing the degrees of contextualization taking place in Asia, and providing a number of examples of these contextualizations. I will conclude with an example of my own work.

Asia covers a huge area, and contains thousands of ethnic groups as well as a rich diversity of cultures. There are no easy ways of classifying the forms of contextualization, but to help make sense of the diversity we can roughly categorize Asians into three basic types: forks, chopsticks, and fingers/spoons. The first Asian dean of the Southeast Asia Graduate School of Theology, Kosuke Koyama, suggested in his well-known book *Water Buffalo Theology* that all the professors in his institution are people of two cultures, "fork and chopsticks."[4] I interpret him as categorizing the modern educational orientation of his faculty members according to their way of eating or handling food: chopsticks for Asian-oriented education, and forks for Westernized education.

While this may be an oversimplification of the day-to-day reality in which many people use both forks and chopsticks, this analysis remains a useful metaphor for understanding the relationships between Western and Asian ideas. For our analysis and understanding of Asia as a whole I add another category: "fingers/spoons." Most of the indigenous peoples in many parts of Asia, especially those in South Asia, Southeast Asia, and the Pacific, eat with fingers and/or spoons. They are also the ones who have kept their traditions, being less influenced from the West.

Let me explain how these three types of food consumption are related to musical styles and their contextual practices.

Forks. This term refers to Asians who, because of their Western education, tend to subscribe to Western cultural expressions and value systems. They appreciate Western music, but may be ignorant of their own culture; some of them might even look down on their own native culture and music. There are two subcategories here: Asians learning to use a fork, and Asians creating new pieces in the Asian fork style.

Let me cite one example of Asians learning to use a fork, that is, Asians learning to sing Western songs. Korean folk music is usually in compound time, 9/8 or 6/8, and tends not to repeat the same note in the melody; Koreans are also fond of anticipating the next tone. When missionaries introduced the hymn tune *Nettleton* ("Come Thou Fount of Every Blessing"), the Koreans were unable to sing it exactly the way they were taught; they had to change the song to

EXAMPLE 1

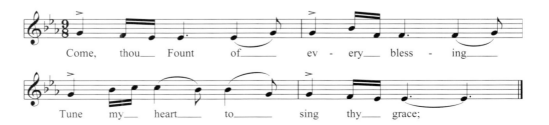

fit their native song style, changing the time and anticipating the next tone[5] (see example 1).

They not only changed the rhythm and the time signature, and anticipated the next tone on the weak beat (the last eighth note), but also removed the seventh degree of the scale (*si*), because it is not in the traditional five-tone scale. This is an example of a Western song but not

sung according to a Western manner. The song was changed to fit a native idiom.

There is also an "Asian fork style" that mostly follows the Western concept of composition and is treated with Western harmony. The Japanese melody, "Gathering Round the Table of the Lord" (see example 2) has only a slight Asian flavor.

EXAMPLE 2

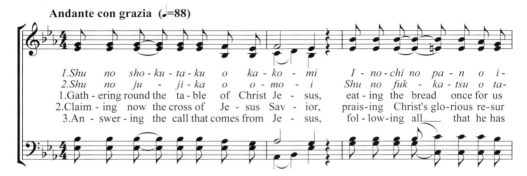

Gathering Round the Table of the Lord
(Japanese: Shu no shokutaku o kakomi)

I have had arguments with people who claimed this tune as very Japanese, but when I asked them to sing it in English they could not identify the Japanese elements. It seems that the

language has made it seem Japanese, and the reiterated eighth notes may also sound Japanese, but the setting in Western traditional four-part harmony has turned this into an Asian fork style.

EXAMPLE 3

God Is Here As We Your People Meet
(Mandarin: Shen zai dian zhong, xintu chong-jing)

Chopsticks. The second type of Asian uses chopsticks. Culturally and geographically this refers to Northeast Asian countries, namely Japan, Korea, China, Taiwan, plus all the cultural Chinese in Southeast Asia (Singapore, Malaysia, Indonesia, and Indo-china). Most of them are proud of their own traditional culture, but many still look up to the Western "fork" culture as their ideal. Musically, they may be divided into two groups.

Group 1 includes those who can perform or appreciate their own traditional high art music. Group 2 includes those who have acquired certain Western musical ideas and skills but who have little or no knowledge of their own music. They equate modernization with Westernization. Here we find the phenomenon of hybridization or syncretism, that is, composing melodies in ethnic styles but harmonizing in a Western way. This is more Asian than the Asian fork type, because the melody demonstrates a stronger Asian character, but at the same time it still uses Western harmonies. In a sense it is half Asian and half Western. So far, this is the most popular practice, enjoyed by composers, singers and listeners. Let me cite two examples here.

F. Pratt Green's "God Is Here As We Your People Meet," has been set to a melody in Chinese style: *Shen zai dian zhong* (see example 3).

EXAMPLE 4

O God of Great Love
(Korean: Sarangui Chunim)

The composer, Dr. Daniel Law of Hong Kong, uses a C natural minor with a pentatonic scale, concluding the A section at the end of the second system in its relative major. Then without modulations he starts with G minor, introducing two new tones, D and A, to create a contrast and sense of modulation, and returns back to the opening motive for the conclusion. Here we can see typical Chinese melodic progressions harmonized in a constantly moving counterpoint with contrary motions, almost Bachian in style. This shows the ideal of many Asian composers today for mixing two cultures together in a hymn.

Another example of an Asian melody with partial Western harmonization may be found in Yong-cho Lee's *Sarangui Chunim* (see example 4).

The text is an earnest prayer for guidance, based on the words of one of the criminals nailed on the cross who begged Jesus to remember him when he came into his kingdom (Luke 23:42). The melodic line and rhythm show a strong Korean character. The harmony is somewhat ambiguous, because there are hints of both Asian and Western influences, with very Romantic chord progressions.

Fingers/Spoons. The third type of Asian contextualization covers not only the peoples in South Asia, Southeast Asia, and the Pacific, but also the Aborigines in Taiwan. They use fingers and/or spoons in eating; they have also preserved more of their original culture and have less Western influence. Herein lies a wellspring of rich Asian music that awaits investigation.

Let me give you an example. You may be aware that traditional music in India, Pakistan, Sri Lanka, Bangladesh, Nepal, Thailand, Myanmar, and Cambodia is, in general, without harmony. The Indian song called a *Bhajan* is a kind of spiritual song in praise of the attributes of God. It preserves a distinctively Indian composition style, sans harmony. Indian music is characterized by a number of key features,

including the use of drones, ornaments, microtones, rhythmic cycles, and *raga*. The notion of *raga* is very complex.[6] The important tones are *Sa*, the foundation or the tonic of the *raga*, and *Pa*, the dominant. These two pitches are frequently sounded together as drones. The Indian octave is divided into twenty-two *sruti*, that is, microtonal intervals smaller than a half-step. Another important feature is ornaments, without which Indian songs would lose their character. Let us sing a bhajan to demonstrate some of these points. (See example 5).

OM is a mystic syllable of ancient origin. It is the combination of three sounds A-U-M, symbolizing the beginning, the middle and the end of life.[7] *Bhagawan* refers to the name of God. This is a very clear example of the use of entirely indigenous music to express a Christian idea. The melody, the rhythm, and all the other elements are Indian in their origin. This song breaks the Western flowerpot. Unfortunately, this *bhajan* has not been generally accepted by all the Indian churches, because the mystical sound OM is a Hindu, not Christian, expression. The Indian name of God, *Bhagawan*, could also be helpful in contemplating the attributes of God. I hope that in due time Indian theologians may be able to come up with more convincing interpretations of their own theologies.

We have just seen some examples of how we can characterize Asian contextualization. Let us turn now to an example of how contextualization is expressed through non-lexical syllables.

Non-lexical syllables. Some cultures in Asia like to sing songs with non-lexical syllables. They are vocables or "untalkables," words or syllables without specific meaning. They gain meaning from the title, the purpose or context, words sung before or after, or the singer's own mood and imagination. I propose that singing in non-lexical syllables may be comparable to St. Paul's idea of "sighs too deep for words" (Rom 8:27); that is, one may express something that

EXAMPLE 5

O Praise the LORD
(Hindhi: Om Bhagawan)

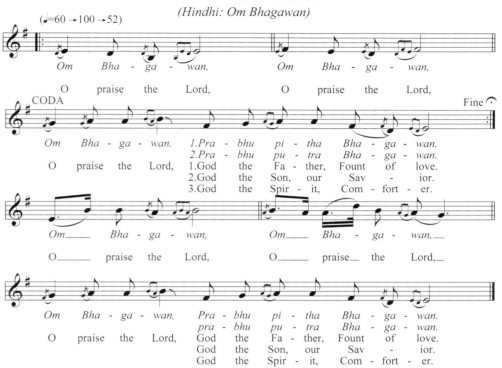

Om   Bha - ga - wan,   Om   Bha - ga - wan,
O   praise   the   Lord,   O   praise   the   Lord,

CODA   Fine

Om   Bha - ga - wan.   1.Pra - bhu   pi - tha   Bha - ga - wan.
                          2.Pra - bhu   pu - tra   Bha - ga - wan.
O   praise   the   Lord,   1.God   the   Fa - ther,   Fount   of   love.
                               2.God   the   Son,   our   Sav   -   ior.
                               3.God   the   Spir - it,   Com - fort - er.

Om____   Bha - ga - wan,   Om____   Bha - ga - wan,___
O____   praise   the   Lord,   O____   praise_   the   Lord,_

Om   Bha - ga - wan,   Pra - bhu   pi - tha   Bha - ga - wan.
                          pra - bhu   pu - tra   Bha - ga - wan.
O   praise   the   Lord,   God   the   Fa - ther,   Fount   of   love.
                               God   the   Son,   our   Sav   -   ior.
                               God   the   Spir - it,   Com - fort - er.

EXAMPLE 6

From this Time Onwards
(Bunun: Pais ka lau pa ku)

solo   chorus   solo   chorus

1.Pais   ka   lau   pa   ku   u   i   hi,   mal   ma   na   nu   u   i   hi.
2.Ta   atha   ha   li   nga   u   i   hi,   min   sial   is   ang   u   i   hi.
1.From   this   time   on - wards,   u   i   hi,   let's   strive   hard - er,   u   i   hi.
2.Hear   God's   word   to   us,   u   i   hi,   love   each   o - ther;   u   i   hi.
3.God   is   call - ing   us,   u   i   hi,   "Look   to   Je - sus,   u   i   hi.

is inexpressible. This can be further confirmed from the contemporary view of the Jewish tradition, as was pointed out recently by a Jewish cantor who said that the best kind of singing is wordless, which expresses the deepest and inner personal feelings. This may be demonstrated through the next hymn from the aborigines of Taiwan, *Paiska Lau Paku*. (See example 6.)

The Bunun tribe in Taiwan builds its choral singing in overtone series, i.e. *do-mi-sol*. This can be demonstrated by the jew's-harp. When singing the Bunun people naturally divide into four or more parts to sing homophonically. In certain call and response songs, the congregation responds to the soloist with the non-lexical syllables U-I-HI, which do not have a particular meaning but express agreement or approval of the text just sung. These non-lexical syllables can mean "Yes, I agree," or "I support your words," or even "Amen." Note that the final cadence is in an open fifth without the *mi*. This is an authentic way of harmonizing without any Western influence.

The above examples are just a few native or acculturated sounds of worship, using fingers/spoons, chopsticks, or forks. Some are genuinely indigenous; nothing has been added.

Some are syncretic, that is, they mix two styles, with different degrees of Western influence and contextualization.

I am pleased to report to you that the Christian Conference of Asia has published *Sound the Bamboo: CCA Hymnal 2000*, which contains 315 hymns from twenty-two countries in Asia, in forty-four languages, all with singable English translations. Through this collection you will be able to trace and discover some Asian musical identities, and get a general picture of how some Asians are struggling to contextualize our faith in worship.

Some Innovative Sounds

We have looked at examples of the range of contextualizations taking place in Asia. We turn now to focus more on innovation. There are pockets of innovation in Asia, where composers are adding something new, and stretching beyond both native and western tradition to worship God. Let's look at a few examples.

Silence. Silent meditation is important in Asian culture. A composer from Bangladesh, Bart Shaha, made use of silence symbolically

EXAMPLE 7

EXAMPLE 8

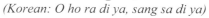

Ohoradiya, In God's Temple, Praise the Lord, God

(Korean: O ho ra di ya, sang sa di ya)

in composing a prayer of confession. His innovation involved the creation of two cycles, six counts each, of total silence. Although the music seems to have stopped, the sound of silence becomes the agent of "a still small voice" (1 Kings 19:12) speaking to us that we can hear only in total silence. This silence may also awaken our conscience to see our true sinful self, thus creating a genuine spirit for confession. As expressed by Madeline L'Engle, "The deepest communion with God is beyond words, on the other side of silence."[8] Let us experience this prayer by looking at "Lord, We Did Not Live Up to Your Teachings. Lord, Forgive Us" in Bengali (see example 7).

Non-lexical syllables. These are used in various styles of music. Some composers are taking advantage of the nature of non-lexical syllables in a Christian context. For example, the Korean song "Ohoradiya" (see example 8) was originally associated with a farmers' dance during festivals. The syllables are shouts of joy and excitement. Geonyong Lee has adapted the singing style, and has transformed the non-lexical syllables *ohoradiya sangsa diya* into the meaning of "Hallelujah" by simply adding a parenthetical "Hallelujah" in the lyrics everywhere that

ohoradiya appears. In this Psalm 150 Korean instruments have replaced all the biblical instruments. The composer has transformed the folk singing style into a hymn of highest praise.

The way to sing this is for the leader to sing the *ohoradiya*, and for the congregation to repeat after. The leader will continue to sing other phrases, but the congregation still responds with the same *ohoradiya*, until the leader introduces a new *ohoradiya*, when the congregation changes accordingly.

The symbolism of sound. Another example of innovation uses an image to guide the development of the motif. The next piece is a mysterious, meditative hymn, marveling at God's creation, its diversity, harmony and perfection. The Filipino author/composer, Francisco F. Feliciano, a Yale graduate, uses an image to explain the symbolism of sound. He says that when one throws a rock into a calm lake it stirs up ripples, first small, then expanding bigger and wider, and finally fading. The composition evolves from this imagery. The melodic construction uses the movement of sound to describe the ripples expanding, then fading. Feliciano is also innovative in utilizing two guitars, one playing only three tones 3 4 6, with

EXAMPLE 9

Still, I Search for My God

With utmost simplicity (♩=60)

1.Still,   I search for   my   God   in   si - lence,   I   mar - vel   at   the
2.Come   lis - ten   to   the   trees,   the   green fields,   the   riv - ers   and   the
3.Yes   I   am   filled   with joy   and breathe   in   the   pre - sence of   the

u - ni - verse, the   world it con - tains, its   beau - ty,   its   har - mo - ny! Cre
morn - ing breeze, the   birds of the   air   all   sing - ing their Mak - er praise! Cre
Lord, my   God,   your   praise I will   sing, your   pow - er   de - clare in chant, and

the other playing accompaniment in arpeggios, all in discords. To my knowledge no other hymns in the West or in Asia are composed with this kind of texture and symbolism. See "Still, I Search for My God" (example 9).

Drones. The following is an example where I have taken the Indian concept of *raga, tala* (rhythmic cycle), and drone, and have added new ideas, which are neither Indian nor Western or Taiwanese. This is my personal ideal of the goal of contextualization as an Asian, not necessarily limiting myself to a single culture.

The function and role of the Holy Spirit is a mystery to many. Shirley Murray, a New Zealander, is one of the best hymn writers today. In her hymn "Loving Spirit" (see example 10) she describes the loving Spirit as a mother, feeding and forming me with her own body;

as a father: protecting me and hoisting me on his shoulder to see the world; as a friend and lover, knowing, comforting, and giving me rest. When I set her text to music I tried to express this mysterious yet intimate feeling of the Holy Spirit with the so-called Gypsy scale of India. The Gypsy scale is organized in two tetrachords, 3 4 #5 6 and 7 1 #2 3, each of which consists of the intervals of a minor 2nd, augmented 2nd, and minor 2nd (similar to the Indian *Bhairav raga* family). I used an additive rhythm, or the South Indian *triputa tala* 3 + 2 + 2. With this variety of melodic intervals, additive rhythm, and ornaments, I could create different melodic lines. As I indicated earlier, Indian music has no concept of harmony. In order to innovate I borrowed the tonic and dominant of the Gypsy scale as drones. These drones, however, move

EXAMPLE 10

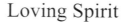

Loving Spirit

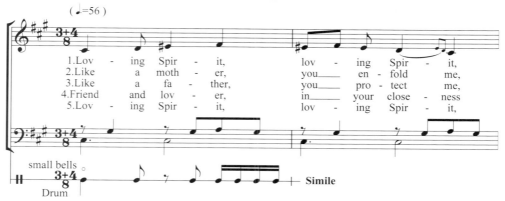

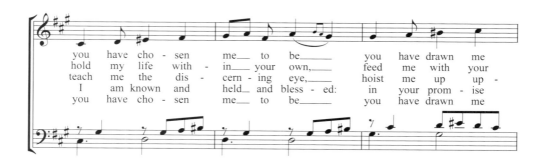

slowly, and gradually develop to a more complex inner melodic line. This creates a mood of mystery, building up to a climax that expresses the "wonder" of the Spirit near the end. The drum and concussion bell accompaniment also adds to the mystery of this hymn. The end of each stanza should leave a cycle of seven beats as interlude.

Two Asian cultures. In this last example, I describe my own work in attempting to fuse musical ideas from two Asian cultures in conflict as a way to symbolize possible unity and reconciliation.

Over four hundred thousand migrants work in Taiwan; they come from the Philippines

and other Asian countries. Some of them have taken jobs that formerly would have been held by Taiwanese aboriginal people. This causes resentment and tension between Taiwanese tribes and migrant workers. When I discovered the New Zealand poet Bill Wallace's hymn "Sound a Mystic Bamboo Song" which vividly depicts Christ in Asian ways of life—wearing tribal cloth, living in a squatter's shed, bending while planting rice—I was deeply moved. I decided to use this text to create a contextualized hymn bringing Philippine and Taiwanese musical cultures into unity. My immediate idea was to use non-lexical syllables to establish the link between the Kalinga people from the Northern Philippines and Taiwanese aboriginal people, both of whom are fond of singing in non-lexical syllables. As I indicated earlier, non-lexical syllables can take on new meaning according to context. I created a new context by putting non-lexical phrases from each culture into the same song. Thus, the Kalinga motive begins the first half of the song, and the Taiwanese tribal motive completes the second half. I hoped that Kalinga and Taiwanese singers and listeners would experience a feeling of unity and reconciliation through bringing the familiar and unfamiliar sounds together. The theology and symbolism behind this composition are that Christ, the Son of God, our Savior, has taken our mortal body, working with us, suffering with us. We, as children of God, in spite of all our differences, are equally loved by Christ. Therefore we can share our burdens, our resources; we can work together, live in harmony, and manifest our unity in Christ. This is my humble attempt in contextualizing with our

Asian sisters and brothers our mutual faith in Christ. (See example 11).

Symbols and Symbolic Acts

So far, I have talked mostly about music in an Asian context. In the last part of this presentation I would like to share with you some of the symbolism used in Asian worship.

Dance and symbolism in Bali. The Protestant church in Bali has stood out as Asians who have been testifying to Christ through various art forms. Their efforts at contextualization may be seen in the following examples:[9]

• The Balinese associate mountains with the presence of God as well as the source of life; this has prompted them to build their churches to resemble mountains.

• In Balinese tradition a temple gate symbolizes coming into the presence of God. Thus, a traditional temple gate is constructed

EXAMPLE 11

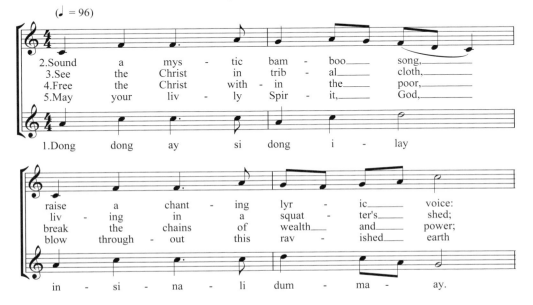

behind the communion table, but a cross is set in the middle affirming that Christ is the Way to God.

• Dance in Bali is "a powerful medium of communicating ideas, emotions and feelings. Their highly-stylized gestures and eye, finger, arm, and foot movements are the keys to understanding Balinese dance, for all these are symbolic representations of something deeper in meaning."[10] For instance dance movements have a traditional meaning that Christians have re-interpreted in a Christian context:

Body Part	Traditional Interpretation	Christian Interpretation
Thumb	Wisdom	God's wisdom, providence
Index	Power, position	God's omnipotence
Middle	Wealth	Richness of God
Ring	Beauty, blessings	God's grace, blessings
Pinky	Trust	Faithfulness, eternal life
Eyes	Heaven, God's watching eyes	Heaven, God's loving care, God's watching eyes
Hands	Human beings	God's children
Feet	World, earth	God's world
Symmetrical movements	Balance between good and evil, right and left	God's justice and mercy, Judgment and grace

All of these new Christian interpretations have added new dimensions in communicating the Gospel to the Balinese through dance.

A famous painter, dancer, musician, and composer, I Nyoman Darsane, composed *Anak Dara* (The Parable of the Ten Virgins) to urge people to prepare diligently and be ready to welcome the sudden coming of the bridegroom. He used the gamelan to accompany singing, which was rare at the time. The parable begins with an overture of dance. It marked the beginning of a new era of Balinese Christian dance and music.

I will mention only a few other symbols and symbolic acts.[11]

Parikrama. Some Christians in South India create a mandala in the sanctuary to pay obeisance to God. A mandala is a space decorated with a vase, pebbles, flowers, etc., to represent the Holy of Holies or the presence of God. When people come to worship they bring gifts of flowers or other objects of God's creation, and walk slowly and meditatively around the mandala, placing the gifts to decorate the mandala, holding their palms together with the sign of namaskar, and slightly bowing the head, which means "I salute the divinity that is in you." It symbolizes thanksgiving, praise and offering. This whole act of worship is called parikrama.[12]

Mat covering. When a Pacific islander wants to show his regret for having seriously offended someone, he has to ask a respected person from his community to take his place. This respected person sits in front of the house of the offended party, covering himself with a mat to express his plea for forgiveness. If someone comes out to remove the mat, it means that the apology has been accepted. If not, this person has to be killed! The church has utilized this act of penitence. During the prayer of confession, one representative of the congregation sits in the middle, covered with a mat. After the assurance of forgiveness the pastor comes down to remove the mat, symbolizing the forgiveness of sins, and the reconciliation between God and people, and between human beings.

Elements for Holy Communion. The liturgy of Holy Communion provides people with ample spaces for imagination. For instance:

• Coconuts are one of the main subsistence foods of Filipinos and many other Asian peoples, and so Filipino Christians have used coconuts to replace bread and wine in the Holy Communion.

One can easily understand the symbolism of one body broken, the meat and juice coming from the same coconut to nourish the people (although some people have problems with the juice, which is not red).

• Taiwan is shaped like a sweet potato. Besides, in the past sweet potatoes were the food of the poor. A recent poem uplifting this Taiwanese spirit reads: "Sweet potatoes, fearless of being rotten under the earth,/ Only yearn for sprouting of leaves and branches for generation after generation." So, we have used sweet potatoes for Holy Communion. The meaning of sacrifice implied in the poem above also reflects the word of Jesus, that when "a grain of wheat falls into the earth and dies … it bears much fruit" (John 12:24).

• Tea is the most important drink in Taiwanese society. It is very meaningful for Taiwanese to serve tea in place of wine or juice in communion.

• Some theologians in Indonesia have done an experiment using chicken meat for Holy Communion, with the following rationale: (1) chicken is the most popular meat for general consumption; (2) chickens only live for people, sacrificing themselves to nourish human beings; (3) a rooster reminds us of the weaknesses in our human nature, warning us of our possible denial of Christ, as did Peter; (4) chickens remind us of God's love as shown in Jesus' lamentation for Jerusalem: "How often have I desired to gather your children together as a hen gathers her brood under her wings …" (Matt. 23:37); (5) chewing the meat makes people experience the actual eating and partaking of "the body."

• Rice wine, a very strong local liquor, is used in place of grape juice.

The sacred flame. South Indian families keep a copper lamp, *Aathari* (sacred flame), lighted at night. The original lamp had a pagan symbol on the top, which is now replaced by a cross. It has five wicks that symbolize five ways to the deity. Christians have given this lamp a new

identity: the *Aarathi* symbolizes the presence of God, or Christ, the light of the world. The flame also stands for the Word, the truth, and eternal life. After a sermon each member of the congregation is invited to come forward to feel the flame. After the first touch they place both hands on top of the head to symbolize receiving the Word or Christ intellectually. After the second touch they place both hands on the eyes, as a prayer for illumination of the mystery and the understanding of the truth. After the final touch the hands are placed on the heart as a sign of receiving Christ and his Word in one's heart with emotion, feeling and love.

Conclusion

These are but a few Asian sounds, symbols, and symbolic acts in worship. They are born out of Asian Christians' genuine search for truth, their glimpses of God's glory. These works, vulnerable as they are, represent humble attempts to comprehend the incomprehensible mystery of God's love and revelation. They may be called religious art that "transcends its culture and reflects the eternal."[13] It is their *imago Dei* responding to the call of the Spirit to participate in the continuing act of God's creation "in us, through us, [and] with us,"[14] whether they use arts, fingers, spoons, chopsticks, or forks to express their incarnated faith. Let us pray that the unique glory of God as shown in God's special gifts to any particular culture will not be lost because of globalization. Let us also keep an open mind, to see through our third eye, and listen through our third ear, to what God may be telling us or revealing to us today through unfamiliar imageries, through the loud sound of gongs, or through a still small voice.

ENDNOTES

1. "Worshiping with Incarnated Music: My Mission" [in Chinese]. *Lam-sin Sin-hak* 2:1 (1991):113-32.

2. Quoted by C. Michael Hawn, *Gather into One:*

Praying and Singing Globally (Grand Rapids: Eerdmans, 2003), 32.

3. "Toward Contextualization of Church Music in Asia," in *Hymnology Annual: An International Forum on the Hymn and Worship*, ed. Vernon Wicker (Berrien Springs, Mich.: Vande Vere, 1991), 1:93.

4. *Water Buffalo Theology*, twenty-fifth anniversary edition, revised and expanded (Maryknoll, N.Y.: Orbis Books, 1999), 176.

5. See Seongdae Kim, *Inculturation in Korean Protestant Hymnody* (Ph.D. diss., Drew University, 1999), 194.

6. The meanings of *raga* can only be explained through the combinations of scale, mode, melodic shape, and tonal center, etc. It is also associated with certain moods, seasons and times of the day. Theoretically there are over seven thousand *ragas*, but even trained musicians would hardly know more than fifty.

7. See Maren C. Tirabassi and Kathy Wonson Eddy, *Gifts of Many Cultures: Worship Resources for the Global Community* (Cleveland: United Church Press, 1994), 74.

8. *Walking on Water: Reflections on Faith & Art* (Wheaton, Ill.: Harold Shaw, 1980), 128.

9. See I-to Loh, *Kristus Sundaring Bali (Christ the Light to Bali): A Collection of New Balinese Hymns* (Manila: Asian Institute for Liturgy and Music, 1988), 7-8.

10. Loh, *Kristus*, 14-15.

11. For the details of these symbols and symbolic acts, see I-to Loh, "Asian Worship" in *The Complete Library of Christian Worship*, vol. 7, *The Ministries of Christian Worship*, ed. Robert Webber (Nashville: Star Song, 1994), 217-21.

12. See Choo Lak Yeow and John C. England, *Doing Theology with People's Symbols and Images*. ATESEA Occasional Papers (Singapore: ATESEA/PTCA, 1988), 21.

13. Madeleine L'Engle, *Walking on Water*, 49

14. *Walking on Water*, 81.

Born in Taiwan, I-to Loh received the M.Div. from Tainan Seminary, the SMM from Union Seminary, and the Ph. D. at UCLA. He has taught Asian and Global Church Music, Ethnomusicology, and Worship in Manila and Taiwan, and compiled over 20 collections of hymns, including Sound the Bamboo: CCA Hymnal 2000. *He has published over one hundred original hymns and anthems,* Teach Us to Praise, *and many academic essays, and has led music and worship at WCC and CCA assemblies and conferences. I-to Loh retired from the presidency of Tainan Seminary in 2002, and is currently editing a hymnal and writing a companion to* Sound the Bamboo.

Authors' Perspectives

Reluctant Partners: Art and Religion in Dialogue, edited by Ena Giurescu Heller (New York: The Gallery at the American Bible Society, 2004)

The collection of essays, *Reluctant Partners: Art and Religion in Dialogue,* was intended as a "reference and methods" volume. The authors are all involved, in various capacities, in shaping the current discourse on Judeo-Christian art and religion. They were brought together in a three-year research project organized by The Gallery at the American Bible Society (now the Museum of Biblical Art); sponsored by the Henry Luce Foundation, it was titled *New Directions in the Study of Art and Religion.* The purpose of the project was an attempt to define the parameters—past, present and future—of scholarly and public dialogue on the interrelation of art and religion. In our symposia we set out to explore basic questions about the field, such as these: Has our discourse about religion, and in particular religious art, changed in recent years (or even historically)? How do we conduct this discourse in classrooms and museums today? What are the limitations of the current approaches? Finally, how do we see the future: how would we like, in an ideal world, to see the relationship between art and religion being explored, exhibited, and taught? What changes in research and teaching, what new partnerships and collaborations, what new tools would be necessary or useful? As we delved into these questions, a need for a written assessment of the state of the field and the current methodologies employed by scholars, museum professionals, and educators working in different disciplines became evident.

Reluctant Partners was devised to fill that need. All the essays included in the section *Art and Religion: Facets of Dialogue* are derived from presentations given at the symposia. Each of them illustrates a different method of connecting art and religion. Robert Nelson discusses the historical course of academic discourse on the relationships—including indifference, antagonism, and conflict—of art, architecture, and art history with religion, starting in the mid-nineteenth century. My essay tracks the evolution of the dialogue proposed by museums, pointing to recent developments that indicate a new interest in exploring the religious in art. Vivian Mann proposes a revision of the common yet misguided belief that, in accordance with the Second Commandment, there is no Jewish art. Doug Adams offers a good example of borrowing other disciplines' methods to expand and refine our understanding of religious art, applying the literary-and-biblical-studies method of intertextuality to an analysis of Rembrandt's "The Return of the Prodigal Son." Marcus Burke also addresses other fields of study by looking at issues surrounding religion and the arts from a theological perspective.

Together these essays show that the tone of the discourse, and the specific research methods employed, vary according to a number of factors. Primary among them is the intended audience. An art history lecture given at a secular university will have a different approach from one intended for students at a theological seminary. Presenting sacred art to a museum audience requires a different emphasis than discussing it with a religious congregation. Yet different groups can and should learn from each other. The disciplines of theology, art history, and museology put their distinctive stamp on these studies; read together, they illustrate the variety of possible roads to take when investigating the religion in art, or the artistic components of religion.

The two essays in the section *Art and Religion: The State of the Field,* by David

Morgan and S. Brent Plate, were commissioned specifically for this volume. They respond to the need, expressed by students and scholars alike, for a systematic historiography, and for a vision of the future of the field. These essays act as bookends to the others by creating a larger context for art and religion as a field of study at this particular time. Or, to be more exact, they try to answer the question, posed by Morgan, of whether "there is, in fact, a history of art and religion *as a field of study.*" Morgan's study answers that question with a nuanced yes, and traces its first systematic historiography, accompanied by comprehensive bibliographic notes. Plate's essay turns to the future by outlining a number of theories and themes currently at the forefront of religion-and-the-arts scholarship. While these themes propose possible future directions of inquiry, we hope that they can also be considered a starting point for a discussion about other, equally possible, avenues of investigation.

 Reluctant Partners was conceived primarily as a tool to be used in the classroom, and I am happy to report that this past year it was one of four textbooks for the required first-year course on Art and Religion at Graduate Theological Union in Berkeley. We hope that the combination of theoretical essays and test-cases offers a useful framework for students and scholars alike. At the same time, we hope that the volume may act as a springboard for further research. By sketching the historiography and the current landscape of our discourse on art and religion this effort may offer a starting point for a more engaged dialogue between scholars of different disciplines, who represent different types of institutions. Ultimately it may contribute to the coalescing of an integrated community of scholars, practitioners, students, and an interested general public.

 As Sally Promey has aptly noted, our field continues to be characterized by a "historical absence of interdisciplinary collaboration

between those invested in the academic study of art and religion—and especially the disinclination of art historians to come to scholarly terms with religion."[1] We hope that *Reluctant Partners,* by bringing together the descriptive approach of historians and the prescriptive method of theologians, has laid the foundations for creative, constructive dialogue in the future.

 Ena Giurescu Heller
 Executive Director, Museum of Biblical Art
 Friend of the Institute

ENDNOTES

1. See Sally M. Promey, "The Visual Culture of American Religions: An Historiographical Essay," in *Exhibiting the Visual Culture of American Religions,* ed. David Morgan and Sally M. Promey (Valparaiso, Ind.: Brauer Museum of Art, 2000), 5.

City, Temple, Stage: Eschatological Architecture and Liturgical Theatrics in New Spain, by Jaime Lara (Notre Dame, Ind.: University of Notre Dame Press, 2004).

The thought of "reviewing" my own book makes me uneasy. After all, how objective can I be with something that cost me nine years of my life in research and writing? After the gestation period and the subsequent birth, I have to admit that I like the offspring that I have produced.

Back in the 1980s, while traveling throughout Latin America, and particularly Mexico, I started to notice buildings, religious rituals, and Spanish words that reminded me of what I had learned in my medieval studies. I began to understand that sixteenth-century Mexico was really a continuation of the Middle Ages on this side of the Atlantic Ocean, and that in order to understand the Hispanic experience I had to apply a sort of medieval template; then I could see that experience through the medieval lens that formed what we call New Spain (present-day Mexico).

The book is a direct outcome of those interests and experiences. In addition, I realized that the book of Revelation (the Apocalypse), and millennial thinking, was a large part of the mind-set of the missionaries. The mendicant friars (Franciscans, Dominicans, Augustinians) who evangelized the New World a century before the arrival of the first Puritans were anticipating a proximate end of the world and/or a golden age of religious renewal and reform prior to the return of Christ for the last judgment. Political historians of America have almost totally overlooked this crucial aspect of the "conquest" and Christianization.

As an art/architecture historian and a student of liturgics, I wanted to see if I could demonstrate and "prove" my thesis by visual and ritual evidence. Little if anything was written in this vein, and I soon found myself mulling over the original diaries and chronicles, and sleuthing the dusty shelves of colonial libraries in Mexico. Insights started to jump out, and I think that my three hundred and twenty photos, and the text, make the point that more was going on in the New World than words like "conquest," "domination," and "political hegemony" allow. I think that I have also helped to uncover some of the creative energy that appeared as native Americans accepted and adapted Christianity to an Aztec worldview.

For the book I chose to unpack three paradigms or architectural metaphors: the city, the temple, and the theatrical stage. Each was actually built in stone and mortar; each had both Aztec and European precedents; and each was used in religious, ritual, and eschatological ways. In the introduction I laid out my method in the light of cultural anthropology and church history, addressing issues like millennial expectations, the Lost Tribes of Israel, and church reform at the middle of the second millennium. In chapter one I described the architecture of conversion, the so-called "fortress monasteries" or evangelization centers that were created all across Mexico. In the second chapter I looked at how the book of Revelation was envisioned throughout the Middle Ages, and how that vision passed to the Americas. Then I considered the city of Jerusalem—the real and ideal Jerusalem—as a model for utopian city planning. I returned to look at iconographic details of the conversion centers, especially the huge stone crosses, as proof of a medieval and eschatological mentality, and then turned my attention to the Christian rituals that were performed in these architectural substitutes for the Aztec pyramid-temples. Finally, I wanted to demonstrate how many of these same rituals and worldviews were ingeniously incorporated into a truly inculturated Christianity and Christian liturgy, and how they continue until today.

The University of Notre Dame Press did
a wonderful job with the photos and layout, on
high quality paper — so much so that the book
has been nominated for a graphic arts award.
Whether or not the text and the author's theories
deserve the same praise is for the reader to
decide.

I have finished a second and related book
which deals with the Christian worship of the
first converts, and their sacramental practice.
*Christian Texts for Aztecs: The Liturgical Conquest
of Mexico* will appear next year, with translations
from the first Latin ritual books brought to the
Americans, and from the Nahuatl (the ancient
Aztec language) bibles, breviaries, psalm books,
hymns, etc., created for and by the neophytes. It
will of course have images, about one hundred
in color, that I hope will demonstrate that the
sixteenth-century in the New World was a time
of tremendous creativity and enthusiasm. In
many ways it was the meeting of the best of both
worlds, Old and New.

[And all this happens as the ISM is
planning a tour of Mexico in May 2006....]

> *Jaime Lara*
> *Associate Professor of Christian Art and
> Architecture*
> *Chair of the Program in Religion and
> the Arts*

Beyond Ritual: Sacramental Theology after Habermas by Siobhán Garrigan (Abingdon: Ashgate, 2004).

Several goals spurred me to write Beyond Ritual. The main one was personal: I wanted to begin to articulate something about God, or more precisely, our relationship with God, that has been emerging in my studies, in my prayer, in meals around tables, in relationships, in life's very fabric over many years. It needs fleshing-out beyond this book's scope, or my present wisdom-level, allow, but the book is a first attempt to say: God is more radically intersubjective than we have previously imagined.

My second goal was an academic one: I wanted to add a little to the literatures of feminist and practical theology, the disciplines that formed me. I wanted to say: we need to stretch to claim as theological voices and situations that have long been ignored, and stretch to talk about them in ways that, crucially, let them stay true in interpretation. I was, in short, impatient with academic cap-doffing to "marginalized" contexts, offended by gestures that tended to either pedestalize or patronize poor and excluded peoples, and challenged by my own communities of accountability to say something that would make sense to them.

The third goal was a methodological one. I wanted to find ways for scholars to access what happens, theologically, when people get together. My work focuses on Christian worship, and is based on the wager that if you want to see people negotiating their theology in its primary form, look at what they do when they gather for liturgy. The problem facing contemporary liturgical studies is that we realize we have to take account of the actual experience of the liturgy and not just its rubrics if we are to interpret worship theologically, but as yet we have far less rigor in our interpretation of experience, far fewer methods at our disposal, than we do in our interpretation of texts. What we end up with is subjective-posing-as-normative theology, which tends to be rather reductive.

To put it another way, the problem I face as a liturgical theologian is how do I, the scholar, hear, see, or otherwise know what people's self-understanding is of the things they do in liturgy? To know about the forms of Christian liturgy I can study its historical texts; to know about the doctrine that both informs and derives from Christian worship, I can study both polity and teaching; but what am I do to in order to know what another person or a community in situ understands of God in the work of ritualizing?

I don't pretend my book solves this problem. But it does raise the question in a clear way (it starts with a comprehensive assessment of liturgical studies' recent forays into Ritual Studies/Theory) and -- and this is the bit I like most about it -- it tries to dig a new interpretative avenue. To do so, I take Jürgen Habermas's theory of communicative action and adapt it for theological ends (Habermas is an atheist – his theory was construed for the law and politics). I try to explain all my moves in ways that make Habermas understandable to a philosophically lay readership, and I admit the things Habermas cannot help us to do as well as the things he can.

I was tempted to stop there, having named the problem, adapted the model, and given serious theological treatment to Habermas's work (mine is, I think, the first theological monograph to engage Habermas). But I was very curious to actually do now what I was suggesting others do eventually, that is, to look at a community's worship through a Habermasian lens and note the theologies that emerge.

To do this I undertook a two-year-long study of six congregations' worship. The results are given in chapter 4, which analyses what I witnessed in a "mainstream" Irish Roman Catholic parish's worship, and chapter 5, which interprets the theologies of five "marginal" communities' worship. These five case studies are composed of a group of gay people who have gathered for worship and fellowship for twenty-five years in Dublin; a geographically isolated, Irish-speaking church in County Galway; a Protestant church in a 98% Catholic neighbourhood in Ireland; and an ecumenical and a feminist worship group, and which I traveled to the USA because, although there are such groups in Ireland, they are yet not secure enough (politically or communally) to be written-up and published about.

My method requires the recording and analysis of what is said. It is extremely limited, therefore, because most communication is non-verbal. Nonetheless, it is a step further than we have previously gone, because it attempts to uncover the shared understanding that exists (or doesn't) between the speakers and hearers in a conversation as they themselves know it.

It is probably worth giving a very brief synopsis of the theory at this point.

Habermas proposes that when we speak we raise "validity claims," meaning that when we say something we include little signals to persuade the person who is listening to us that what we are saying should be believed. Once we have done this we can examine the "conditions of possible understanding" that are latent in the exchange, upon which, indeed, the exchange depends. Generally speaking, there are three sorts of validity claims: claims to the truth of what we are saying, to the rightness of our saying it in this context, and to our own trustworthiness; while all are present in all interactions, only one is usually being explicitly aired. It sounds simple: I speak, I assure you that what I am saying is valid, you hear, we understand one another. But it is not so simple;

indeed there are potential problems every step of the way. I may not have the right to speak (or I may be to inhibited to speak), what I am saying may not be appropriate to this context, I may not know to what I need to appeal in order to persuade you of my trustworthiness (or I may not be trustworthy), you may not hear me, we might be engaged in a complex web of manipulation or coercion which renders "understanding" null and void.

When a speaker raises a validity claim, the hearer has the right to ask questions and expect answers; without this, there can be no process of coming to mutual understanding. Most interactions proceed this way (e.g., I don't like cottage cheese. Why not? Because it makes me sick. Do you mean to look at it? No, I mean that when I eat it I vomit), but only if both parties have an equal and unrestrained opportunity to talk. The example I give is mundane, but you can easily imagine that at the level of law and politics, whether or not speakers and hearers have uncurtailed opportunity to query and respond until understanding is reached, is far from a given. Situations in which the speaker does not have the right to speak fully, or the hearer to query, are easy to spot in situations that we identify as tyrannies, but they arise in subtler forms too — just think of the potential restrictions on understanding between a Hispanic working-class woman standing before a mostly white, mostly male, mostly middle class jury.

One of the things *Beyond Ritual* raises is how Christian liturgies are prey to the dangers of such "distorted communication." By looking not at what is scripted but what is actually said, my case studies reveal how many subtle, but significant, power-plays are operational in the local context, which might either enable or limit the conditions of possible understanding. The simplest example was, perhaps, the church in which when the priest said, "The Lord be with you," the people did not say, "And also with you." The most extreme example was, perhaps, the church in which the assembly left the building while the priest was speaking. But most examples of distorted communication (just like most examples of its opposite, communicative action) came in more subtle forms and had several potential interpretations. It is these interpretations which, I suggest, are of enormous value to theology because they reveal the conditions of possible understanding of God that a community knows within its relationships and other symbols.

The closest theological category I know for such a notion is "sacramentality." The whole book I have cast as an attempt to construct a contemporary sacramental theology. Throughout the book you can hear an ongoing conversation with Louis Marie Chauvet, whose work on symbolism and the body is, I think, going to keep us theologians in conversation for many years to come. Where Habermas's theory allowed me to make explicit self-understandings that would otherwise be implicit, Chauvet's

theological categories allowed me ways of interpreting them within the Christian sacramental tradition. Sacramentality remains, I suggest, a profoundly articulate theological concept as long as we enhance our notion of the intersubjective nature of its emergence in our lives as well as the radically intersubjective nature of the God it mediates. Such notions require the elimination of all forms of domination and oppression, even those that are made apparent in the smallest liturgical gestures, like not saying "and also with you," or something like it, when offered the peace.

Note: My book is horribly expensive. Please encourage your library to buy it: if enough libraries buy it, the publisher will issue a paperback edition and the people whose voices the book records will be able to actually buy it!

Siobhán Garrigan
Assistant Professor of Liturgical Studies
Assistant Dean for Chapel

Psalms in Community: Jewish and Christian Textual, Liturgical, and Artistic Traditions, edited by Harold W. Attridge and Margot E. Fassler (Leiden: Brill; Atlanta: Society for Biblical Literature, 2004)

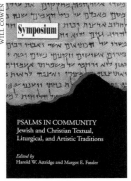

As part of its mission the Yale Institute of Sacred Music supports many publications, recordings, and films written and created by its faculty; this faculty, in turn, commonly carries out its work in partnership with colleagues outside the walls of the Institute, at Yale and beyond. *Psalms in Community* is a work created in this collaborative spirit: the book grew out of a conference hosted by the ISM along with other Yale schools and departments, but physically located in synagogues and churches in New Haven and its environs as well. A team of scholars and practitioners planned the conference and brought the lectures and performances to hundreds of people, always intending to reach out to many more through a later publication. The book, written about a variety of communities, was produced by communities, both of learning and of faith.

In addition a film, *Joyful Noise*, the second in a series concerning the nature and styles of Psalm singing found in Christian, Jewish, and Muslim communities, will appear this fall. It joins *Work and Pray*, a DVD about the Psalms as lived with the nuns of Regina Laudis, Bethlehem, Connecticut. Much of *Joyful Noise* was shot on location during the conference, and so relates directly to the many subjects treated in the book. The scholars, performers, choirs, and congregations involved in the book and the film have prepared a feast of psalmody, inviting teachers and students, classrooms and congregations, to learn more about this great subject: the Psalms. In the future other films will appear until we have a full witness to contemporary practices of sacred song, one that will complement the historical and textual studies of the book. The conference, book, and films are supported by a grant from the Lilly Endowment, Inc.

The Psalms are the great touchstone for the People of the Book. As lived texts they breathe in as many translations as there are liturgical languages, and so the Hebrew Psalms, the song book of Second Temple Judaism, have shaped practice as practice reshapes them. The masterful opening essays of the book are a study in contrast, and establish tensions sparking the entire conversation. Robert Taft's essay documents various erosions of Christian Psalm singing in the late antique Christian world, pointing to how the texts were overwhelmed in practice by later additions and the loss of congregational proclamation, which he deems essential to using the texts as vehicles for communal prayer. Larry Hoffman finds the psalms to be the exegetical glue that grounds the dialogue between the people, their worship leaders, and God. He, like Robert Taft, longs for communal appreciation and understanding of the process and its innate power to sustain us in a frightening and uncertain world: "with ears now deadened to textual intricacies, we moderns no longer hear the psalms as our ancestors did. They are still there…we rarely notice them…"

The following sections of the book respond to these initial pleas for better understanding and a resurgence of attention to practice centered on the psalms. Esther Menn offers a portrait of David and the tradition of his prophetic authorship as developed in Second Temple Judaism. In his "Amazing Grace" John Collins explores the Thanksgiving Psalms of the Dead Sea Scrolls, finding them to be new compositions based on the Psalms but most likely intended for personal devotion. Patrick Miller proposes a theological framework for the canonic Psalter, and then shows how reading and praying it establishes an individual and communal doxology. Scholars who work with the Christian New Testament expand upon these ideas. Harold Attridge begins with Esther Menn's suggestion that the Psalms are the most cited portion of the Old Testament in the New, explains why this is so, and what this tells us about the worship lives of early Christians. Adela Collins then lays out an early Christology based upon the psalms and Christian use of them in practice and in thought. Diana Swancutt looks at a specific group of texts, those that invoke God as "Rock," and transports us to the world of St. Paul and the liturgical practice of psalm singing.

Essays on the way the psalms shaped both practice and theological thinking in the late antique period follow. Peter Jeffery relates how Philo's description of the worship of a first-century Jewish community, the Therapeutai, was later taken as a description of a Christian group, and so determined the nature of Christian practice in its turn. Brian Daley looks at the daily bread of Psalm singing in early Christian thought, exploring "God's music," and how it was their "sweetness" that enabled these sung texts to transform people. Bryan Spinks offers a note on the use of the Psalter of the Syriac Bible in evening prayer where it forms "the heart in pilgrimage."

From the centuries of the formation of these texts and their use by ancient peoples and communities the book takes the reader on a journey through later Christian communities. Here the editors lament that some Jewish scholars contacted to speak and write for the book were unable to be present because of illness. If they had this would not be a Christian section; medieval and early modern Judaism carried on an intense encounter with the Psalms, one we wish were studied here. My own paper on the centrality of the Psalms in Christian monastic practice puts one of its greatest practitioners, Hildegard of Bingen, back in the context of Benedictine prayer. Walter Cahn,

in a paper that forms a visual counterpart to that by Brian Daley, explores the illuminations in medieval Psalter commentaries as part of a broader pedagogical agenda. This same pedagogical theme resonates in the paper of Jaime Lara with its intriguing title "Feathered Psalms." With striking visuals Lara demonstrates the ways in which the texts were brought to sixteenth-century Mexico, forcing an encounter between Old World and New, and Christian and indigenous liturgical understanding. Two papers explore various aspects of the Psalms as used for worship in Calvinist communities in Geneva. Serene Jones speaks of the reenactment of the Psalms as they become essential tools for dealing with problems of violence and chaotic displacement. Carlos Eire looks at the ways in which the ungodly are shunned in the Psalm texts and treated by worshipping communities as justification for a new "chosen" people, the Genevans, who saw themselves as the spiritual children of an ancient covenant.

The final sections of the book include case studies of contemporary practices. These are so varied that it seems best to turn to living examples of textual arts made by individuals in and for communities. Gilbert Bond describes the psalmody of an African American church in Atlanta and roots its practice in earlier traditions. Mark Kligman, an ethnomusicologist, explores the traditions of Sabbath prayer among Syrian Jews in Brooklyn, noting various styles of singing and the musical prominence of the Psalms. Alexander Lingas outlines the place of psalm singing in Byzantine liturgical traditions, and then turns to various attempts at renewal in modern practice. Richard Clifford speaks of the ways Roman Catholics have wrestled with their Psalm texts for worship, advocating a look at "register," and noting the challenge of translating a liturgical language in which male metaphors for God abound. Elliot Stevens addresses translations by looking to midrashic commentary as a way of adding new understanding yet remaining faithful to tradition. Gordon Lathrop says that the language of the Psalms in worship matters so much because of the meaning of assembly: "there is no rank here, no gender preference, no inside track." He lays out the rules followed by those who translated the psalter for the *Book of Common Prayer*. Peter Hawkins reveals through carefully chosen texts the great influence of the psalms on contemporary poetry, setting modern-day authors on the shoulders of great English poets, and closing with the beautiful and poignant "I (Handiwork/Glory)" by Jacqueline Osherow, who writes as a Jew whose gifts have not been silenced by the horrors of Auschwitz. She makes a new Psalm 150 for this age. Two preachers,

Rabbi Margaret Moers Wenig and Rev. Ellen Davis, end the collection offering commentaries on the Psalms for congregations of their own traditions.

"Taste and see," the Psalmist says. This book invites, challenges, demonstrates, and persuades, broaching a myriad of themes surrounding the one hundred fifty texts of the Psalms. The point is their centrality to both Jewish and Christian traditions. Here we see not only why this has been so, but engage with the reasons for continuing it.

Margot E. Fassler
Tangeman Professor of Music and Liturgy

Student Presentations

2003–2004 Student Presenters

MASTER OF DIVINITY
Grace Burson
Nunzio D'Alessio
Mary Jane Donohue
Jane Huber
Caleb Maskell
Andrea Olsen
B. J. Owens
Sidney Symington

MASTER OF ARTS & RELIGION
Audrey Lin
Melanie Ross

MASTER OF SACRED THEOLOGY
Philip Corbett
Carol Wade

MASTER OF MUSIC IN CHORAL CONDUCTING
Joseph Gregorio
Christopher Hossfeld
Evan Wels

MASTER OF MUSICAL ARTS IN
CHORAL CONDUCTING
Richard Gard
Charles Kamm

MASTER OF MUSIC IN ORGAN
Kyle Babin
Daniel Hahn
Christopher Jennings
Iain Quinn
Jason Roberts
Daniel Sullivan

MASTER OF MUSICAL ARTS IN ORGAN
Paul Weber

ISM Colloquium Presentation Abstracts
Spring 2004

Kyle Babin
The Organist as Liturgist in Post-Reformation Germany

In my presentation I examined the various roles of the Lutheran church organist in Post-Reformation Germany. Some of these roles included accompanying congregational singing of chorales, improvising and performing pieces based on those chorales, and performing in alternatim with the congregation. I presented a brief performance of this type of alternatim practice by improvising short organ versets between sung verses of the Magnificat in Mode V. I posited the idea that by molding and shaping a musical idea (like the chorale) that was deeply impressed on the minds and hearts of Post-Reformation Lutheran worshippers, the Lutheran organist acted as a liturgist. Through his improvisations, he was able to react to specific and spontaneous aspects of the liturgy. In essence, he became a musical preacher.

Questions:
1. How can the organist today, as in the 16th and 17th centuries, react through improvisation to a particular liturgy? Give an example.
2. What expectations and skills were required of Post-Reformation Lutheran church organists when applying for church positions?
3. How would you like to see these principles applied to church musicians in their roles in worship today?

Grace Pritchard Burson
Furry Dances and Wassailing Trees: The Survival of the English Ritual Year

The traditional English agricultural ritual year is a legitimate cultural expression, worthy of being revived, especially in rural and Anglican churches. It consists of a cycle of celebrations tied to the natural and liturgical years, many of which involve dressing up, song and dance, food and drink, begging from house to house, bonfires, and blessings of crops and animals. These traditions have been preserved or revived in many places. They can be fun and meaningful traditions in the parish if done with respect for their integrity.

Three Questions:
1. What does this set of traditions have to do with the Anglican liturgical tradition or the English choral tradition?
2. Can you say a little more about the Mummers' Play and the other traditions involving dressing up and playing parts? Can these be described as "liturgical drama"?
3. Can you explain what you mean about the way these celebrations work as far as involving both children and adults and creating parish tradition?

Philip Corbett
Benediction of the Blessed Sacrament: A Devotion for the Modern World

In my presentation I discussed the origins of the service of Benediction as well as its use within the Anglican Church. I described the structure of the service and played some of the music that might be used. I was keen to show how the service might be used in the life of a parish. I tried to illustrate how it might be used following Evensong or as a Station of the Resurrection, a 15th Station of the Cross. It is my hope that the service might be used as a time of silent focused prayer for a worshipping community, perhaps focusing on a particular issue (in some churches for example long periods of sacramental exposition occur with Pro-Life issues in mind).

I was keen to point out that the service is one of equality: all are equal before the sacrament.

1. Might there be different designs for the monstrance, perhaps relating to the modern world and modern liturgy?
2. What scope is there for musical diversity or improviation in the service? Is it possible to use music from around the world in the service or must there always be Gregorian Chant?
3. Can the service relate to many churches' desire for outreach in the community and to deal with issues of social justice?

Nunzio D'Alessio
Old World Forms, New World Content: Puebla, Padilla, and the Prophet

To most people who have ever traveled there Mexico is a cultural backwater, its music nothing more than Mariachi umpah bands, and its food all too spicy. Scholarship has followed this popular trope by setting apart Latin America from the rest of the New World, judging its history as "other" or inferior. Mainstream musicology has concurred, seeing in New Spain no Josquin, no Bach, no Mozart. While some scholars have been challenging this received paradigm, their efforts have been directed at either the "spiritual conquest" of the 16th century or the beginning modernity of the 18th. The long established view is that the 17th century is the "colonial siesta," the "silver age," and the "century of depression." By this time Roman Catholicism is firmly established on all levels of society in New Spain, and the land is riddled with seminary colleges, cathedrals, and religious houses. In short, it is said to be a time of consolidation rather than innovation. In this paper I seek to challenge this opinion by focusing on the work of the "distinguished maestro," singer, priest, and instrument maker at Puebla Cathedral, Juan Gutierrez de Padilla (c. 1590–1664). Drawing on recent reorientations

within the field, I emphasize the social, economic, religious, and political matrices in which a musical culture might flourish. I address four topics: the baroque backdrop of New Spain, the urban context of Puebla, an introduction to Padilla's life and work, and finally his *Lamentatio Ieremiae Prophetae* for Holy Thursday. My conclusion is that far from merely exploiting the "conventional wisdom" of peninsular composers, the sacred music of Padilla is an example of *mestizaje*, the mixing of two elements in such a way that something new is created. To include a chapelmaster like Padilla in our music histories and performance halls means to subject the writing of music history to interrogation, and calls for an expansion of the canon to include Western music. In that process we come to see — and hopefully hear — how shared musical practices transmit social knowledge and identity. Old forms, yes; but what magnificent new content!

Mary Jane Donohue
Practical Implications of the Life of the Collective Unconscious in Entrance and Initiation Rites

According to psychoanalysts at the Tavistock and Grubb Institutes in London, much of the irrational and apparently chaotic behavior we see in groups can be viewed as springing from basic assumptions common to all their members. Wilfred Bion (1897-1979) distinguished three sets of unconscious group assumptions that give rise to distinct constellations of feelings, thoughts and behavior: basic assumption dependency, basic assumption fight-flight, and basic assumption pairing.

It is a street-level truism that in most local congregations roughly 80% of the work is done by 10% of a church's membership. I suspect that one of the reasons for the persistence of this phenomenon is a proliferation of anti-task behavior which can be conceptualized in Bion's Basic Assumption models. It is my contention that understanding these defenses and how to address them liturgically might help us to promote healthier, integrated group functioning.

In my address I asked the question, what happens at the front door, at the literal entrances to our weekly celebrations and the ritual entrances to our communities, that may be perpetuating Bion's non-work group states in our churches? I offered a number of liturgical examples from more contemporary Anglican texts (New Zealand Prayer Book, England's Common Worship) that offer clues for American textual reform, and suggested some localized non-textual ritual actions that might work against these unconscious group forces.

1. Are there ways that the patterns of the collective unconscious could be (and are) mobilized in positive contribution to our primary communal tasks, however defined?
2. What practical, extra-liturgical suggestions do I have for helping a community define its primary task: to aid in resisting unconscious anti-task functioning?
3. Why have the insights of the Tavistock and Grubb Clinics been embraced by certain parts of the Anglican Communion (England, New Zealand, Australia) and not others? Why has this way of thinking about group/church life not resonated with American ecclesiology?

Richard Gard
Dance Topics in the Chorale Cantatas of J.S. Bach

During the years 1723 and 24 Bach experimented with a compositional technique using a noble dance (usually the sarabande) in the penultimate movement of some chorale cantatas. The technique was refined during his second Leipzig cycle, and Bach continued to use it as long as he composed chorale cantatas. The technique is connected with images of heaven, Advent, and Jesus as the bridegroom.

Joseph Gregorio
Lasso's Lamentations for the Bavarian Court

[abstract not available]

Daniel Hahn
"Dear Christians, one and all, rejoice": The Chorale Fantasias of Dietrich Buxtehude

Dietrich Buxtehude's *Nun freut euch lieben Christen g'mein*, BuxWV 210, is one of the prime examples of the chorale fantasia genre. This form represented the highest quality of organ playing in 17th century Germany and was inextricably linked to the philosophies of rhetoric of the day. Rhetorical procedures are found particularly in the use of figures corresponding to rhetorical formulas, and forms corresponding to the scheme of speeches. The genre also appealed to non-musicians, functioning as a type of organ sermon in which the organist was free to interpret at length the text and music of a chorale.

1. How popular was the chorale fantasia genre, and from which other composers do examples survive?
2. What role does registration play in the interpretation of the chorale fantasias?
3. What are the modern uses of the chorale fantasia genre?

Jane Huber
Rereading Sacred Texts

Rereading Sacred Texts was a short film created for use as a teaching tool for adult education in the church. The film documented the rehearsal of music transcribed from the Feast of the Assumption as found in a 12th century breviary with focus on: the process of rehearsal; the architectural space in which the music was rehearsed; comments from observers; and the visual contrast of sacred to secular space. In its focus on music from a particular historical period, the film was intended to provide a context for the broader discussion of contemporary understandings of the liturgy by different members of the Riverside Church, an interfaith community located in New York City. Through the documentation of elements of a particular liturgical event, the focus of the film on re-reading sacred texts was also intended to provoke conversation about the relationship between individually held theological convictions and their corresponding liturgical practice.

Further questions:
1. What production/direction considerations determined the making of the film?
2. Did rehearsal of the music affect the written transcription?
3. The film was made to provoke response from an inter-faith, multi-cultural audience, but was presented to an academic, interdisciplinary audience (also inter-faith, multi-cultural); were the "audiences" given adequate consideration?

Christopher Hossfeld
Benjamin Britten's Curlew River

The presentation explored the opera, its origins, and the themes that permeate it. Of particular interest was the combination of Asian and medieval English influences masterfully acheived by Britten in this adaptation of a Japanes Noh play. A more in-depth look at the music revealed the chant melodies interwoven in the musical texture.

Questions:
1. Could you please comment on why Britten chose to have men play all the roles in Curlew River?
2. How did you deal with this particular gender issue in your production of Curlew?
3. How did Britten's homosexuality affect his interpretation of *Sumidagawa*, the Japanese play on which Curlew River is based?

Christopher Jennings
Ora Labora: The Unique Heritage of the Anglican Choral Tradition and its Calling in the 21st Century Church

This presentation discusses the history of the Anglican Choral tradition, and, most notably the role of children in the choirs of the great cathedrals of England, and now in parish churches in America as well. It presents ideas for founding a chorister program as well as the benefits of doing so. The most important benefits of these programs for parishes is the way in which they draw children to the church—children become a proactive part of the parish as they make a vital contribution to the liturgy in the lifting up of their voices in song. By the end of their time as choristers they become professional musicians, but not without rigorous training and discipline. This is not to say that chorister programs cannot and are not fun, rather the opposite is true. When working with children, one always has to think on one's feet and one is always surprised at the ways in which children enrich the lives of those around them through their own gifts as members of the household of God. They are not the "future" of the church, but a vital part of the church TODAY, and when they are given the tools with which to work, they will do amazing things.

As a follow-up to this presentation, I am currently just beginning a new full-time job as organist and choirmaster at St. James's Episcopal Church, West Hartford, Connecticut, where I have been hired to rejuvenate the chorister program. The parish has amazing potential for a successful chorister program but lacks focus, energy, and drive, and so I have been called there to put my study into action!

1. Why do we need children as part of the liturgy?
2. What are some ways of recruiting?
3. What are the physical differences of the boys' and girls' vocal cords and what are the benefits of having them sing separately?

Charles Kamm

Where East Meets West: Two Sacred Works from the Baltics— Arvo Pärt's Berliner Messe *and Einojuhoni Rautavaara's* Vigilia

The incorporation of musical elements and artistic ideals of Eastern Orthodoxy, specifically from Russia, are considered in sacred choral works from the northern boundaries of Eastern and Western Christianity. Brief biographies of Arvo Pärt and Einojuhani Rautavaara highlight their personal intersections with Orthodoxy. Recorded examples of Byzantine chant and Russian bell-ringing, as well as images of Orthodox icons, illuminate the compositional goals and musical structures in Pärt's *Berliner Messe* and Einojuhani Rautavaara's *Vigilia*.

Questions

1. How do the trends discussed affect the total output of each composer?
2. Is this music used liturgically? If so, in what tradition?
3. Does the Lutheran music of that corner of Europe influence music in Russia?

Audrey Lin & Caleb Maskell

(Extra)ordinary: The Worship Life of the Hyde Park Vineyard Church

The presentation given by Audrey Lin and Caleb Maskell was a multimedia attempt at constructing a liturgical theology of the Hyde Park Vineyard Church in Chicago, Illinois. The presentation showed film footage of formal elements of the service space and of the service itself, as well as extensive interviews with members of the congregation. With all of this, we attempted to show the tight connections between the worship life of the HPVC and the Christian self-understanding of the church members. The service is, in the aspect which we highlighted, a reflection of the "ordinary" of life outside the walls of the church meeting. People come to the Vineyard just as they would come to school, or to a meeting with friends. Inside

this constructed "ordinary" the Vineyard seeks, in each aspect of its service, to embody, teach, and celebrate the manner in which ordinary life is rendered extraordinary by the Gospel of Jesus Christ.

1. How do leaders of the musical worship prepare to lead, and can you tell as more about what are they trying to do as they are leading the worship?
2. How is the prayer ministry team recruited and trained, and what kind of expectations do they and the people who come forward for prayer have during the prayer ministry time?
3. What significant impact did your time at the church have on your lives?
4. What are the psychological and/or theological implications of the absence of concrete liturgical formulae? Are you gnostics?

Andrea Olsen

Marriage, Sacrament, and Identity in Byzantium: A Case Study

In my presentation for the ISM Colloquium I addressed three issues regarding Byzantine marriage jewelry and its relationship to the liturgy. First, I pointed out the transitional nature of jewelry dated to the third through the fifth centuries, which indicates a Christianization of Roman customs such as the *dextrarum iunctio* ("joining of right hands," as for a pledge or contract). Second, I drew attention to the correspondence between the iconography of the jewelry and the Christian marriage liturgy, highlighting the importance of the crowning ritual in Byzantine marriage ceremonies. And third, I proposed an iconographic connection between a group of rings bearing scenes from the life of Christ and the Syrian Orthodox marriage rite.

B. J. Owens

*"We may not keep silent…": The Barmen
Declaration and the Rhetoric of the Confessing
Church*

"The old has passed away. The new has emerged.
The church's political struggle is past. Now
begins the struggle for the soul of the people."[1]
Reich Bishop Ludwig Muller, July 1933

In the years leading up to the Second
World War, many thousands of German
Protestant Clergy and lay church leaders – at
times constituting a majority of Protestant
leadership – sought to synthesize National
Socialist ideology with Christian theology.
Those leaders called themselves the "German
Christians." In May of 1934, Protestant
opponents gathered in Barmen to respond to the
German Christians, whose influence had become
widespread and catastrophic. The crisis was
deeply theological and profoundly rhetorical: the
conveners and leaders of the Barmen Synod –
among them Karl Barth, Martin Niemoller,
and Dietrich Bonhoeffer – gathered to respond
confessionally to what the church in Germany
had become. The result was the Theological
Declaration of Barmen, a theological and
exegetical response to a specific rhetorical
situation.

This paper will first clarify what is meant
by speaking of the Barmen Synod as a rhetorical
situation. This is not to say that it was a moment
for speech and not action, or to suggest that such
speech is vacuous. Rather, to study rhetoric is to
study the relationship of language and action, it
is to study how persuasion is crafted to the level
of art, and it is to study how speech demands
reaction and response.

The task at hand is first to study carefully
the theological rhetoric of the German
Christians in order to understand what about
it was so compelling to so many thousands
of Christian leaders at that time, and second,
to study the conditions and arguments of the
response by the Confessing Church in order
to gain insight into discourse that is both

theological and rhetorical. To that end this paper
will first give a brief historical background of the
German Christians, followed by a study of the
theological foundations of the German Christian
movement. Finally, it will look carefully at the
confessional response to see what conclusions
can be drawn.

The Barmen Synod responded that given
its current loyalties "the Church ceases to be the
Church and the German Evangelical Church, as
a federation of Confessional Churches, becomes
intrinsically impossible…We may not keep
silent"(italics added).[2] Barmen was crafted as
an exegetical response to a crisis of catastrophic
isogesis: the church had become "intrinsically
impossible" because it no longer sought to
build a communal foundation upon revelation.
Rather, the German Christian "church" tailored
revelation to the foundation they had devised.

Barmen's response was, ultimately, an
exercise in what Thomas B. Farrell calls "the
rhetoric of critical interruption," in which a
cultural and national reappraisal could take
place on both civic and ecclesiological terms.[3]
Specifically, the interruption called attention
to the nominally "Christian" foundations upon
which the Nazi state was built.

In consideration for Barth, however,
who did not hold the principle of "rhetoric as
revelation" in high regard, and who helped to
craft Barmen not as a definition of "us" or even
"them," but instead as a definition of who God
is, this paper will finally consider Barmen not
only as an example of the rhetoric of critical
interruption, but as a homiletic of critical
interruption as well.

ENDNOTES

1. Ulrich Mauser, "The Theological Declaration
of Barmen Revisited." *Theology Matters* 6 (2002),
4.

2. *The Theological Declaration of Barmen*, 8.07,
8.08

3. Thomas B. Farrell, *Norms of Rhetorical Culture.*
New Haven, London: Yale University Press, 1993.
p.258

Three questions I would like to have been asked:

1. What can an evaluation of a rhetoric/ homiletic of critical interruption teach us about discourse and controversy among faithful person and groups?
2. In what ways is rhetorical culture made manifest in church bodies and parishes? How are we as ministers, musicians, and theologians called to shape, guide, and participate in that discourse?
3. The immediate "result" of Barmen was not stellar: the government came down even harder on the churches, and the global conflict inflicted by German was in no way averted. Even decades later, how do we evaluate the success of something that didn't work at the time but informs our theological understanding in the present?

Iain Quinn
The Founding and Development of the Trinity Chorister Program

The Trinity Chorister Program (Trinity Episcopal Church, Hartford, Connecticut) was founded in September 2000 to provide children from the Greater Hartford region with an opportunity to sing the finest sacred music written for treble voices in weekly services. Currently there are 23 children enrolled in the program which meets every Monday and Thursday for rehearsals and each Sunday for the 10:30 am service. The children are attracted to the program from a wide variety of backgrounds, and since the beginning of the program a significant outreach of the parish has been served with many families joining the church as a result.

The choristers sing repertoire ranging from Gregorian chant to contemporary works. They represent the parish at regional and national courses of the Royal School of Church Music and this summer will represent both the diocese and the state as they sing the liturgies at the National Cathedral, Washington D.C., for "Connecticut Day."

1. What are the plans for the program in the future?
2. What has been the greatest challenge since the program was founded?
3. What has been the greatest success since the program was founded?

Jason Roberts
Secular Music in a Sacred Setting: Luther and Early Reformation Contrafacta

Most of Luther's chorales were contrafacta: that is, they placed a new text over an existing melody. I examined the sources for Luther's tunes and found that he borrowed almost exclusively from sacred sources. A repertory of popular religious folk songs served as his greatest resource. I also posed the question of what can be learned from Luther's attitudes about sacred and secular music.

Three Questions:

1. Why is there no equivalent today to the popular, sacred repertory of Luther's time?
2. How was such "popular" music received in church at the time?
3. What connotations do today's popular styles carry with them in contrast to the styles of Luther's time?

Melanie Ross
Liturgical Theology through an Evangelical Lens

[abstract not available]

Daniel Sullivan
J.S. Bach's Goldberg Variations

Through a very incomplete and cursory examination of Bach's *Goldberg Variations* this presentation sought to introduce the audience to some of the most elementary and basic organizing principles of western art music as well as to situate the *Goldberg Variations* within this privileged form of art as one of its most spectacular and monumental achievements.

Three questions you WISH you had been asked following your presentation
1. What is the point of making music; or why did and do people compose it?
2. Why do you make music?
3. What is the role or purpose of music as you see it?

Sidney Symington
Thespian Theology

This talk explores and celebrates the connections between the performance of narratives and their spiritual power. Mr. Symington advocates development and prioritization of theatrical activity in faith communities as a sublimely affective tool for theological exploration and community enrichment. He notes the loss of intrapersonal integration brought about by scientific achievement; whereas the several areas of human consciousness once came together in the venues of our faith traditions, modern lives are increasingly splintered. Mr. Symington admonishes faith communities to nurture art programs, especially drama, as a vital element of spiritual formation.

1. How does doing drama in the faith community prepare people for their lives outside in society?
2. What if people are shy, have stage fright, or just don't like performing in front of a group?
3. Could you say more about embodied theology, especially from a Christian persepctive? What is it about Christianity that demands doing beyond word and worship?

Paul Weber
Messiaen the Theologian

This presentation dealt with the use of religious symbolism in the music of Olivier Messiaen. Messiaen described his own musical language in theological terms, and this project attempted to examine the use of this musical language to communicate a theological message in the *Messe de la Pentecôte* of 1950. The presentation gave a summary of Messiaen's chief compositional tools before focusing on the third movement of the *Messe*, entitled "Consecration."

Questions:
1. Can music have meaning in and of itself?
2. What is significant about the delivery of a theological message through the medium of music?
3. How does extra-musical meaning enhance inherent musical meaning?

Evan Wels
Bernstein and His Chichester Psalms: The Fine Line from Times Square to Lincoln Center

[abstract not available]